Masculinity and the Trials of Modern Fiction

How do lawyers, judges and jurors read novels? And what is at stake when literature and law confront each other in the courtroom? Nineteenth-century England and France are remembered for their active legal prosecution of literature, and this book examines the ways in which five novels were interpreted in the courtroom: Gustave Flaubert's *Madame Bovary*, Paul Bonnetain's *Charlot s'amuse*, Henry Vizetelly's English translation of Émile Zola's *La Terre*, Oscar Wilde's *The Picture of Dorian Gray* and Radclyffe Hall's *The Well of Loneliness*. It argues that each of these novels attracted legal censure because they presented figures of sexual dissidence – the androgyne, the onanist or masturbator, the patricide, the homosexual and the lesbian – that called into question an increasingly fragile normative, middle-class masculinity. Offering close readings of the novels themselves, and of legal material from the proceedings, such as the trial transcripts and judicial opinions, the book addresses both the doctrinal dimensions of Victorian obscenity and censorship, as well as the reading practices at work in the courtroom. It situates the cases in their historical context, and highlights how each trial constitutes a scene of reading – an encounter between literature and the law – through which different forms of masculinity were shaped, bolstered or challenged.

Marco Wan is Associate Professor of Law and Honorary Associate Professor of English at the University of Hong Kong.

Masculinity and the Trials of Modern Fiction

Marco Wan

Routledge
Taylor & Francis Group
LONDON AND NEW YORK

First published 2017
by Routledge
2 Park Square, Milton Park, Abingdon, Oxon, OX14 4RN

and by Routledge
711 Third Avenue, New York, NY 10017

First issued in paperback 2018

Routledge is an imprint of the Taylor & Francis Group, an informa business

British Library Cataloguing in Publication Data
A catalogue record for this book is available from the British Library

Library of Congress Cataloging-in-Publication Data
Names: Wan, Marco, author.
Title: Masculinity and the trials of modern fiction / Marco Wan.
Description: Abingdon, Oxon ; New York, NY : Routledge, 2017. |
Series: Discourses of law | "A Glasshouse book." | Includes
bibliographical references and index.
Identifiers: LCCN 2016020594 | ISBN 9781138684195 (hbk) |
ISBN 9781315544083 (ebk)
Subjects: LCSH: Trials (Obscenity)—France—History. | Trials
(Obscenity)—England—History. | Law and literature—France—History. |
Law and literature—England—History. | Sexual freedom in literature. |
Masculinity in literature.
Classification: LCC KJC67.O27 W36 2017 | DDC 345.42/0274—dc23
LC record available at https://lccn.loc.gov/2016020594

ISBN 13: 978-1-138-60616-6 (pbk)
ISBN 13: 978-1-138-68419-5 (hbk)

Typeset in Baskerville by
Keystroke, Neville Lodge, Tettenhall, Wolverhampton

To my family

Contents

Acknowledgements

This book has been a long time in the making, and I have benefited enormously from the knowledge, patience, kindness and intelligence of many people over the years. I would like to thank Jan-Melissa Schramm, Mary Jacobus and Yota Batsaki for guiding my PhD thesis and for showing me what it means to be a rigorous and ethical scholar. Jeremy Tambling and Maria Aristodemou sharpened my thinking about the relationship between law, literature and gender. Nicola Lacey generously took the time to read the manuscript in the final stages of the project and provided many insightful comments. Peter Goodrich has been, and continues to be, an inspiration. Andrew Counter read every word I wrote with love and care. The project has also been enriched by conversations with Peter Brooks, Johannes Chan, Janet Halley, Elaine Ho, Chris Hutton, Douglas Kerr, Janny Leung, Bill MacNeil, Daniel Matthews, Paul Raffield, Mitra Sharafi, Andy Tucker, Scott Veitch, Gary Watt and Kenji Yoshino. Finally, I would like to thank my family for their continuing love and support.

Part of Chapter 1 was published in *Law and Humanities* (Volume 2(2), 2008), and a section of Chapter 4 was published in the *Oxford Journal of Legal Studies* (Volume 31(4), 2011). I would like to thank the editors for permission to reuse the material. I would also like to acknowledge the support of the General Research Fund (GRF) from the University Grants Committee of Hong Kong, which provided teaching relief and therefore valuable writing time.

Introduction: legal interpretation, gender and the novel

On 3 April 1895, the Old Bailey was transformed from England's Central Criminal Court into the venue for a literary event. Oscar Wilde was suing the father of his lover for libel, and the courtroom was as packed as the opening night of some of his plays. When Edward Carson, the lawyer for Wilde's opponent, raised the question of whether *The Picture of Dorian Gray* could be interpreted as a 'sodomitical book', Wilde found himself in the surprising position of having to defend his work in a trial that he himself had initiated.[1] Carson also demanded to know whether Wilde thought that an exchange between Dorian and the artist Basil Hallward in the novel 'would suggest that what they were talking about was a charge of sodomy' when the passage was 'taken in its natural meaning'.[2]

I begin with this moment from the Wilde trials because at its core are two interconnected questions which I will explore in this study. The first is the question of gender; the figure of the sodomite constituted one of several sexual identities that were particularly unsettling in the late nineteenth century because they put pressure on a normative bourgeois masculinity that was already under strain. The second is the question of interpretation. Carson appeared to assume a direct correspondence between *Dorian Gray*'s content and the life of its author, and the cross-examination proceeded on the basis that the novel can be construed as evidence of Wilde's sexual desires and practices. To a literary critic, Carson's approach to literature seems curious at best; as Wilde tried to tell him during the trial, a text does not allow for any easy access to a pre-discursive reality.

My aim is to investigate the processes of interpretation that take place when legal readers – lawyers, judges, jurors – encounter literature in the courtroom, and the ways in which such interpretive processes take part in the formation of gendered identities in literature and law. By approaching the trials themselves as texts that deserve to be *read*, I will examine the assumptions legal readers make about literary texts, the arguments used when counsel on the opposing sides

1 Merlin Holland (ed), *Irish Peacock and Scarlet Marquess: The Real Trial of Oscar Wilde* (London: HarperCollins, 2004) 81.
2 Ibid. 102.

advance competing interpretations, the blind spots of such readings and the ways in which 'legal' language can itself be considered to have 'literary' qualities or significance.

The period from the mid-nineteenth century to the early twentieth century is a particularly fruitful period of investigation because it was a time of intense censorship. Michel Foucault famously argued against the view of the Victorian period as a time of prudery and repression, and his ground-breaking work has shifted our focus from the top-down model of legal prohibition to the circulation of power amongst multiple discourses.[3] Nevertheless, if we examine the nature and quantity of the legal rules promulgated in that period, it remains true that it was one of the most repressive in literary history: the modern definition of obscenity in English law, which is still operative today, was first formulated in the 1850s; the French edicts regulating literary and journalistic publications became increasingly stringent as the century wore on; and governments uncompromisingly intervened in literary production in the name of protecting the moral health of the nation.[4]

A large number of literary trials, in which writers or their publishers were brought to the dock because of fiction or poetry that was allegedly indecent, obscene or transgressive, took place between the 1850s and the 1930s, and they constitute particularly illuminating instances of how literature is interpreted through the eyes of the law. In this study, I shall examine five of these court cases, including those concerning Flaubert's *Madame Bovary* (1856); Paul Bonnetain's narrative about a compulsive masturbator, *Charlot s'amuse* (*Charlot Plays with Himself*) (1883); Émile Zola's *La Terre* (*The Earth*) (1887), whose English translator and publisher, Henry Vizetelly, was prosecuted for obscenity in the English courts; Oscar Wilde's *The Picture of Dorian Gray* (1890) and Radclyffe Hall's novel about lesbianism, *The Well of Loneliness* (1928).

I call these cases 'literary trials' not because I assume that the texts were necessarily considered of great aesthetic value at the time of the prosecution, or that 'literature' embodies any timeless, incontestable standard of beauty. On the contrary, I call them 'literary trials' because they are events which turned on the very question of what constitutes 'literature' in the first place. Even though this question was rarely explicitly articulated in the courtroom, it hovered just below the surface, always ready to emerge during the proceedings, as when a writer sought to defend the 'literary' merit of his or her writing, or when a lawyer contended that a novel should be construed as 'filth' or 'trash' rather than literature. Elisabeth

3 Michel Foucault, *The History of Sexuality, 3 vols* (Richard Hurley (trans), London: Penguin Books, 1978) I.

4 For a discussion of nineteenth-century censorship in England and America, see Walter Kendrick, *The Secret Museum: Pornography in Modern Culture* (Berkeley: University of California Press, 1987) 67–95. For a discussion of nineteenth-century French censorship, see Nicholas Harrison, *Circles of Censorship: Censorship and its Metaphors in French History, Literature, and Theory* (Oxford: Clarendon Press, 1995) 19–35.

Ladenson has highlighted the vicissitudes of the term 'literature' in her work on literary obscenity, arguing that books which were considered obscene in the nineteenth century became accepted as literature in our own time because 'realism' and 'art for art's sake', two ideas which were then regarded as 'avant-garde heresy . . . gradually became accepted clichés, and then grounds for legal defence'.[5] She demonstrates that as literary styles which were 'unmentionable' gained acceptance, so did the works that were written in those styles.

The terms 'realism' and 'art for art's sake' (or aestheticism) are also central to my study, and I will return to them in the following pages, and especially in the chapter on the Wilde trials. At the same time, I will broaden the scope of inquiry by showing that the question of what constitutes 'literature' with which all of these cases were implicitly concerned intersected with a number of other issues, such as the relationship between literature and the visual arts, the 'scientific' basis of fiction, the distinction between literature and pornography and the intertwined epistemologies of law and literature.

The nineteenth and early twentieth centuries were also a crucial period in the history of gender and sexuality. In recent years, some of the most productive work on 'law and literature' studies, especially those with an explicit historical focus on the period, have examined the relationship between women, literature and the law, revealing the patriarchal assumptions behind legal discourse and underscoring how literature questioned conventional legal notions of femininity.[6]

In this study, I build on the existing scholarship on law, literature and gender, but shift the focus from femininity to masculinity to examine the ways in which the legal reading of literature bolstered, interrogated and subverted orthodoxies about normative male identity of the time. The middle-class belief about the desirability and normality of a procreative, conjugal and familial masculinity, established in the first half of the nineteenth century, became increasingly challenged from the second half of the century. As the foundation of this male identity became less and less secure, a number of literary works whose plots revolved around characters that did not fully conform to gender expectations were placed under legal scrutiny. Their writers or publishers were prosecuted for publishing obscene material, or had their desires and beliefs publicly put on trial.

5 Elisabeth Ladenson, *Dirt for Art's Sake: Books on Trial From Madame Bovary to Lolita* (Ithaca: Cornell University Press, 2007) xv.

6 See Maria Aristodemou, *Law and Literature: Journeys from Her to Eternity* (Oxford: Oxford University Press, 2000); Kristin Kalsem, *In Contempt: Nineteenth-Century Women, Law & Literature* (Columbus: Ohio State University Press, 2012); Christine L. Krueger, *Reading for the Law: British Literary History and Gender Advocacy* (Charlottesville: University of Virginia Press, 2010); Nicola Lacey, *Women, Crime and Character: From Moll Flanders to Tess of the d'Urbervilles* (Oxford: Oxford University Press, 2008); Martha C. Nussbaum and Alison L. LaCroix (eds), *Subversion and Sympathy: Gender, Law, and the British Novel* (Oxford: Oxford University Press, 2013); Ian Ward, *Law and the Brontës* (Basingstoke: Palgrave Macmillan, 2012); Ian Ward, *Sex, Crime and Literature in Victorian England* (Oxford: Hart Publishing, 2014).

The courtroom became a site where the battle between legal and literary representations of masculinity took place.

The act of interpretation played a critical role in this battle: when a lawyer argued that a work should not be proscribed, he was on some level arguing against the illegitimacy of the gender categories posited in the text. Alternatively, when a lawyer interpreted a novel as containing (for instance) 'sodomitical' messages, he was drawing on the popular association of sexual deviancy, social transgression and immorality, at the very moment when the 'homosexual' was coming into being as a distinct medical and psychological category. Questions that seem purely *legal* in nature, such as whether a text could be used as evidence against its author or whether it should be considered obscene, played an important role in shaping the wider *cultural* understanding of masculinity.

I posit that the legal arguments, as well as judicial opinions, in the trials are texts that deserve close reading, as the rhetorical strategies through which they are formulated are indicative of the interpretive assumptions underpinning them, and these assumptions in turn have a strong influence on the discursive formation of gender. Finally, I will show how a psychoanalytic mode of interpretation could bring to the forefront the gender implications of the legal arguments.

Studies on the trials of modern fiction have tended to approach the court cases as stages in the development of the modern law of obscenity, portraying each trial as a step in the long march towards greater freedom of expression, a freedom which supposedly reaches its peak in our own time.[7] Ladenson's work questions this teleological narrative and contends that the history of obscenity is constantly 'repeating itself in such loud and insistent tones that we can only sit back and listen to its incoherent tale'.[8] She cautions against adopting an attitude of 'chronological chauvinism', whereby we assume our own time to be more permissive and morally enlightened than the past.[9] Ladenson's work helpfully shifts the focus away from changes in doctrine to the literary texts themselves. However, it takes the centrality of the history of obscenity for granted in its analysis of literary trials, even as it revises the linearity of this history. In other words, it remains premised on a long, sweeping historical view of obscenity doctrine, even though it reconsiders the established accounts of this history. In this book, I focus less on the long-term temporal trajectory of any one area of law, be it the law of obscenity or otherwise, and more on the ways in which literature is interpreted by legal readers in individual cases at a particular historical moment.

I will further argue that the scenes of reading in these trials can shed light on how literary and legal discourses are related. One of the greatest contributions of

7 See C.H. Rolph, *Books in the Dock* (London: Deutsch, 1969); Geoffrey Robertson, *Obscenity: An Account of Censorship Laws and Their Enforcement in England and Wales* (London: Weidenfeld & Nicolson, 1979) 15–45; Donald Thomas, *A Long Time Burning: the History of Literary Censorship in England* (London: Routledge & Kegan Paul, 1969).

8 Ladenson (n 5) 16.

9 Ibid. xvi.

'law and literature' studies is the dialogue it has established between the seemingly disparate disciplines. Richard Weisberg has proposed a 'poethics of reading' through which literature can provide an emotive, moralistic supplement to an overly rational and technical method of legal reasoning.[10] Martha Nussbaum has similarly argued that literature enables judges to adopt the perspective of a 'judicious spectator' which in turn allows them to empathise with people inhabiting a space outside their realm of racial, sexual, and economic experience.[11]

More recently, critics have enabled a conversation between legal philosophy and literature by highlighting the jurisprudential dimension of literary texts. For instance, William MacNeil has demonstrated that fiction engages with key legal-philosophical concepts such as sovereignty, rights and justice, and that the 'novelistic rendering of legal theories complicates, challenges and calls the juridical imaginary to account'.[12] In a similar vein, Desmond Manderson has demonstrated that D.H. Lawrence's *The Kangaroo*, a novel which has seemingly little to do with legal issues, can embody a new vision of the rule of law.[13] This study furthers the current debate about the relationship between law and literature by approaching the literary trials as moments when the two discursive fields come into contact in the courtroom. It demonstrates that each trial constitutes an encounter between 'law' and literature' which highlights their common linguistic structures, reconfigures their discursive boundaries and reveals them to be intertwined discourses that repeat each other's problems of representation. Each of the cases I discuss in this book brings to the forefront a discursive affinity between law and literature that has been insufficiently acknowledged.

The novels and the legal cases in this book generated intense interest amongst writers and in the wider reading public in their time. Writing to his brother Achille, Flaubert noted that the French Government's decision to prosecute him caused so much publicity that 'the courtroom was packed' on the day of the trial.[14] As we shall see, Bonnetain's trial was regarded by many French naturalist writers as nothing less than the trial of naturalism itself. In England, translations of Zola's novels became the target of the National Vigilance Association and also led to a debate in the House of Commons on the urgency of curbing the circulation not only of his novels, but of French fiction in its entirety. The impact of the Wilde trials is reflected in the scope of their reportage: virtually all the major newspapers devoted both news and editorial space to the trials, and the *Illustrated Police Budget*

10 Richard Weisberg, *Poethics, and Other Strategies of Law and Literature* (New York: Columbia University Press, 1992).

11 Martha C. Nussbaum, *Poetic Justice: The Literary Imagination and Public Life* (Boston: Beacon Press, 1995) 72–77.

12 William MacNeil, *Novel Judgements: Legal Theory as Fiction* (Abingdon: Routledge, 2012) 11.

13 Desmond Manderson, *Kangaroo Courts and the Rule of Law: The Legacy of Modernism* (Abingdon: Routledge, 2012).

14 Gustave Flaubert, *The Letters of Gustave Flaubert, 1830–1857* (Francis Steegmuller (ed and trans), London: Belknap Press, 1980) 227 (30 January 1857).

obsessively followed Wilde's movements to ensure maximum news coverage. Finally, the theatrical metaphor which one of Hall's biographers used to describe the *Well of Loneliness* trial attests to its social impact: she notes that on 9 November 1928, the magistrates' court 'looked like a first night. So great were the crowds that a notice was placed on the door saying "Court Full" long before the proceedings began'.[15]

The novels also constitute paradigmatic instances of the major intellectual and artistic currents in modern literature: mid-nineteenth-century realism, late-nineteenth-century naturalism and aestheticism, and early-twentieth-century modernism. At the same time, the starting and end points of this study serve as a reminder that any delineation of temporal contours is to some degree provisional, and one should avoid uncritical reliance on literary labels. Flaubert was regarded as the master of realism both in his time and in much contemporary scholarship, but the free indirect discourse and the focus on interiority in *Madame Bovary* are part of a distinctly modernist mode of narration. Similarly, Radclyffe Hall's novel was published in 1928, a year which is commonly regarded as falling squarely within the high modernist period and which witnessed the publication of Virginia Woolf's *Orlando*, yet *The Well of Loneliness* has a distinctly realist tenor.[16] As we shall see, Flaubert's 'modernist' style and Hall's 'realistic' depiction of lesbianism were critical to the ways in which the legal readers interpreted *Madame Bovary* and *The Well of Loneliness* in the courtroom.

Most importantly, the novels I discuss can all be said to present figures of gender dissidence which courted legal controversy: such figures include the androgyne, the onanist, the patricide, the homosexual and the lesbian. To argue that gender representations that we recognise today already existed in the literary discourse of the time is not, of course, to argue that such figures are timeless or universal; the work of historians of gender and sexuality have alerted us to the specific historical circumstances under which gender identities emerged. Rather, the following analysis of figures of gender dissidence represented in fiction acknowledges that they were either coming into existence or were causing peculiar concern in the cultural imaginary at the particular moment in time at which the novels were brought to the dock, and examines the historical, political and cultural circumstances under which these figures were constituted or understood in the courtroom and in the broader cultural domain.

Throughout this study, the focus will be on the clash between legal and literary representations of masculinity, the rhetorical dimension of arguments put forward in court, the implications of the legal interpretation of fiction for gender identities in the nineteenth and early twentieth centuries and the epistemological connections between literature and the law.

15 Sally Cline, *Radclyffe Hall: A Woman Called John* (London: John Murray, 1997) 259.

16 For a comparative discussion of the modernist style of *Orlando* and the realism of *The Well of Loneliness*, see Adam Parkes, 'Lesbianism, history, and censorship: *The Well of Loneliness* and the suppressed randiness of Virginia Woolf's *Orlando*' (1994) 40 *Twentieth Century Literature* 436–60.

(I) Procreation, family and hegemonic masculinity

To make clear what was at stake in the way the novels were interpreted in the courtroom, I will situate the literary trials in relation to the anxieties, paradoxes and pressures exerted on normative masculinity in England and France from the mid-nineteenth to the early twentieth centuries. In this section, I will discuss the nature and the inherent contradictions in middle-class male self-identity in this period, and will examine the major forces challenging its dominance. The discussion here will provide the background to my study of how lawyers, judges and jurors read literature, and of the gender implications of such legal readings.

R.W. Connell's concept of 'hegemonic masculinity', one of the foundational terms of men's studies, has energised the historical study of masculinity and provides a useful starting point of analysis.[17] Connell first posited this concept in the 1980s, and later revisited it in light of its inter-disciplinary impact and the debates it generated.[18] Connell defines hegemonic masculinity as the embodiment of the 'most honoured way of being a man'.[19] Society is created in the image of this masculine form, and men who do not conform to it, as well as women, are placed in disempowered or marginalised positions. Its primacy 'is maintained not only by force, but by cultural means . . . which establish many of the assumptions of hegemonic masculinity in the realm of "common sense", where they are particularly difficult to dislodge'.[20] Connell notes that the concept has a strong normative force, in part because it sets the standard of masculine behaviour and thereby requires 'all other men to position themselves in relation to it', either explicitly or implicitly.

In nineteenth-century England and France, hegemonic masculinity took the form of a dominant bourgeois identity premised on procreation, fatherhood and family. Marriage, children and paternal authority were prerequisites for full manhood. Conjugal love was understood to be 'pleasurable' as well as 'ethical, selfless, life-affirming', and a man who could not ascend to the institution of marriage, or worse, who rejected it, was seen as morally suspect.[21] A number of factors accounted for the consolidation of this form of masculinity, one of which was the influence of religion. As Catherine Hall has pointed out, 'Evangelical

17 R.W. Connell, *Gender and Power: Society, the Person and Sexual Politics* (Stanford: Stanford University Press, 1987) 183–91. See also the elaboration of this concept in *Masculinities* (2nd edn, Cambridge: Polity Press, 2005).

18 R.W. Connell and James W. Messerschmidt, 'Hegemonic masculinity: rethinking the concept' (2005) 19 *Gender & Society* 829–59.

19 Ibid. 832.

20 John Tosh, 'Hegemonic masculinity and the history of gender' in Stefan Dudink, Karen Hagemann and John Tosh (eds), *Masculinities in Politics and War: Gendering Modern History* (Manchester, Manchester University Press, 2004) 41–61 at 42–43.

21 Judith Surkis, *Sexing the Citizen: Morality and Masculinity in France, 1870–1920* (Ithaca: Cornell University Press, 2006) 1.

morality was probably the single most widespread influence in Victorian England'.[22] Prominent Christians such as Henry Thornton and William Wilberforce, who believed that one of their missions was to reform the manners and morals of the nation, championed male authority by insisting that women should withdraw from the public sphere and function as 'supportive backcloth, helpmeets to their husbands'.[23]

Evangelical ideology advanced the understanding of the male role as primary, active and public by making the female role secondary and private. The Church of England's attitude towards sexual relations was a multi-faceted one: the husband was at once his wife's superior, her lord and master, and her equal, her caring and benevolent companion.[24] This equilibrium became increasingly hard to maintain as women's rights progressed in the second half of the century. In France, the Catholic Church also dictated that a man's sexual energy must be directed to sentimental, familial purposes, and insisted even more firmly on the procreative dimension of marriage than English Evangelicalism. Corbin's survey of nineteenth-century French Catholic confessional manuals reveals that many of them were devoted to stamping out non-reproductive practices between married couples.[25] For instance, the manuals singled out 'conjugal onanism', or masturbation between married partners, as a particularly heinous practice, because it was solely for pleasure and had no reproductive function.[26]

The scientific discourse also played an important role in establishing the normative model of masculinity. Thomas Laqueur has traced the emergence of a 'two-sex model' under which men and women were regarded as 'incommensurable'.[27] Robert Nye similarly notes that biological sex became the 'primordial category' for understanding the relations between the men and women, and the conception of sexual dimorphism, whereby the *raison d'être* of each gender was to perform its physiologically ordained role in the perpetuation of the human species, formed a basis for the construction of masculinity and femininity at this time.[28] Women were biologically designed to conceive, and the ideal male was one who, 'through his power and his fertility', knew 'how to satisfy his spouse's ardent wish to be a mother', whilst at the same time carefully avoiding succumbing to sexual

22 Catherine Hall, 'The early formation of Victorian domestic ideology' in Robert Shoemaker and Mary Vincent (eds), *Gender and History in Western Europe* (London: Arnold, 1998) 181–97 at 181.

23 Ibid. 192.

24 See Ben Griffin, *The Politics of Gender in Victorian Britain: Masculinity, Political Culture and the Struggle for Women's Rights* (Cambridge: Cambridge University Press, 2012) 37–65.

25 Alain Corbin, *L'Harmonie des plaisirs: les manières de jouir du siècle des Lumières à l'avènement de la sexologie* (Paris: Flammarion, 2010) 331–61.

26 Ibid. 331.

27 Thomas Laqueur, *Making Sex: Body and Gender from the Greeks to Freud* (Cambridge: Harvard University Press, 1990) 153.

28 Robert Nye, *Masculinity and Male Codes of Honor in Modern France* (Oxford: Oxford University Press, 1993) 5.

indulgence.[29] A man's mission was, 'above all else, to ensure the continuation of his species by inseminating a woman'.[30]

This understanding of the male body further entrenched the alignment of masculinity, marriage and reproduction, and led to a conflation of physical and behaviourial characteristics: a man, 'like his genital organs', was believed to be 'turned outward', in the sense that he was always ready to tackle the challenges coming from the external world.[31] He was therefore expected to be, amongst other things, predisposed to action, unafraid of hard work and eager to prove his courage.

Although the conceptions of normative masculinity in England and France were similar, they took different inflections in the two countries. As John Tosh has shown, masculinity in Victorian England was inextricably tied to domesticity. It consisted of three intertwined processes: *establishing* a home, which was a 'crucial stage in winning social recognition as an adult, fully masculine person'; *protecting* the home, which 'underpinned the association of masculinity with physical self-reliance and personal bravery' and *providing* for the home, which was tantamount to assuming the 'responsibility' of a fully grown man.[32]

Marriage and family were preconditions to the establishment of male authority: patriarchy, in its literal meaning of 'father-rule', was the only acceptable framework for governing the household. It was also the key to 'masculine self-respect'; a husband who did not have mastery over his wife's sexual conduct risked ridicule by his friends, uncertain paternity of his children and the loss of property to an outsider.[33] A man's status was also in part dependent on the manly standing of his sons; a father's fulfilment of his parental duties was regarded as an indicator of his social standing.

In France, this domestic masculinity, whilst important, was coupled with a 'martial masculinity' inherited from the Napoleonic era, according to which 'the epitome of manhood' resided in 'the French soldier and the martial virtues he possessed'.[34] After France's defeat in the Franco-Prussian War, the French people recognised that the glory of the nation depended to a great extent on a strong army, and the valorisation of soldierly virtues as masculine virtues became even clearer. It is not an accident that the soldier was defined by his 'virility and aggressive heterosexuality', for his procreative potential was regarded as the

29 Alain Corbin, Jean-Jacques Courtine and Georges Vigarello (eds), *Histoire de la virilité, 3 vols* (Paris: Éditions du Seuil, 2011) II, 22.

30 Ibid. 17.

31 Ibid. 19.

32 John Tosh, *A Man's Place: Masculinity and the Middle-Class Home in Victorian England* (New Haven: Yale University Press, 2007) 3.

33 Ibid.

34 Michael J. Hughes, 'Making Frenchmen into warriors: martial masculinity in Napoleonic France' in Christopher E. Forth and Bertrand Taithe (eds), *French Masculinities: History, Culture and Politics* (Basingstoke: Palgrave Macmillan, 2007) 67–85 at 52.

driving force behind his military prowess and his devotion to the *patrie*. In his discussion of the revival of the practice of dueling in the Third Republic, Nye observes that the understanding of bourgeois masculinity was largely based on the soldierly ideal. A man who refused to enter into a duel, or who showed signs of cowardice during the contest, was labelled as dishonourable and therefore as unmanly. The notion of honour, so central to what it meant to be a man, is a concept that has its roots in the 'military virtues' of the nobility.[35] The courage, resolution and quickness of action associated with dueling, as well as the virility and energy of the soldier, were defined as positive and manly qualities, largely because of their association with the model of martial masculinity.

However, the procreative, conjugal and familial model of masculinity was 'at once presumed and problematic', its hegemony both incontestable and besieged. Its status as the standard, the ideal and the norm of what it meant to be a man at this time was increasingly questioned in the second half of the century.[36] One important challenge arose from the advancement of women's rights from the 1850s. Masculinity and femininity are relational categories, and an improvement in the status of women necessarily entails a reassessment of their male counterparts' status, authority and self-perception. These changes took place on several fronts, including women's right to divorce, their ownership of property, as well as their education and job opportunities. In England, the Matrimonial Causes Act 1857 made divorce easier and cheaper, and a series of Acts passed in 1878, 1886 and 1895 established further grounds for a wife to terminate her marriage. The 1857 Act, together with legislative changes in 1870 and 1882, also gave married women greater control of their property.[37]

These changes were not uncontroversial in their time, and the 1857 Act in particular was strongly opposed by such figures as William Gladstone and Samuel Wilberforce, the Bishop of Oxford. Their vocal concerns testified to the anxieties about attempts to alter the balance of power between the sexes. Divorce had been officially abolished in 1816 in France and, despite strong opposition, it was reintroduced in 1848 through the efforts of a small but influential group of people, including the jurist Amable Félix Couturier de Vienne and Alexandre Dumas, *fils*. The drive for reform culminated in the *Loi Naquet* of 1884, which recognised four new grounds for a woman to end her marriage: adultery, physical violence, *injures graves* (a flexible category which amounted to virtually any kind of moral cruelty) and *condamnation afflictive et infamante*, which applied to, say, a spouse sentenced to life imprisonment.[38]

35 Nye (n 28) 217.

36 Surkis (n 21) 11.

37 For a detailed discussion of the legislative changes, see Lee Holcombe, 'Victorian wives and property: reform of the Married Women's Property Acts, 1857–1882' in Martha Vicinus (ed), *A Widening Sphere: Changing Roles of Victorian Women* (London: Methuen & Co., 1980) 3–29 at 12.

38 James F. McMillan, *France and Women 1789–1914: Gender, Society and Politics* (London: Routledge, 2000) 152–53.

As Nicholas White points out, the law marked a turning point in the history of the French nuclear family because it 'signalled the fragility of state-sponsored idealism about the indestructibility of the married couple' and questioned the presumption of a woman's happiness in marriage.[39] French women also moved towards financial independence as they gained the right to open a bank account in the 1880s, first without the need for their husband's assistance and then without the need for their husband's consent.

Education and employment ceased to be under the exclusive purview of men in this period. Frances Mary Buss founded the North London Collegiate School, the first all-girls secondary school in England, in 1850, and the rapid expansion of all-girls schools in the years that followed meant that, by the end of the 1890s, it was no longer unusual to assume that girls would attend school or board away from home.[40] When Agnata Ramsey took the only first-class degree in the Classics Tripos in 1887 at Cambridge and, three years later, when Philippa Fawcett was classed above the senior wrangler in the Mathematical Tripos, they provided incontrovertible proof that women were not of inferior intellect to men.

In France, the Falloux Law of 1850 made it a requirement for communes with a population of more than 800 people to build a primary school for girls, and the push for female education intensified in the 1870s as France's defeat in the Franco-Prussian War was partly attributed to the weakness of the French education system. In both countries, a higher level of education for women made it harder for men to justify their exclusion from employment, and the greater supply of female labour undermined the conception of the workplace as an exclusively male domain. Such legislative and social changes were of course liberating for women but, as Annelise Maugue has rather colourfully noted, they also 'heightened anxieties kindled in men by modernity' by making every man reconsider whether he could live up to 'the grandiose ambitions that his sex condemns him to conceive for himself'.[41] As we shall see, such an unprecedented challenge to male authority in the family home, the school and the workplace led to efforts to defend it that, in turn, had a repressive influence on identities that did not conform to the heterosexual, conjugal model of gender.

Whilst the challenges were similar on both sides of the English Channel, the ways in which bourgeois male identity became destabilised again took different forms in the two cultural contexts. In England, its discontents related specifically to its domestic nature. First, it was not unusual for men to feel alienated or dissatisfied within the family despite, or perhaps because of, its overwhelming

39 Nicholas White, *The Family in Crisis in Late Nineteenth-Century French Fiction* (Cambridge: Cambridge University Press, 1999) 5.

40 David Rubinstein, *Before the Suffragettes: Women's Emancipation in the 1890s* (Brighton: Harvester Press, 1986) 185.

41 Annelise Maugue, 'The new Eve and the old Adam' in Geneviève Fraisse and Michelle Perrot (eds), *A History of Women in the West, 5 vols* (Cambridge: Belknap Press, 1993) IV, 515–33 at 532. See also A. Maugue, *L'Identité masculine en crise au tournant du siècle* (Paris: Éditions Rivages, 1987).

centrality to their lives; even though the home was supposed to provide a refuge from the pressures of work and the temptations of the outside world, it was also associated with *ennui* and feminine restraint. It was therefore common for men to seek regular company with other men, rather than succumb to the '"tyranny of five o'clock tea"'.[42] Clubs and taverns drew husbands away from their domestic duties and constituted 'the forum in which masculine standing was appraised and recognised, and often a means of reinforcing gender privilege'.[43]

Moreover, Eve Kosofsky Sedgwick's demonstration that desire does not operate according to a binary logic, but could subsist in seemingly non-sexual relationships between men, implies a need to rethink the sexual dynamic of such venues. Whilst the clubs and taverns fostered masculine camaraderie in a way that was supposedly devoid of sexual charge, their aggressive proscription of male–male desire arguably betrays Victorian anxieties over a man's possible movements along that ambiguous and conflicting middle stretch of the homo-social spectrum.[44]

Secondly, domestic life clashed with the spirit of freedom, discovery and exploration which was increasingly marketed as an alluring part of the imperialist adventure through storybooks, magazines and other reading material aimed at boys and young men.[45] The view that a man who was devoted to his wife and children was in fact living an 'unglorious, unfulfilling and – ultimately – unmasculine' life haunted the ideal of English normative masculinity.[46] The profession of the typical family man was often regarded as incompatible with the bravery and unbridled energy of these imperialist men of adventure: with a nod to Thomas Carlyle, Tosh notes that bourgeois domestic men were '"captains of industry" but hardly captains of men'.

Finally, even though a man was supposedly the head of his household, the perception of the domestic sphere as the private sphere, and hence as the woman's domain, meant that his decisions there were sometimes seen as an encroachment on the wife's realm of influence and resented by her. The Evangelical basis of the family dictates that the wife occupy a subordinate place in relation to her spouse, but at the same time the Church's recognition of 'the power of the moral mother as the foundation of a godly family life' meant that 'the spiritual standing of the wife was bound to rise', to such an extent that 'it was an open question whether the bedtime prayer of mother and child was not more important than the family prayers led by the father'.[47] As Valerie Sanders has noted, the *paterfamilias'* place at the head of the table at mealtimes may be guaranteed, but 'his domestic role the

42 Tosh, *A Man's Place* (n 32) 7.

43 Ibid. 6.

44 Eve Kosofsky Sedgwick, *Between Men: English Literature and Male Homosocial Desire* (New York: Columbia University Press, 1985).

45 Joseph Bristow, *Empire Boys: Adventures in a Man's World* (London: Unwin Hyman, 1991).

46 Tosh, *A Man's Place* (n 32) 7.

47 Ibid. 73.

rest of the time evades definition'.[48] She describes this tension as 'the central paradox of Victorian fatherhood'.[49] The normativity of English domestic masculinity seemed to be put in doubt by forces emanating from all directions.

In France, tensions arose because of the clash between the model of domestic masculinity and the earlier model of martial masculinity, and became more and more pronounced as the century progressed. This domestic, or civic, middle-class masculinity was characterised by more refined manners, a high level of education, professional work that is cerebral rather than physical in nature, material comfort and a sedentary lifestyle. As this newer form of identity became more prevalent, there emerged concerns that it could give rise to social conditions that would not only make 'many noble and middle-class men ill-suited to the rigours of war', but could also lead to the feminisation of French men.[50] There were fears that, if left unchecked, the swerve away from the martial model could 'create beings whose gender was undecidable under any circumstances'.

Moreover, whilst French policy-makers and moralists professed confidence in the benefits of marriage and procreation, they worried about the long-term viability of the normative model, and were engaged in a constant act of policing and maintaining its boundaries. Judith Surkis demonstrates that as all men acceded to political rights in the Third Republic, which was founded in 1870 on the principle of universal male suffrage, conjugal love and commitment became the criteria guaranteeing the moral character of the male citizen. The ideal Frenchman was someone whose citizenship was presumed to be congruent with his manhood. People who did not conform to the ideal, such as young men who did not marry, men who channelled their sexual energies towards self-pleasure rather than procreation, men who acted upon their sexual desire for other men and adulterers who carried with them the mark of venereal disease, were regarded as threats to the social and moral order.

As we shall see below, novels that depicted such non-normative figures were precisely those that the law targeted in both England and France. As women's rights progressed and men's status became challenged, the very recognition of the precariousness of masculinity fuelled and justified the state's efforts to enforce its normative effects all the more stringently, and one way in which this enforcement took place was through the proscription of non-conformist gender identities in the courtroom.

48 Valerie Sanders, *The Tragi-Comedy of Victorian Fatherhood* (Cambridge: Cambridge University Press, 2009) 5.

49 Ibid. 6.

50 Christopher E. Forth, '*La Civilisation* and its discontents: modernity, manhood and the body in the early Third Republic' in Christopher E. Forth and Bertrand Taithe (eds), *French Masculinities* (Basingstoke, New York: Palgrave Macmillan, 2007) 85–103 at 89.

(II) Law, literature and masculinity

As the normative force of bourgeois masculinity waned in the mid-nineteenth to the early twentieth centuries, law and literature emerged as two discourses critical to the representation of gendered identities. A number of critics have, either explicitly or implicitly, acknowledged the combination of complicity and antagonism which marked the relationship between the two in this period. Jan-Melissa Schramm has argued that the competition between them stems, paradoxically, from the very similarity in their modes of presenting reality: the Victorian assumption that fiction, like law, 'must be tied to a paradigm of evidentiary realism' created 'the conditions for the conflict of literature and the law'.[51]

Schramm highlights the enactment of the Prisoners' Counsel Act, the legislative instrument which gave counsel the right to speak or to represent the thoughts and intentions of the accused, as a pivotal event in this conflict. After the passage of the Act, lawyers and writers found themselves in the similar position of claiming the right to narrate the mind of another, be it a literary character of their own creation or a client whom they defended. She notes that this commonality generated a profound anxiety about the possibility of manipulating evidence and falsely depicting a state of affairs on the part of both parties. The result was that: 'each profession . . . sought to justify its model of reality by accusing the other of "misrepresentation", or a failure to present evidence responsibly'.

Like Schramm, Lisa Rodensky focuses on the criminal law and she argues that, whilst legal discourse presumes a continuity between action and intention and 'does expect a wicked act to tell the story of a wicked mind', in literature the narrator's direct access to a character's mind can expose moments of slippage or incongruity between a mental state and a physical deed, hence raising the question of how guilt and innocence should be determined in the mind of the reader.[52] Rodensky's analysis shows that, whilst nineteenth-century fiction did not overtly subvert the law's paradigms, it did put pressure on the assumptions underpinning them and threw into question firmly entrenched ideas in the criminal law.

Literature can thus be said to constitute what Kristin Kalsem calls 'outlaw texts', which, whilst 'not considered official legal texts and thus "out" of the purview of much legal inquiry', shared some of its key concerns and could 'imagine new possibilities for law and justice' from a different vantage point.[53] The work of Schramm, Rodensky and Kalsem reveals the complex and multifarious interactions between law and literature at his time.

Literary trials, in which writers or their publishers are brought to the dock because of the publication of literary works, constitute especially revealing

51 Jan-Melissa Schramm, *Testimony and Advocacy in Victorian Law, Literature and Theology* (Cambridge: Cambridge University Press, 2000) 183.

52 Lisa Rodensky, *The Crime in Mind: Criminal Responsibility and the Victorian Novel* (Oxford: Oxford University Press, 2003) 39.

53 Kalsem (n 6) 7.

instances of such interactions: the appearance of a literary text in the legal setting of a courtroom can be considered as a moment in which literature literally comes into confrontation with the law, or an occasion of inter-disciplinary contact which leads us to think anew about epistemological similarities and divisions between them. Moreover, in light of the contradictions and challenges to normative masculinity, these trials can potentially shed light on how literature responded to, bolstered or challenged the law's representation of masculinity.

A number of historico-legal studies have highlighted the gendered dimension of law. Angus McLaren has shown that the nineteenth and early-twentieth century courtroom was often a place in which the boundaries of acceptable masculine behaviour were policed. He points out that a significant number of criminal trials turned on whether a defendant had acted in a 'manly' manner, so that what was at stake was not only the question of whether a specific legal rule had been infracted but of how to differentiate between normal and deviant male behaviour. The work of the courts thus consisted not only of drawing 'a clear line between the criminal and noncriminal worlds', but also of determining whether 'certain types of men had forfeited their right to be treated as human beings'.[54]

Martin Wiener's study of Victorian criminal justice and male violence is premised on a similar vision of the alliance between law and normative masculinity: the changes made to the criminal law guaranteeing greater protection for women against male violence were also giving form to the belief that 'the law-abiding, self-disciplined, marriage-and-woman-respecting Englishman (and Scotsman)' were the 'cultural ideal' and the 'archetype' of masculinity.[55] The channelling of juridical energies to marriage reform and women's rights, which at first glance seems to disrupt the alignment between law and normative masculinity, meant that men who shunned marriage, who did not desire women, who engaged in male–male sexual practices or who were insufficiently self-disciplined to devote their sexual energy to the reproductive cause became increasingly regarded as reprehensible in the eyes of the law.

Even trials that did not exclusively deal with the question of what constituted manliness or acceptable male behaviour could be grounded in a gender dynamic. The trial of Alfred Dreyfus for treason is a case in point. In 1894, Dreyfus was convicted of selling military secrets to the Germans and exiled to Devil's Island, off the coast of French Guyana. Christopher Forth has demonstrated that the trial became the focal point of a debate about the place of Jews in France that was suffused with metaphors of gender, and brought to the forefront prejudices rooted not simply in racial difference but more specifically in a supposed Jewish unmanliness. He notes that there was an assumption that 'Jewish men, whether due

54 Angus McLaren, *The Trials of Masculinity: Policing Sexual Boundaries, 1870–1930* (Chicago: University of Chicago Press, 1997) 13.

55 Martin Wiener, *Men of Blood: Violence, Manliness and Criminal Justice in Victorian England* (Cambridge: Cambridge University Press, 2004) 29.

to age-old customs or congenital factors, were bookish, sedentary beings, whose weakness, cowardice, and effeminacy rendered them unfit for military service'.[56]

They were therefore often depicted as the opposite of the brave, nation-loving soldier. Alfred Dreyfus was put on trial not only for the specific crime of treason, but for his lack of manly attributes. Forth notes in particular how the courtroom audience and the press were outraged at his stoicism in face of the accusations, a stoicism that had paradoxically been ingrained in him through years of education in the French school system. They construed his lack of emotion as a kind of feminine passivity, and expected 'a true man of honour' to have actively and 'spontaneously rebelled against the humiliation of public degradation'.[57] Dreyfus did not have his name cleared until 1906, when he was officially exonerated by the *Cour de Cassation*. Forth's analysis shows that, even though the treason trial was not concerned with questions of manliness on strictly legal grounds, its outcome was very much dependent on the conflation of Frenchness and masculinity, and on the concomitant perception of Jewishness as the signifier of passivity, femininity and emasculation.

The work of McLaren, Wiener and Forth together indicates that, in a legal trial, the law often defends the normative constructions of masculinity and becomes part of a social infrastructure bolstering conventional ideas about what it means to behave in a 'manly' fashion. Whilst it is difficult, if not impossible, to generalise about the ideological dimension of the law in all cases at all times, these studies suggest that it is important to be vigilant about the assumptions about masculinity underpinning legal provisions that are purportedly gender neutral, especially in a historical period when the established form of hegemonic masculinity was increasingly challenged, and different gendered identities jostled for legitimacy and cultural supremacy.

The ideological work that literature performs is no less complex. Commentators have been unable to agree on whether literature reinforces cultural norms or whether it undermines them. On the one hand, critics such as Jonathan Dollimore have argued that art, including literature, 'constantly transgresses the limits which define what it is to be decently human', a central part of which could be said to be the determination of what constitutes acceptable male desire and behaviour.[58] Dollimore has further noted that literature constituted a form of 'dangerous knowledge', a vision of humanity that society refuses to acknowledge because of its potential to undermine existing structures and sanctioned identities.[59] He concludes that literature is by definition culturally insubordinate, and has the potential to expose and overturn normative identities.

56 Christopher E. Forth, *The Dreyfus Affair and the Crisis of French Manhood* (Baltimore: Johns Hopkins University Press, 2004) 18.

57 Ibid. 31.

58 Jonathan Dollimore, *Sex, Literature and Censorship* (Cambridge: Polity, 2001) x.

59 Ibid. xii.

In a classic essay, Hans Robert Jauss makes a similar point about literary transgression: he posits that literature enacts a shift in the readers' 'horizon of expectations', creating an aesthetic distance between 'the familiarity of previous aesthetic experiences' and its literary innovation, and that this distance places a demand on readers to reassess their existing relationship to the text.[60] For Jauss, there is something inherently anti-conformist and unsettling about literature; it is the disturbance or disruption of orthodoxies, conventions and states of knowledge enacted by a text that constitutes its literary quality.

On the other hand, D.A. Miller has famously argued against the 'subversive hypothesis' of critics such as Dollimore and Jauss. Miller contends that literature, in so far as it is an integral part of culture, must at least to some degree reproduce and conform to the ideology of that culture. As such, literature does not so much undermine the existing cultural economy as take part in the formation of 'a subject habituated to psychic displacements, evacuations, reinvestments, in a social order whose totalizing power circulates all the more easily for being pulverized'.[61] In other words, instead of making any easy assumptions about the subversive potential of literature, it may be more productive to take any claim about its subversive power as precisely, and unwittingly, reinforcing the social order of which the literary text forms a part.

In this study, I will not attempt to adjudicate between these opposing views, and I will avoid making any presumptions about the nature and function of literature. Instead, I hope to allow the individual novels and trials examined here to speak for themselves. In other words, my argument about the work of literature, and about the engagement between law and literature in the construction of gendered identities, will proceed on a case-by-case basis, through a close reading of the most significant literary-legal events of the time. Such an approach leads to the conclusion that, even though not all fiction of the period could be considered subversive in gender terms, it is undeniable that novels which were deemed legally questionable, such as *Madame Bovary*, *Charlot s'amuse*, *La Terre*, *The Picture of Dorian Gray* and *The Well of Loneliness* posited visions that interrogated, challenged and undermined established gender structures and deeply entrenched sexual hierarchies in the nineteenth and early twentieth centuries, even if their visions were still influenced by ideas and norms about proper masculine desires and behaviour of the time. Normative masculinity was arguably based on a 'bourgeois script', which enforced 'compulsory heterosexuality and compulsory matrimony' and which permitted few deviations; the novels showed how the narrative of masculinity could be written differently, and their rewriting of the 'bourgeois script' was a key factor triggering the heavy-handed legal response.[62]

60 Hans Robert Jauss, 'Literary history as a challenge to literary theory' (1970) 2 *New Literary History* 7–37 at 14.

61 D.A. Miller, *The Novel and the Police* (Berkeley: University of California Press, 1988) xiii.

62 Herbert Sussman, *Victorian Masculinities: Manhood and Masculine Poetics in Early Victorian Literature and Art* (Cambridge: Cambridge University Press, 1995) 16.

The figures of the androgyne, the onanist, the patricide, the homosexual and the lesbian in the novels all questioned values or assumptions inherent in the procreative, familial model of bourgeois male identity, and constituted alternative or even dissident ways of thinking gender. The high-profile prosecutions with which the law reacted to the publication of these novels or the allegedly indecent behaviour of their authors indicates that an integral part of the texts' literary effect was the disruption of the boundaries between hegemonic and marginalised identities, normal and abnormal behaviour, and respectable and vilified modes of existence, even if these prosecutions did not necessarily result in convictions, given the specific circumstances of the cases. To disregard the subversive potential of these novels is to disregard a significant dimension of their literary quality, as well as a crucial aspect of the legal response to their publication.

I will focus specifically on the confrontation between fiction and the law because the novel was the most popular literary genre of the nineteenth century. A number of socio-economic factors contributed to its generic dominance at this historical juncture, including the expansion in the middle and lower middle-class population, a rising literary rate, the expansion of railway travel – leading to greater demand for reading material on train journeys – and an increasing amount of middle-class leisure time brought about by the hiring of domestic servants. For the working class, reading, especially fiction reading, provided an escape from the tedium of the workplace.[63]

Partly because of its wide readership, the novel became a source of great anxiety amongst moralists and jurists. As Patrick Brantlinger has shown, works of fiction were frequently depicted as 'poisonous' books, which exerted a corrupting influence on the minds of their readers.[64] Schramm has similarly argued that there surfaced in the 1840s a fear that 'criminal acts may somehow be transmitted through space and adhere to those who do not want to own them' through reading novels; it was believed that a mimetic textual effect could cause the reader to re-enact any transgressive behaviour that was depicted in fiction.[65]

There were particular concerns over the potential effect that the genre would have on young people, especially young women, as reflected by the episode in *Madame Bovary* in which Charles's mother attempts to restrict Emma's access to novels by cancelling her subscription to the lending library in Rouen. Worries about female reading were rooted in 'the prevalence of assumptions about women's greater sensitivity and sensibility', assumptions that were believed to have 'biological grounds' because a woman's body was organised differently from that

63 Richard D. Altick, *The English Common Reader: A Social History of the Mass Reading Public, 1800–1900* (Columbus: Ohio State University Press, 1957) 81–99.

64 Patrick Brantlinger, *The Reading Lesson: The Threat of Mass Literacy in Nineteenth-Century British Fiction* (Bloomington: Indiana University Press, 1998) 22.

65 Jan-Melissa Schramm, '"The anatomy of a barrister's tongue": rhetoric, satire, and the Victorian bar in England' (2004) 32 *Victorian Literature and Culture* 285–303 at 298.

of a man.[66] Specifically, it was thought that a woman's instincts of child-rearing and her instinctive capacity to develop close ties with her children meant that 'such instincts as sympathetic imagination, and a ready capacity to identify with the experience of others' were 'unalterable facts about her mental operations, and hence, by extension, about her processes of reading', making her especially susceptible to the influence of undesirable reading material.[67]

The cultural anxiety about the impact of fiction reading on young women was also registered by the law. In the *Charlot s'amuse* trial, the Director of Public Prosecutions in Paris decided to initiate proceedings against Bonnetain in part because of a letter from an anonymous writer underscoring the dangers that the novel posed to young women. The letter stated that it was freely available in a *cabinet de lecture* and could easily 'fall into the hands of children and young girls', especially if their mother or guardian had not read the novel themselves and had left it lying around.[68] The letter triggered a legal process ending in Bonnetain's conviction for obscenity.

Even though much discussion centred on the adverse effects of novels on young women, there were also widespread fears about their impact on young men. Oscar Wilde alludes to this fear in the only novel that he wrote, *The Picture of Dorian Gray*, in which Henry Wotton gives Dorian a 'yellow book', a French novel whose plot seems distinctly similar to that of Joris-Karl Huysman's *À Rebours* even though, as we will see later on, Wilde denied the link between his own novel and that of the French writer when he was put on trial. The narrator describes the novel's effect on the young man in the following way: 'the mere cadence of the sentences, the subtle monotony of their music . . . produced in the mind of the lad, as he passed from chapter to chapter, a form of reverie, a malady of dreaming, that made him unconscious of the falling day and creeping shadows'.[69]

As its influence on Dorian intensifies, 'the heavy odour of incense seemed to cling about its pages and to trouble the brain'. Its impact is here described as a disturbance of mental and sensory faculties. Novels were dangerous to young men because they were, to return to the metaphor which Brantlinger highlighted, 'poisonous'. As the status of procreative, conjugal masculinity came under increasing strain, the possible perverse influences which novel reading was imagined to have on the male readership caused great concern in both England and France.

Interpretation played a key role in the understanding of the literary and legal representations of gendered identity in these trials. The arguments of both the prosecution and the defence lawyers were premised on competing interpretations of the novels: the lawyers representing the author or the publisher would attempt

66 Kate Flint, *The Woman Reader, 1837–1914* (Oxford: Clarendon Press, 1993) 54.
67 Ibid. 57.
68 Anonymous letter, Dossier D2U8 174, Archive de Paris.
69 Oscar Wilde, *The Picture of Dorian Gray* (1891) (London: Penguin Books, 2003) 121.

to deflect accusations of obscenity or gross indecency through their readings, whilst the lawyers on the opposing side would put forward more hostile interpretations of the same text. Since the courtroom was a forum for the competition between gender identities, the legal interpretation of fiction which formed the crux of the trials not only determined whether specific legal rules had been infringed by the publication of the novels, but performed the wider cultural work of bolstering, shaping or challenging different forms of masculinity in the nineteenth and early twentieth centuries.

The more favourable readings of the novels often argued for the acceptance of alternative conceptions of gender, yet lawyers eager to secure an acquittal at times reinforced existing norms by muting the subversive voice of the text. As Dollimore has pointed out, 'those who love art the most also censor it the most', in that writers, academics and lawyers who defend art against conservative critics often unwittingly and paradoxically reproduce the censoring effect of these conservative critics.[70] Hostile readings of the novels often reiterated the more conventional ideas about masculinity of the legal establishment, although, as we shall see, they sometimes inadvertently revealed points of commonality between the discursive formations of identity between literature and law.

The link between literature, legal reading and gender is a complex and multifaced one. This book will therefore focus on the reading process of the lawyers and judges in the trials and examine their implications for gender normativity. The 'law and literature' enterprise has traditionally been divided into the study of 'law in literature', or the study of the representation of legal institutions, concepts and agents within a literary text, and 'law as literature', or the interpretation of legal material through the lens of literary theory.[71] The analysis here could be considered as a study of 'literature in law', or the way fiction was interpreted within a legal setting. One way in which the gender dimension of the trials could be examined is through the mode of analysis most attuned to the ways in which close readings of rhetorical symptoms in a discursive field can contribute to revealing hitherto unrecognised, repressed or disavowed dimensions of gender and sexuality, that of psychoanalytic cultural criticism.

(III) Psychoanalytic cultural criticism or the interpretation of legal interpretation

Writing in the context of the *Madame Bovary* trial, Dominick LaCapra notes that it is important to distinguish between the novel's 'ordinary crime', the infraction of

70 Dollimore (n 58) 96.

71 Helpful introductions to the 'Law and Literature' enterprise include Ian Ward, *Law and Literature: Possibilities and Perspectives* (Cambridge: Cambridge University Press, 1995); Kieran Dolin, *A Critical Introduction to Law and Literature* (Cambridge: Cambridge University Press, 2007) and Austin Sarat, Matthew Anderson and Cathrine O. Frank (eds), *Law and Humanities: An Introduction* (Cambridge: Cambridge University Press, 2009).

a specific legal rule or doctrine and its 'ideological or political "crime"', or its disturbance to the wider cultural conditions which underpinned the impulse to prosecute.[72] LaCapra argues that the novel's disruption of these conditions may be less readily detectable to the critic than the specific doctrinal issues at stake in the trial. This study takes its cue from LaCapra and approaches the trials of modern fiction on two levels: on the level of doctrine and on the level of the less readily perceivable, but no less critical battle of gender hegemony taking place in the courtroom. It will examine the alleged infringement of specific legal rules, such as the common law definition of obscenity laid down in the case of *R v Hicklin*[73] in Victorian England or the provision on 'outrage against public and religious morals' under which Flaubert was prosecuted in mid-nineteenth-century France. It will further examine, in detail, the legal attempt to maintain and reinforce gender norms and the novel's interrogation of those norms beyond the surface operation of doctrine.

In light of the two inter-related yet distinct dynamics in the trials – one more apparent and doctrinal, the other less readily detectable, but perhaps precisely for this reason more significant – it is necessary to ask how one could analyse the latent, second-level processes at work. With what methods of interpretation, through what critical lens can we approach the anxieties about literature's interrogation of normative masculinity underlying the legal interpretation of the novels? Tosh's observation that the ways in which hegemonic masculinity legitimises itself are 'often unconscious' gestures towards an answer: one way of addressing this issue could be through psychoanalytic literary and cultural criticism, the set of hermeneutic practices concerned with giving form to, amplifying and understanding precisely the meanings of a text that are not fully expressed, or are expressed in a distorted manner.[74]

Robert Ferguson notes that 'the surface narrative of a courtroom transcript is not unlike the consciousness of an individual; both offer the official record of what passes for explanation, and both know themselves to be under distinct pressure from other levels of explanation that need to be contained'.[75] The ways in which fiction draws on, revises and subverts the hegemony of a conception of masculinity as heterosexual, conjugal and familial is arguably one of the 'other levels of explanation' through which to understand the literary trials, and this study will draw on psychoanalytic modes of reading as a means of bringing them to the forefront. The intangible, invisible, yet pervasive forces shaping gender constructions in the courts can also be said to constitute a juridical unconscious, a dimension which could be meaningfully discussed through the concepts, vocabulary and framework of psychoanalysis.

72 Dominick LaCapra, *'Madame Bovary' on Trial* (Ithaca: Cornell University Press, 1982) 7.
73 (1868) LR 3 QB 360.
74 Tosh, 'Hegemonic masculinity and the history of gender' (n 20) 44.
75 Robert A. Ferguson, 'Untold stories in the law' in Peter Brooks and Paul Gewirtz (eds), *Law's Stories: Narrative and Rhetoric in the Law* (Yale University Press, New Haven 1996) 84–99 at 89.

The analysis presented in the following pages is inspired by Peter Goodrich's pioneering work on interpreting the law in a psychoanalytic frame. Goodrich claims that for the law to establish itself as a determinate discourse and discipline, it required 'its own effigy, its own paternity, its own forms of legitimacy or familial identity and role'.[76] That is to say, the law 'writes so as to have a past, it writes so as to lay claim to an identity'; it actively forges a form for itself as law by establishing a lineage, a history, a transmission of traditions, knowledge and insignia, which differentiates it from other discourses. Part of this forging of disciplinary and institutional identity is the process of differentiating itself from everything that it deems unsuitable, and then repressing them to prevent their existence as alternative possibilities of law. The basis of the law can thus be regarded as a forgetting of the commonalities it shares with other discourses.[77]

The attentive critic can locate the points at which the forgotten alternatives to the law return to challenge its disciplinary unity. Goodrich's most powerful move is to posit a mode of reading that focuses on rhetorical tropes in a legal text such as antonomasia, allegoria and synecdoche as symptoms through which the critic can retrieve the repressed of the law. It is thus a mode of analysis which is premised on close reading, the practice of which is also fundamental to literary criticism. By paying careful attention to the rhetorical dimension of the trials, his work gestures towards a way in which the level of meaning determination that lies beyond the conscious, doctrinal surface of the case can be accessed.

Goodrich's hermeneutic praxis closely models itself on Freud's own mode of interpret-ation. Freud believes that a patient's symptom carries 'a psychical significance, a meaning'.[78] The symptom's meaning is not fixed, but 'is lent to it, soldered to it . . . and in every instance the meaning can be a different one, according to the nature of the suppressed thoughts which are struggling for expression'.[79] Goodrich's work innovatively incorporates psychoanalytic thinking into legal analysis: the interpret-ation of rhetorical tropes as symptoms is faithful to the Freudian hermeneutic method, but since the symptom is always overdetermined as a signifier, Goodrich also avoids the charge of dogmatism and reductionism that is often directed at psychoanalytic criticism.

I will approach the second-level dynamic of gender construction in the legal cases through a close reading of the novels, the trial transcripts and the judicial opinions in a psychoanalytic frame. Throughout this study, metaphors, repetitions and other narrative structures in the law are approached as points of entry into

76 Peter Goodrich, *Oedipus Lex: Psychoanalysis, History, Law* (Berkeley: University of California Press, 1995) 25.

77 Ibid. 27.

78 Sigmund Freud, 'Fragment of an Analysis of a Case of Hysteria' (1905) in James Strachey (ed and trans), *The Standard Edition of the Complete Psychological Works of Sigmund Freud, 24 vols* (London: Vintage, 2001) VII, 3–125 at 40.

79 Ibid. 41.

overlooked, unacknowledged or repressed dimensions of gender and sexuality. For example, in the *Madame Bovary* trial, the prosecution lawyer repeatedly described Flaubert's novel as a 'lascivious painting'. This metaphor, so insistently relied upon in the case, has been curiously overlooked in the existing scholarship on the novel or the trial. I will demonstrate in the next chapter that reading the metaphor in relation to Freud's essays on fetishism can shed light on the prosecution's attempt to suppress the gender transgression enacted by *Madame Bovary*, which was taking place beyond, and at the same time as, the prosecution of Flaubert on the doctrinal grounds of obscenity.

Finally, by drawing on this psychoanalytic paradigm, I will demonstrate that the trials not only shed light on the ways in which literary and legal discourses confronted each other over the definition of masculinity, but constitute scenes of reading – encounters between legal readers and literary texts – which point towards a new way of understanding the relationship between law and literature. The psychoanalytic literary critic Mary Jacobus has argued that scenes of reading 'involve concepts or unconscious phantasies of inner and outer, absence and boundaries', and 'the transmission of thoughts and feelings' between self and other.[80] To this list of terms whose binary opposition is problematised in the reading counter we could add that of law and literature.

By reading the legal and literary texts next to, and across, one another, I will posit that the law repeats the very questions and problems of representation of the literary texts that are condemned under specific legal provisions. The analysis of the five trials reveals that law and literature are intertwined discourses. Even though they seem to be in an antagonistic relationship in the courtroom and align themselves with competing models of masculinity, both the legal text and the literary text are underpinned by common tropes and structures. As Goodrich has argued, the law 'is a literature that denies its literary qualities'; it will not acknowledge that its modes of argumentation and reasoning are forms of narrative because that would mean undermining its distinctive discursive identity.[81]

In each of the five cases in this study, the juxtaposition of the legal text and the literary text in the courtroom leads to a reconfiguration of the boundary between the two discourses. The turn to psychoanalytic concepts will be especially clear in Chapters 1, 3 and 5. Chapters 2 and 4, although drawing on the vocabulary of psychoanalytic methodology less explicitly, are attuned to the uncanny resemblance or double-ness of the two discourses in part because of the wider psychoanalytic frame of this study. When law and literature are brought together, the disciplinary certainty of the law also comes under challenge and the latent similarities begin to come to light. The following chapters will show that the law unknowingly shares many of the characteristics of the novels it so loudly denounces.

80 Mary Jacobus, *Psychoanalysis and the Scene of Reading* (Oxford: Oxford University Press, 1999) 9.

81 Peter Goodrich, *Law in the Courts of Love: Literature and Other Minor Jurisprudences* (London: Routledge, 1996) 112.

In Chapter 1, I will argue that the publication of Flaubert's *Madame Bovary* led to legal prosecution not simply because it is a novel about adultery, but because Emma's 'androgyny', as highlighted by the poet Charles Baudelaire, challenged the very distinction between 'male' and 'female' so central to French society at the time. Flaubert's narrative style does not allow for an unequivocal gender identification on the part of the reader. I will interpret the novel as the site of a radical gender mobility that the prosecution attempted, unsuccessfully, to arrest through its recourse to the rhetoric of realist art. I will further demonstrate the ways in which the defence highlighted the novel's radical textual plurality as a strategy of advocacy.

Charlot s'amuse, Bonnetain's narrative of a man's indulgence in a sexual act which the medical discourse represented as anti-social, morally harmful and, most importantly, depletive of a man's reproductive capacity, unsurprisingly received a hostile reading in the courtroom. In Chapter 2, I will situate Bonnetain's novel, and the obscenity trial, in the context of the late-nineteenth-century medical discourse on onanism, and will examine how anxieties about declining male fertility, although not explicitly articulated, were nonetheless registered in the courtroom. In light of the defence's argument that the novel could be read as a scientific treatise on onanism, I will also reopen the question about the relationship between naturalist fiction and science.

In Zola's *La Terre*, the Oedipal conflict at the heart of the narrative not only disturbs the myth of 'father-rule' within the family, but suggests that murderous impulses directed by the son against the father in fact lurk beneath the thin veneer of civilisation in every family. In Chapter 3, I examine the structure of repetition underpinning both the novel and the trials, and I argue that the law operates with the same violence which it finds reprehensible in literature.

Wilde's trials for gross indecency reveal anxieties over homosociality, which Sedgwick has underscored; the possibility that a man who is married with two children, and who at least outwardly appeared to conform to the model of domestic masculinity, could desire other men necessarily puts pressure on the question of what constitutes masculinity. In Chapter 4, I will examine the trials as a clash between two different modes of reading literature by the lawyer and man of letters, as represented by the barrister Edward Carson and Wilde himself, respectively.

Finally, Hall's novel presents the mannish lesbian as an unprecedented challenge to masculinity in that the heroine, Stephen Gordon, competes with the heterosexual male for single women in the marriage market and triumphs over him, even though she chooses to give up her prize. Chapter 5 completes my examination of the gender implications of fiction within the law and of literary-legal relations by bringing the discussion into the twentieth century. In that chapter, I will draw on the notion of the return of the repressed to highlight the dynamic of silencing in both the literary and the legal discourses in the trials. The figures posited by the novels in this study – the androgyne, the onanist, the patricide, the homosexual and the lesbian – presented alternative models of gender whose existence raised the possibility that the entrenched distinction between hegemonic masculinity and other identities could be reconfigured, and that the normative basis of the domestic model of manhood could not be taken for granted.

The rhetorical structures of the legal arguments presented in court provide entry points into the interpretive assumptions behind the law's response to the literary representations of gender. The confrontation of literature and law also constituted scenes of reading that revealed the interconnections and cross-overs between the two fields. Against the background of the destabilisation of the reproductive, familial mode of bourgeois male identity that was already gathering pace, the battle for legitimacy between hegemonic and peripheral gendered categories, the clash of interpretative tactics between some of the most famous lawyers of the period and the confrontation between literary and legal discursive formations combined to make the drama of the court cases as riveting as the novels which gave rise to them.

Chapter 1

The *Madame Bovary* trial: the lascivious painting of Flaubert's androgyne

Flaubert's *Madame Bovary* occupies a central place in the history of modern fiction; it is both a quintessential nineteenth-century 'realist' novel and a precursor of the early twentieth-century 'modernist' novel. This duality would play an important role in the obscenity trial of 1857, which took place because of the novel's alleged lasciviousness. Flaubert was admired by some of his contemporaries as the master of realism, an artistic vision characterised by a resolute focus on contemporaneity, a turn away from classical models and high personages in favour of the representation of ordinary people and experiences, a commitment to truthful depictions of reality and an interest in the immediate and the transitory over the eternal or the universal.[1]

Literature and visual art are closely related in French realism: intellectual and personal exchanges between artists and writers were frequent; similar subjects from the less aristocratic walks of life recurred in the novel and the visual arts, and realist fiction was frequently compared with paintings in the mid-nineteenth century. The parallels between realist fiction and art are so strong that Peter Brooks has suggested that realism should be understood as a representation that 'turns crucially on its visuality'.[2] As we will see, the critique of the visuality of realist fiction formed the crux of the prosecution's argument in the trial.

Flaubert himself was strongly averse to being labelled a 'realist' writer: 'I execrate what is commonly called "realism", even though I'm regarded as one of its high priests'.[3] He wanted *Madame Bovary* to be 'dependent on nothing external' and for it to be 'held together by the internal strength of its style'.[4] The novel's focus on style over content and its textual independence from 'external' reality

1 See Peter Brooks, *Realist Vision* (New Haven: Yale University Press, 2005) 1–21. For an early study that continues to resonate, see Bernard Weinberg, *French Realism: the Critical Reaction, 1830–1870* (London: Oxford University Press, 1937).

2 Ibid. 71.

3 Letter to George Sand dated 6 February 6 1876 in Francis Steegmuller (ed), *The Letters of Gustave Flaubert, 1857–1880* (London: Belknap Press, 1982) 230–31 at 231.

4 Letter to Louise Colet dated 16 January 1852 in Francis Steegmuller (ed), *The Letters of Gustave Flaubert, 1830–1857* (London: Belknap Press, 1980) 154.

arguably gives it a more distinctively modernist echo. Moreover, Flaubert's *style indirect libre* – a mode of storytelling whereby the narrative viewpoint shifts between the thoughts and impressions of the characters and of the narrator without any signposting – looks forward to the turn towards interiority characteristic of the modernist novel: in his lectures Vladimir Nabokov identifies Flaubert as a key influence on Franz Kafka, and speculates that: 'without Flaubert there would be no Marcel Proust in France, no James Joyce in Ireland'.[5]

As I will show, Flaubert's defence lawyer would advance an argument which foregrounded the novel's modernist style. *Madame Bovary*'s position as simultaneously the epitome of mid-nineteenth-century realism and a curiously anachronistic instance of literary modernism makes it an apposite starting point for a study of literary trials and literary-legal relations in the modern period.

In this chapter, I will examine the ways in which *Madame Bovary* was read in the courtroom, and combine historicist and psychoanalytic approaches to investigate the construction of gender in both fiction and the law. The first section focuses on the novel and interprets it as the site of mobile, indeterminate gender identifications whose textual effects challenged the conventional notions of gender in mid-nineteenth-century France. Central to this section is the notion of androgyny: the novel's construction of the androgyne can be understood as one cause of the obscenity trial in that it threatened to undermine the entrenched distinctions between masculinity and femininity of the period.

The second section studies the ways in which *Madame Bovary* was read in a legal setting; it brings the method of close reading usually associated with literary criticism to bear on the text of the trial transcript, focusing on the courtroom rhetoric to explore the ways in which the law attempted to contain the novel's subversive force. It argues that the prosecution presented the novel in visual terms in an attempt to arrest its free play of gender identifications through the dynamic of fetishism. The defence, on its part, paradoxically adopted the radical mobility of gender in the novel as the basis of its counter-argument by demonstrating the same mobility on the level of form. It was this intertextual reasoning that determined the outcome of the trial in Flaubert's favour; the novel's very radicality that led to legal censure in the first place was also the element which secured Flaubert's acquittal.

(I) Two kinds of androgyny: reading *Madame Bovary*

French androgynies

Madame Bovary appeared in six instalments between October and December 1856 in the *Revue de Paris*, a liberal publication founded by, amongst others, Flaubert's

5 Vladimir Nabokov, *Lectures on Literature* (Fredson Bowers (ed), London: Weidenfeld and Nicolson, 1980) 147.

friend Maxime Du Camp.[6] Even though Du Camp kept the promise to publish the novel which he had made to Flaubert five years previously, he was attuned to the pressures of censorship and advised the author to allow his text to be 'pruned' by the editors: 'Be brave, close your eyes during the operation, and have confidence – if not in our talent, at least in the experience we have acquired in such matters and also in our affection for you'.[7]

Flaubert was furious at this intervention; he scrawled '*Gigantesque!*' on Du Camp's letter, threw it into a drawer and did not deign to reply. There were further disputes between the two friends, and eventually a compromise was reached: the novel would be published, but a long passage about a cab journey through the streets of Rouen, in which the movement of the vehicle was suggestive of the love-making of Emma and her lover Léon inside it, would be omitted. As serialisation proceeded, however, the *Revue* became increasingly worried by complaints amongst its subscribers about the novel's immorality, and also learned that the government censor had initiated proceedings against the magazine and Flaubert for breaching the obscenity laws of the Second Empire. The editors expunged another passage from the December instalment and advised Flaubert to make further cuts. Flaubert refused to do so on the basis that such excisions would only 'weaken' the novel: 'I will not make a correction, not a cut; I will not suppress a comma; nothing, nothing!'[8]

The disagreement intensified to such a degree that Flaubert insisted on the cancellation of the final instalment, but it eventually reached its readers with a preface in which Flaubert disclaimed responsibility for the published version. The *Revue*'s efforts ultimately did little more than antagonise the author and failed to pre-empt the legal proceedings: on 30 January 1857, Flaubert, along with representatives from the *Revue,* appeared before the *Tribunal Correctionnel* in Paris charged with having committed an 'outrage against public and religious morals, or against decency' (*outrage à la morale publique et religieuse, ou aux bonnes moeurs*) under a law originally passed on 17 May 1819. Ernest Pinard, the deputy prosecutor at the imperial court, represented the French Government, and Jules Sénard represented the author and the publisher.[9]

In his perceptive analysis of the *Madame Bovary* trial, Dominick LaCapra argues that the court 'processed as ordinary crime what was, in significant and special ways, ideological or political "crime" '.[10] In other words, even though the allegation ostensibly concerned the outrage to public morality and religion which *Madame*

6 For an interpretation of the exchanges between Flaubert and his editors as a process for the construction of authorship, see Ramona Naddaff, 'Confronting the frugal editors: the *Revue de Paris*' *Madame Bovary*' (2007) 3 *Law, Culture and the Humanities* 266–92 at 291.

7 Letter dated 14 July 1856 in Steegmuller, *Letters 1830–1857* (n 4) 219.

8 Letter to Léon Laurent-Pichat dated 7 December 1856 in Steegmuller, *Letters 1830–1857* (n 4) 221.

9 For a helpful discussion of the events leading up to the trial, see René Dumesnil, '*Madame Bovary*' *de Flaubert: Étude et Analyse* (Paris: La Pensée moderne, 1968) 253–83.

10 Dominick LaCapra, '*Madame Bovary*' *on Trial* (Ithaca: Cornell University Press, 1982) 7.

Bovary incited, the real issue at stake was the ways in which the novel challenged 'the validity of the norms, categories, and criteria tacitly assumed by the trial as the basis of understanding and judgment'.[11] LaCapra identifies three interrelated components to the "crime": the novel dismantled the opposition between marriage and adultery, it undermined the difference between the sacred and the profane, and it provided no reliable or coherent centre of narration. It is this final, stylistic, element of the novel which receives the most sustained analysis in LaCapra's reading.

The *style indirect libre* of *Madame Bovary* has received much critical attention.[12] LaCapra's contribution lies in identifying the political and ideological significance of Flaubert's style in the context of the trial. He argues that since Emma's story is told in 'a dual mode involving both proximity and distance – empathy and irony – in the relation of the narrator to the character or narrated object', it becomes impossible to tell whether the author is critical or sympathetic of his heroine's behaviour.[13] In the words of Pinard, the prosecution lawyer: 'Who is able condemn this woman in the book? Nobody. Such is the conclusion. In the book there is not one character that is able to condemn her'.[14] The absence of a clear authorial stance gives rise to two incompatible interpretations of *Madame Bovary*, as represented by the opposing sides in the trial. For the prosecution, Pinard argued that Flaubert was sympathetic to Emma, read the novel as a glorification of infidelity, and claimed that it ought to be subtitled 'History of the Adulteries of a Provincial Woman'.[15]

For the defence, however, Sénard interpreted the novel as a cautionary moral tale and argued that Emma's suffering was a warning to its readers not to succumb to illicit desire. In response to Pinard's accusation that Flaubert had written 'adulterous poetry', Sénard contended that the writer aimed to cultivate virtue by instilling a horror of vice.[16] The exculpating interpretation which Sénard posited is a familiar one in the history of literary realism: the preface to Daniel Defoe's

11 Ibid. 31.

12 Of the numerous works on Flaubert's style, I have found the following most useful: Erich Auerbach, *Mimesis: The Representation of Reality in Western Literature* (William R. Trask (trans), Princeton: Princeton University Press, 1953) 482–92; Victor Brombert, *The Novels of Flaubert: A Study of Themes and Techniques* (Princeton: Princeton University Press 1968) 37–92; Gérard Genette, 'Silences de Flaubert' in *Figures: essais* (Paris: Éditions du Seuil, 1966) 223–45; Christopher Prendergast, *The Order of Mimesis: Balzac, Stendhal, Nerval, Flaubert* (Cambridge: Cambridge University Press, 1986) 180–212; Marcel Proust, 'A Propos du "style" de Flaubert' in Pierre Clarac and Yves Sandie (eds), *Contre Sainte-Beuve; précédé de pastiches et mélanges et suivi de essais et articles* (Bibliothèque de la Pléiade, Paris: Gallimard, 1971) 586–99.

13 LaCapra (n 10) 59.

14 Gustave Flaubert, *Madame Bovary* (1856/57) Margaret Cohen (ed), Eleanor Marx Aveling and Paul de Man (trans), New York: W.W. Norton, 2005) 334. This edition of the novel includes a translation of the trial transcript. All translations of the novel and the trial transcript are taken from this edition unless otherwise indicated.

15 Ibid. 338.

16 Ibid. 325.

Moll Flanders (1722) provides a similar justification of the novel's depiction of criminal and immoral behaviour by explaining that giving 'the history of a wicked life repented of, necessarily requires that the wicked part should be made as wicked as the real history of it will bear, to illustrate and give a beauty to the penitent part'. It is 'the moral' that wicked action will not go unpunished, rather than 'the fable' of the action itself, which is the point of the tale.[17]

The preface itself makes reference to the history to this defence when it notes that the 'advocates for the stage have, in all ages, made this the great argument to persuade people that their plays are useful'.[18] Sénard interpreted *Madame Bovary* as a moral tale by reproducing this 'great argument', and Pinard interpreted it as the glorification of licentiousness by positing the absence of authorial condemnation as a narrative endorsement of her behaviour. The novel was thus presented to the court as both 'poison and antidote to the larger sociocultural complex' of mid-nineteenth-century France.[19]

LaCapra rightly identifies indeterminacy and undecidability as the central problem in the trial, but his exclusive focus on the narrator's morality – on how the narratorial presence fails to present itself clearly as 'a centre of value and judgment' – leaves unexamined the link between gender identity and Flaubert's *style indirect libre*, as well as the ways in which the construction of gender via the novel's mode of narration could constitute another political or ideological 'crime'.[20] LaCapra's analysis thus provides the starting point for a further discussion, which brings into focus the subversive potential of the novel's representation of gender.

A number of critical works have productively analysed Emma Bovary's gender under the rubric of hysteria, a focus which is no doubt influenced by Freud's speculations on the subject and also by the famous appellation of Emma as an 'hysterical poet' by the poet and critic Charles Baudelaire in his review published in *L'Artiste*.[21] However, as Jan Goldstein notes in an influential article, Baudelaire only 'slips in' the category of hysteria towards the end of his review.[22] She further points out that the central paradigm in his review is not hysteria, but androgyny: Baudelaire highlights the complexity of Emma Bovary's gender identity by describing her as a 'bizarre and androgynous creature'.[23]

17 Daniel Defoe, *The Fortunes and Misfortunes of the Famous Moll Flanders* (1722) (Juliet Mitchell (ed), Harmondsworth: Penguin Books, 1988) 29.

18 Ibid. 30.

19 LaCapra (n 10) 149.

20 Ibid. 56.

21 See Janet Beizer, *Ventriloquized Bodies: Narratives of Hysteria in Nineteenth-Century France* (Ithaca: Cornell University Press, 1993) 77–169. See, more generally, Jann Matlock, *Scenes of Seduction: Prostitution, Hysteria, and Reading Difference in Nineteenth-Century France* (New York: Columbia University Press, 1994) 123–99.

22 Jan Goldstein, 'The uses of male hysteria: medical and literary discourse in nineteenth-century France' (1991) 34 *Representations* 134–65 at 144.

23 Charles Baudelaire, '*Madame Bovary*, by Gustave Flaubert', reprinted in *Madame Bovary* (n 14) 408. Jean-Paul Sartre also discusses Emma's androgyny in *L'Idiot de la famille, 3 vols* (Paris: Gallimard, 1971) I, 708–712.

In the paragraph immediately following his statement that Emma possesses traits 'characteristic of the hysterical poet', Baudelaire notes that 'in women, it [hysteria] acts like a stifling ball rising in the body . . . while in nervous men it can be the cause of many forms of impotence as well as of a limitless ability at excess'.[24] By controversially positing that hysteria has both female and male manifestations, he undermines the conventional understanding of hysteria as a specifically female illness and underscores its androgynous nature. For Baudelaire, Emma is a complex and bizarre mix of the male and the female: she has 'male blood' in her female veins and 'the seductiveness of a virile soul within the body of a beautiful woman'.[25]

This gender duality, which constitutes Baudelaire's interpretation of Emma Bovary's behaviour and her 'hysteria', enables Goldstein to highlight the primacy of androgyny over hysteria: 'Baudelaire's hysteria seems to refer not merely to supposedly feminine component of Emma's behaviour in the convent but, more broadly, to her very coupling of male and female traits; *it seems to be the expression of her "bizarre" androgyny*'.[26] She concludes that 'Flaubert uses hysteria as the vehicle of androgyny, as the liminal ground where ordinary gender boundaries can be transgressed'.[27] The discussion below accordingly shifts the focus of Emma's gender identity from hysteria to androgyny, and interprets the latter as the core of the novel's literary subversion.

How was the concept of androgyny understood in mid-nineteenth-century France, and what does Baudelaire's appellation reveal about the novel's 'ideological or political "crime" '? In this section, I will show that the French discourse on androgyny around the time of the trial established and perpetuated conservative, rigidly demarcated gender categories, and that Emma's own 'androgyny', which is characterised by flux, mobility and indeterminacy, constituted a challenge to the entrenched ideas about gender at this historical juncture. Despite the law's references to morality and religion, it was the incompatibility of Emma's androgynous quality with contemporary conceptions of gender which constituted the underlying cause of the government's attempt to suppress the novel.

The discourse on androgyny of course existed prior to the nineteenth century. Its origin is usually traced back to two sources: the creation of Eve from Adam in the biblical narrative of *Genesis* and the separation of androgynes into two entities as punishment for their assault on the gods in Plato's *Symposium*.[28] However, as A.J.L. Busst points out in the essay which remains the most comprehensive discussion of the subject, it was in the nineteenth century that the figure of the androgyne became marked 'above all by important historical, social and even

24 Ibid. Baudelaire 408.
25 Ibid. 407.
26 Goldstein (n 22) 144 (my italics).
27 Ibid. 146.
28 Plato, *The Symposium* (J.A. Brentlinger (ed), S.Q. Graden (trans), Amherst: University of Massachusetts Press, 1970) 60–69.

political associations'.[29] By the time of the *Madame Bovary* trial, it had already become 'a vast social symbol' in France.[30]

Kari Weil echoes Busst's argument when he notes that the androgyne 'moved out of the realm of pure ideas and entered practical treatises concerning the social order and social "progress"' as its popularity spread to France at the height of the romantic movement.[31] He argues that in the aftermath of the French Revolution and the promulgation of the Napoleonic Code, which 'dislodged class, family and sex status', the line between traditional notions of gendered identity began to blur. The French discourse on androgyny represented a conservative reaction to political upheaval by attempting to restore strict demarcations between the male and the female; the figure of the androgyne became a structuring principle for maintaining the existing patriarchal gender hierarchy in nineteenth-century France.

As Busst and Weil recognised, the theological writings of Pierre-Simon Ballanche are emblematic of this French discourse on androgyny. Ballanche was a writer and counter-revolutionary philosopher whose work earned him a place in the French Academy in 1841, six years before his death. In *La vision d'Hébal*, his eponymous character watches the progression of humanity from its earliest times until the date of the text's publication. In that text, Ballanche polemically reinterprets the biblical narrative of Adam and Eve as the justification for male superiority and female subordination. According to this reading, the division of the universal man, the original androgyne, into two distinct sexes is not simply a distant historical event which can be dismissed as a myth of origin. Instead, it is 'a cosmogonic law', which explains and justifies contemporary divisions in society; it is the underlying event that structures and sustains difference:

> This cosmogonic event, this decay and rehabilitation, this dogma so deeply buried in the mystery of origins, results in the separation of the sexes, the attributions of castes and classes, and the distinct characters of races.[32]

In Ballanche's narrative, social inequality based on gender, caste, class and race are depicted as the natural result of the original division of the sexes by Providence. That women are 'the passive sex' and men are 'the active sex' is explained not by mutable social perceptions or prejudices, but by divine ordainment. Any challenge to the status quo of gender division, or indeed any other division, is therefore regarded as a challenge to the divine order itself. Ballanche's theology is not a

29 A.J.L. Busst, 'The image of the androgyne in the nineteenth century' in Ian Fletcher (ed), *Romantic Mythologies* (London: Routledge & Kegan Paul, 1967) 1–97 at 39.

30 Ibid. 19.

31 Kari Weil, *Androgyny and the Denial of Difference* (Charlottesville: University of Virginia Press, 1992) 68. See also Frédéric Monneyron, *L'Androgyne romantique* (Paris: ELLUG, 1994).

32 Pierre-Simon Ballanche, *La vision d'Hébal* (1831) (Paris: Librairie Minard, 1969) 138. All translations of this text are my own.

simplistically misogynist one, for he concedes that the passive sex 'will no doubt attain equality with the active sex, because it belongs to the same original essence'.

Yet despite the seemingly progressive stance, it is reactionary at heart, for he believes that this equality 'will never be perfect, because physiological difference will continue to exist'. Since Providence has created woman with a different physiology – one could say a physiology of lack, or incompleteness, or weakness – her passivity and her unequal social status are inscribed on her body from the very moment of her creation. Ballanche's interpretation gestures towards a final overthrow of the gender order through his vision of the reunification of the split androgyne, but this utopia seems to be forever out of reach. In the meantime, a divinely-ordained patriarchal order remains firmly in place.

The work of the philosopher and political economist Pierre Leroux provides a further instance of the androgyne as the perpetuation of a rigid gender distinction. Leroux's rereading of *Genesis*, like that of Ballanche, posits the biblical text as the justification for a patriarchal societal structure, and Eve's role in introducing Adam to the forbidden fruit is crucial to the political implications of gender in his work. In *De l'humanité*, Leroux argues that God increased woman's daily toils and her suffering during childbirth as a punishment for her sin of corrupting Adam. Significantly, he also relegates her desire to a supplement of her husband's, and ordains that the man will always dominate in the relationship. His discussion of the consequences of Eve's punishment is worth quoting in full:

> In the animal world, the sexes offer a sort of equality which an egoism tied to science, an enlightened and wise egoism, has completely destroyed in humanity. *Woman has become the slave of man. That was her fate in all of antiquity and in the Orient; even in the West, and in the modern period, equality of the sexes has not yet been proclaimed or included.* This slavery of the woman is of course the fruit of egoism united with knowledge. Egoism united with knowledge engenders evil.[33]

The woman's subordinate status is the result of her own fall into temptation and her fault in leading Adam into temptation. As with Ballanche, Leroux believes that the original division of the androgyne justifies and structures current gender inequality, yet he explains the imbalance of power between the sexes in even more polemic terms: whilst Ballanche at least gestures towards a utopian state of gender equality, however unattainable it may be, Leroux unequivocally argues that women are not merely subordinate to men in his own time and society, but are destined to remain so across time and across cultures. As further evidence of this claim, he contrasts the state of the human world with the purported gender equality in the animal world. 'The woman, as the weaker sex, is a slave; man, the tyrant': the

33 Pierre Leroux, *De l'humanité* (1840) (Paris: Fayard, 1985) 388 (my italics).

formulation is given so succinctly that it almost seems to take on the status of a divine law within Leroux's philosophy.[34]

The work of Ballanche and Leroux shows that the figure of the androgyne in the nineteenth century perpetuated a patriarchal system in the name of an original, biblical, separation between two halves, and hence functioned as the discursive containment of potential gender trouble in French society.

Emma Bovary as androgyne

Madame Bovary challenged the conservative, dualistic discourse in the mid-nineteenth century through its representation of a radically different androgyny, and within the framework of gender analysis, it is arguably this challenge which led to the law's attempt to suppress the novel. As we have noted, the hallmark of the *style indirect libre* is the impossibility of assigning a fixed narratorial or moral position to the subject. The correlation of this impossibility is the radical indeterminacy of the subject's *gender* position: since it is impossible to tell who is speaking, it follows that the reader cannot unequivocally state whether the narrator is male or female. One could go further and argue that the very possibility of gender is thrown into disarray, for the subject could be male, female, both or neither at any point in the novel. This problematisation of gender identity in the novel in turn leads to an impossible gender identification by the reader. The '*moi*' or 'I' in the famous, if possibly apocryphal, proclamation '*Madame Bovary, c'est moi*' is multiple and oscillating, and the fixity of gender positions is everywhere undermined within the text.

This fantasy of radical gender mobility is given its modern, psychoanalytic, formulation in Jean Laplanche and Jean-Bertrand Pontalis's seminal essay on phantasy, in which they argue that 'the subject, although always present in the fantasy, may be so in a desubjectivized form, that is to say, in the very syntax of the sequence in question'.[35] The subject is always in a state of flux, present everywhere and yet never fully occupying any single position within the phantasy. In Flaubert's novel, the dispersal of the subject through the chain of signification is effected by the multiple, indeterminate positions opened up by the free indirect mode of narration. The gender implications of this 'absence of subjectivization' are articulated via the scenario of the daughter's seduction by the father discussed by Freud.[36]

For Laplanche and Pontalis, the scenario is one 'with multiple entries, in which nothing shows whether the subject will be immediately located as *daughter*; it can as

34 Ibid. 389.

35 Jean Laplanche and Jean-Bertrand Pontalis, 'Fantasy and the origins of sexuality' in Victor Burgin, James Donald and Cora Kaplan (eds), *Formations of Fantasy* (London: Methuen, 1986) 5–28 at 26.

36 Sigmund Freud, 'A Child is Being Beaten' (1919) in James Strachey (ed and trans), *The Standard Edition of the Complete Psychological Works of Sigmund Freud, 24 vols* (London: Vintage, 2001) XVII, 175–204.

well be fixed as *father*, or even in the term *seduces*'.[37] Reading *Madame Bovary* from a psychoanalytic perspective, we could say that the gendered identity in the novel is radically indeterminable because it is inextricably tied to the troubling of the very syntax and sequence through which identity is constituted. Like the subject in the scene of seduction above, narratorial presence in *Madame Bovary* cannot be unequivocally located in the subject of any single utterance: it can equally exist in the object, in the verb or anywhere else in the text. There is therefore no determinate gender position which the reader can occupy.

Jonathan Culler has polemically argued for an interpretation of Flaubert's work as 'a text which is simply *written*; a series of sentences which pass before the reader'.[38] Culler is right in pointing to the textual quality of novels such as *Madame Bovary* and highlighting the primacy of sequence and syntax, yet it is not necessary to conclude, as he does, that Flaubert's works are a form of pure writing without an author, or 'a text in which no one speaks'. Rather than completely evacuating the text of its narratorial presence, it is possible to follow Laplanche and Pontalis to argue that the language of the text continues to construct a narratorial subjectivity, even though the mode of narration precludes the possibility of unambiguous gender identification. The androgyny of *Madame Bovary* can be understood as the mixing or dismantling of conventional notions of gender, and therefore as the disruption of the stability and certainty of categories, which writers such as Ballanche and Leroux sought to maintain. Flaubert's androgyne constituted a disturbance in the 'horizon of expectations' in mid-nineteenth-century France by challenging the constructions of gender and the possibility of unequivocal gender identification.[39]

The following passage on the encounter between Emma and Léon, chosen by Pinard as an instance of Emma's immoral behaviour, illustrates the dynamic of the novel's gender subversion. Following the consummation of their passion in the carriage, the couple chooses a hotel room for their regular rendezvous. The reader is given a description of the interior: 'The bed was a large one, made of mahogany and shaped like a boat. The red silk curtains which hung from the ceiling, were gathered together too low, close to the lyre-shaped headboards'.[40] At first glance, the reader seems to be given Emma's vision of the room. Her obsession with luxury and fashion, together with her total disregard for financial considerations, make it natural to assume that she is the character who is surveying the chosen bedroom to ensure that everything is perfectly arranged. Yet the sentence continues: '. . . and nothing in the world was so lovely as her brown hair and white skin set

37 Laplanche and Pontalis (n 35) 22–23.

38 Jonathan Culler, *Flaubert: The Uses of Uncertainty* (London: Paul Elek, 1974) 110.

39 For a full discussion of the concept of the 'horizon of expectations,' see Hans Robert Jauss, 'Literary history as a challenge to literary theory' (1970) 2 *New Literary History* 7–37 at 14. Jauss discusses the *Madame Bovary* trial in passing in this article but leaves its gender implications unexamined.

40 Flaubert, *Madame Bovary* (n 14) 208.

off against that deep crimson colour, when with a gesture of modesty, she closed her arms and hid her face in her hands'.

The reader suddenly realises that the scene is described from Léon's point of view. Between the first and last words of the sentence, the gender identity of the narrator and the subject position of the reader are rendered radically undecidable as the narrative viewpoint slides from one character to another within the same paragraph. The narrative continues: 'The warm room, with its subdued carpet, its frivolous ornaments and its soft light, seemed made for the intimacies of passion'. Here the narrative viewpoints merge, and it becomes impossible to tell whether it is Léon, Emma or some other narratorial figure who is describing the room. As the narrative viewpoints shift, slide and conflate, the possibility of identification becomes increasingly troubled because the gender positions overlap and blur into each other.

A more complex passage provides a further illustration of the dissolution of gender through Flaubert's *style indirect libre*. Emma is thoroughly disgusted with her provincial life, and plans to run away with her lover, Rodolphe. She dreams of a life far away from the banality and boredom of her marriage with Charles. She is described in the following way:

> Never had Madame Bovary been so beautiful as at this period; she had that indefinable beauty that results from joy, from enthusiasm, from success, and that expresses the harmony between temperament and circumstances. Her cravings, her sorrows, her sensuous pleasures and her ever-young illusions had slowly brought her to full maturity, and she blossomed forth in the fullness of her being, like a flower feeding on manure, on rain, wind and sunshine. Her half-closed eyelids seemed perfectly shaped for the long languid glances that escaped from them; her breathing dilated the fine nostrils and raised the fleshy corners of her mouth, shaded in the light by a slight black down.[41]

Pinard highlights this segment as one of 'profound immorality'.[42] Who is speaking in this passage? Given that it appears during one of Emma's amorous sessions with Rodolphe – the reader is told that she pressed herself against his shoulder whilst murmuring words of love two paragraphs before – it seems natural to attribute this vision to him. Moreover, Emma is at her most childish and most hysterical during this meeting, demanding that he abandon everything to run away with her, taking her daughter with them: 'Take me away . . . carry me off! . . . I beg you!'[43] As a man of considerable experience in women and amorous affairs, Rodolphe would find Emma's simplicity and idealism charming. Moreover, his cynicism would explain the observation that Emma's beauty '*n'est que l'harmonie du tempérament*

41 Ibid. 157.
42 Ibid. 325.
43 Ibid. 156.

avec les circonstances' (more accurately translated as 'nothing but the harmonious adaptation of temperament to circumstance').[44]

Finally, the last sentence of the quotation, with its attention to eyes made for 'long languid glances'; 'breathing' voluptuously emitted through 'fine nostrils' and sensuous, full lips, indicates that the vision is that of a lover. When the reader reaches the end of the passage, however, he realises, with some surprise, that the narrator is not in fact Emma's lover, but her husband: 'Charles thought her exquisite and altogether irresistible, as when they were first married'. Within one paragraph, reader identification slides from the lover, who is in full possession of the heroine as an object of desire, to the husband, the most pathetic figure in the story. However, it is still problematic to attribute the narrative voice to him unequivocally. Charles is an exceedingly dull and unimaginative character, and the comparison of Emma with flowers would presumably be beyond the scope of his imagination. Moreover, he is singularly unobservant, and fails to discern Emma's cause of unhappiness during their entire time together. It is therefore unlikely that he would have gazed upon Emma's facial features with as much attention as is implicit in the final sentence of the quotation, or that he would have been able to describe them with those well chosen words.

If the narrator is neither Rodolphe nor Charles, then who else could it be? One possibility is Emma herself. Interpreted as a moment of self-observation, the passage echoes an earlier moment in the text, when Emma catches her own reflection in the mirror: 'when she saw herself in the mirror she wondered at her face. Never had her eyes been so large, so black, nor so deep. Something subtle about her being transfigured her'.[45] In this reading, this phrase would represent Emma's vain indulgence in the idea of her own beauty. However, this attribution is not satisfactory either, for Emma utterly lacks the dispassionate, critical mentality which would have allowed her to recognise that her beauty 'betokens nothing but the harmonious adaptation of temperament to circumstance', or to understand that her expectations are but manifestations of 'illusions of her heart'. The gender identification starts to become problematic; the reader could potentially occupy the subject position of a male character, that of a female character or both at the same time, or that of some other character whose gender remains undetermined.

There are other possibilities that are as credible as the ones mentioned above, although also as problematic. Perhaps the narrator is Félicité, the 14-year-old maid who observes that her mistress is happier and healthier, but who does not know why? Yet surely it would not make sense for Félicité to describe her employer's facial features in the vocabulary of a lover. One could also attribute the paragraph to a simple passer-by in the town, perhaps a farmer or an agricultural worker – hence the references to manure and to nature. Finally, one could of course point

44 Gustave Flaubert, *Oeuvres, 2 vols* (A. Thibaudet and R. Dumesnil (eds), Bibliothèque de la Pléiade, Paris: Gallimard, 1951) I, 657.

45 Flaubert, *Madame Bovary* (n 14) 131.

to an omniscient narrator, although that would beg the question of the narrator's gender and the reasons for describing Emma like a lover.

Rodolphe, Charles, Emma, Félicité, a stranger, the omniscient narrator . . . what the passage highlights is the multiple, conflicting viewpoints inherent in the text and the impossibility of assigning a definitive gendered identity to the narrator. Flaubert's creation is unique amongst the figures of androgyny in nineteenth-century French cultural discourse; here gendered subject positions merge and conflate to such an extent that their boundaries disappear along with the authorial centre. In this light, one could understand the reasons for which the prosecution highlighted the passage on Emma's communion. The reader is told that her religious experience is so intense that: 'her flesh, *lightened of its burden*, no longer weighed her down . . . It seemed that her being, rising towards God, would *annihilate* itself in this love, like a lighted incense that *dissipates in vapour*'.[46]

Pinard interpreted this passage as 'effusions of adultery', but it is also unsettling in another way, for the dissipation of Emma's being can be read as literalising the dissolution of gendered subjectivity which the novel enacts, and which constitutes precisely the 'crime' of challenging conventional gender categories for which its author was prosecuted.

(II) Visuality and intertextuality: reading the trial transcript

Legal fetishism, or the case for the prosecution

The *Madame Bovary* trial can be interpreted as the legal response to the challenge which the novel posed to established gender categories. How did the prosecution lawyer, Pinard, seek to contain this threat, and how did the defence lawyer, Sénard, justify the novel's conception of gender? The publication of Flaubert's novel generated two responses within the courtroom. The prosecution attempted to suppress the novel by discursively arresting its radical gender mobility, whilst the defence capitalised on this radical mobility by putting forward an argument premised on repeating and amplifying it at the level of form. In this section, I will first consider the prosecution's legal rhetoric, and will then explore the defence's strategy, which ultimately secured the acquittal.

Pinard attacked Flaubert's novel through a detailed reading of four episodes: two passages relating to Emma's adultery, one passage on Emma's short-lived religious conversion and the final, lengthy, description of Emma's death. The most persistent and striking metaphor which recurred in his argument is the metaphor of visuality; he constantly compared both the novel and its heroine to realist paintings. Elisabeth Ladenson provides one context for understanding

46 Flaubert, *Oeuvres* (n 44) 649, 659.

the prosecution's use of the term 'realism' as the linchpin of its argument. She notes that, during the Second Empire, the 'officially designated function of literature was to uplift the spirit by good example'. As a result, realism's insistent focus on the baser, more sordid aspects of life embodied an 'obvious anti-idealist agenda' and 'was demonstrably antagonistic to the aesthetic and (therefore) moral status quo'.[47] The prosecution lawyer's accusation was not only that Flaubert's novel failed to live up to its responsibilities, but that it shockingly strove to undermine the very morality it was supposed to defend. Ladenson's discussion helpfully places the term 'realism' in its historical and cultural setting, yet it fails to account for the specifically visual quality of the prosecution's rhetoric: Pinard's objection was not so much that Madame Bovary is realist, but that it is a realist *painting*. The connections between fiction and the visual arts ran deep in mid-nineteenth-century France.

Without repeating the work of art historians here, it is worth noting that much of the debate over realism took place in the domain of art as well as the domain of literature, and that there was much intellectual traffic between writers, critics and painters. When Gustave Courbet's *A Burial at Ornan* and the newly completed *The Painter's Studio* were turned down by the jury of the Exposition Universelle in 1855, he angrily withdrew the 11 paintings which had been accepted and set up his own, alternative exposition at the nearby Avenue Montaigne, with a sign stating 'Du Réalisme. G. Courbet. An exhibition of forty paintings from his work' over the entrance of the building. The catalogue to this alternative exhibition has been regarded as the realist manifesto, but another document which also has the status of a manifesto is the letter to George Sand by the realist author Champfleury, the pen name of Jules Husson, published in *L'Artiste* in September of that year. The letter was a response to Courbet's private exhibition, in which Champfleury admits to siding with those critics who saw Courbet's exhibition as 'an incredibly audacious act', rather than with those who regarded it as a 'scandal'.[48]

The 'anti-idealist' agenda of realist literature which Ladenson highlights as being particularly offensive to the establishment was also present in realist art: as Champfleury recognised, part of the problem of *A Burial at Ornan* was that Courbet gave a subject as unremarkable and bleak as 'a peasant lying in his coffin', surrounded by 'farmers, low-class people', as much pictorial space as 'the magistrates going to the Mass of the Holy Ghost' in Nicolas de Largillière's portraits or the 'Spanish novels, Infants, Infantas' in Velasquez's paintings.[49] What

47 Elisabeth Ladenson, *Dirt for Art's Sake: Books on Trial From Madame Bovary to Lolita* (Ithaca: Cornell University Press, 2007) 22, 26.

48 Jules Champfleury, 'A letter to Madame Sand about M. Courbet' in Linda Nochlin (ed) *Realism and Tradition in Art, 1848–1900* (New Jersey: Prentice Hall, 1966) 36–45 at 37.

49 Ibid. 39.

I am trying to highlight in this brief survey of the connections between literature and art is that the porous boundaries between them contributed to the conceptualisation of realist fiction in visual terms in this period.

Ruth Bernard Yeazell addresses a similar phenomenon by pointing out that nineteenth-century commentators frequently, even ubiquitously, compared the novel to seventeeth-century Dutch painting. She noted that the qualities commonly associated with the realist novel, both in the sense of the formal realism which Ian Watt identifies in *The Rise of the Novel* and the more self-conscious realism of the mid-nineteenth century, 'had their visual analogues in the so-called Golden Age of Dutch painting'.[50] As such, 'many of the images produced by seventeenth-century Netherlandish painters clearly provided an important precedent; and however vaguely they conjured with the analogy, nineteenth-century writers were well aware of the fact'.

Given the centrality of the visual arts to the nineteenth-century novel, the artistic metaphors in Pinard's legal discourse require close scrutiny. The rhetoric of visuality, or the legal representation of the novel and its heroine as paintings, is everywhere apparent in Pinard's speech. When making his argument that Flaubert committed offences against public morality and religion, he claimed that the novel presented the reader with a series of 'lascivious paintings'. At the beginning of his speech, he told the jury that the author 'meant to compose genre paintings, and you shall see what kind of paintings!!!'[51] He claimed that since 'his novel is a painting', it is the jury's duty to 'wonder about the colour and brushstroke' of its creator, just as it is their responsibility to find out 'to which school [of art] he belongs'.[52]

When he presented the four extracts as evidence, he noted that the passages represented 'four scenes, or rather four paintings'. He explicitly equated language and painting when he presented Emma's affair with Rodolphe as evidence: 'Gentlemen, do you know a more expressive language in the world? Have you ever seen a more lascivious painting?'[53] He identified the paintings as belonging to the realist school, a label which Flaubert despised: 'the genre which Mr. Flaubert cultivates . . . is the descriptive genre, it is realist painting'.[54] He argued that by drawing on realist conventions, the defendant could indulge himself and 'paint temptations, and above all temptations to which Mrs. Bovary succumbed'. Moreover, just as the 'lascivious paintings' constituted Flaubert's offence against public morality, the images mixing sacred ideas and practices with those which were voluptuous constituted his offence against religion. Pinard concluded that,

50 Ruth Bernard Yeazell, *Art of the Everyday: Dutch Painting and the Realist Novel* (Princeton: Princeton University Press, 2008) 7.

51 Flaubert, *Madame Bovary* (n 14) 315.

52 Ibid. 319.

53 Ibid. 324.

54 Ibid. 331.

whilst Flaubert might be a talented artist, his novel was 'an atrocious painting from the perspective of morality'.[55]

His deployment of this rhetoric of visuality was noted by some of Flaubert's supporters: Charles Augustin Sainte-Beuve appropriates Pinard's imagery to praise the novel in his review, pointing out that Flaubert is more accurately described as a 'painter' than an author.[56] He further argues that Flaubert succeeds in condensing his vision onto a 'tightly composed canvas', and that his description of Charles's visit to les Bertaux is 'admirably rendered in minute detail . . . like a Dutch or Flemish painting of Normandy'.[57] The appropriation of this rhetoric of visuality by the observers of the trial attests to its centrality to the prosecutorial dynamic at work in the courtroom.[58]

What does it mean for Pinard to describe a novel and its characters as a painting? If, as Roland Barthes points out, the rhetoric of the image proceeds through the interaction of different levels of meaning, then it would be important to uncover the symbolic functions underlying the more literal operations of the rhetoric.[59] What is at stake in the law's elision of the narratorial and the visual in the *Madame Bovary* trial and more importantly, how does the elision relate to the novel's challenge to established gender categories? To phrase the question in another way, what kind of textual effects did the law's rhetoric of visuality produce in response to the textual effects of the literary text which it confronted?

The work of Goodrich provides one point of entry into these questions. Goodrich argues that the law's existence is inextricably tied to its denial of the image, so much so that legal doctrine 'depends upon an antiportrait or negative image' and forges its own identity 'by showing the face, the plurality or void, of evil'.[60] He further notes that the face of this evil is often a female one: the rejected image is usually that of 'an extravagant woman, a perpetual threat of excess, of plurality, and of transgression'.[61] This rejection of the feminine image enables the law to maintain its own legitimacy and to deny its own imagistic qualities: by depicting everything outside its boundaries as 'a spurious surface, a face, an idol, vanity, or lie', the law forges an image of itself as the embodiment of reason and truth without acknowledging that such a representation is itself an image.[62]

The distinctive feature of visual metaphors is that the law both rejects and relies upon them. In this context, Pinard's legal rhetoric of visuality appears as part of

55 Ibid. 328.

56 *Charles Augustin Sainte-Beuve, Madame Bovary, by Gustave Flaubert*, reprinted in Flaubert, *Madame Bovary* (n 14) 392.

57 Ibid. 393–94.

58 On the significance of Sainte-Beuve's review, see Dumesnil (n 9) 253–83.

59 Roland Barthes, *Image-Music-Text* (Stephen Heath (trans), Glasgow: William Collins, 1977) 32–52.

60 Peter Goodrich, *Oedipus Lex: Psychoanalysis, History, Law* (Berkeley: University of California Press, 1995) 49 (my italics).

61 Ibid. 62.

62 Ibid. 42.

the long history of the law's use of images. The law manipulates the image for its own ends through a double movement; it rejects the image and thereby hides its own status as image. Through the use of psychoanalytic modes of reading, the following discussion aims to uncover the operation of this double movement in the *Madame Bovary* trial; Pinard's visual figures both reject Flaubert's depiction of gender and simultaneously, although more subtly, enact the law's own discursive construction of gender.

Pinard's recourse to the metaphor of painting which reframed the indeterminate, mobile gender representations in *Madame Bovary* as an image which could be *seen* provides the starting point for such a psychoanalytic interpretation: as will be discussed below, his rhetorical gesture converted the complex gendered identity of the heroine into an image of licentious femininity and enabled the reader to occupy the position of a male viewer. Pinard's objection to Flaubert's paintings, as he termed them, was that the writer revealed too much of his heroine. He condemned Flaubert for showing Emma Bovary 'without a veil' ('*sans voile*') and contended that his style was not to be tolerated because it was an art form without restraint.[63] For the prosecution lawyer, art without rules was 'no longer art' but was 'like a woman who would take off all her clothes' ('*L'art sans règle n'est plus l'art; c'est comme une femme qui quitterait tout vêtement*').[64] Pinard's aversion to the full display of the heroine's body in the reader's field of vision is epitomised in the following passage:

> Mr. Flaubert knows how to embellish his paintings with all his artistic means, but without the consideration for the tact of art. *In his work, no mist, no veils, it is nature in all its nudity, in all its harshness!*[65]

On one level, Pinard's condemnation of Flaubert's method is based on the objection to the deliberate depiction of undesirable aspects of life (such as adultery), which underlies most denunciations of realism during this period. However, the broader question of the truthful depiction of reality in literature does not exhaust the analysis of Pinard's imagery, for his striking comparisons of fiction to art above suggest that there is something inherently disturbing about a woman who would fully reveal her sexual difference. Pinard did not want to see the woman 'who would take off all her clothes'; nor did he want to see nature (feminine in French: *la* nature) in all her nudity.

The insistence on the need to cover up the female body within this rhetoric of visuality is especially curious given that the novel does not present the reader with any description of what Emma Bovary looks like when unclothed. Indeed, as

63 Flaubert, *Madame Bovary* (n 14) 324.

64 Ibid. 335.

65 Ibid. 328 (my italics): '*M. Flaubert sait embellir ses peintures avec toutes les ressources de l'art, mais sans les ménagements de l'art. Chez lui point de gaze, point de voiles, c'est la nature dans toute sa nudité, dans toute sa crudité!*'

Peter Brooks points out, the reader is not given a full picture of her body at all; the narrative focus is always displaced onto items of clothing or individual body parts.[66] What exactly was Pinard objecting to in his denunciations of Flaubert's purported portraits of female nudity? What, in other words, is so horrifying about the sight of a naked woman?

Freud's notes on the Medusa's head suggest that the horror arises from the male subject's attempt to comprehend sexual difference:

> What happened, therefore, was that the boy refused to take cognisance of the fact of his having perceived that a woman does not possess a penis. No, that could not be true: for if a woman had been castrated, then his own possession of a penis was in danger; and against that there rose in rebellion the portion of his narcissism which Nature has, as a precaution, attached to that particular organ.[67]

Within Freud's narrative, the male subject interprets difference as the result of castration; the sight of an absence on the female body needs to be displaced because it induces the terror of castration. In Freud's formulation: 'To decapitate = to castrate. The terror of Medusa is thus the terror of castration that is *linked to the sight of something*'.[68] The male subject anxiously displaces his vision onto a substitute image, and 'Medusa's head takes the place of a representation of the female genitals'.[69] Freud's speculations on fetishism shed light on the question of mobile gender identifications in *Madame Bovary* because it underscores how the confrontation with sexual difference generates anxiety and necessitates a disavowal of the difference through the return to a more stable representation.

The dynamic of fetishism operates as such a process of stabilisation. Freud not only insists on the anxiety of castration which lies at the core of the terror of Medusa, but also on the apotropaic effect which Medusa's head generates: the hair on her head is frequently depicted as a mass of snakes, and it is a 'remarkable fact that, however frightening they may be in themselves, they nevertheless serve actually as a mitigation of the horror, for they replace the penis, the absence of which is the cause of the horror'. Even though Medusa's snakes may be terrifying, they are ultimately reassuring in that they give form to the otherwise unrepresentable horror of castration. Similarly, even though the sight of the Medusa's head 'makes the spectator stiff with terror, turns him to stone,' it also 'offers consolation to the spectator: he is still in possession of a penis, and the stiffening reassures him of the fact'.[70] In this instance, the spectator's own stiffened body acts as the symbol

66 Peter Brooks, *Body Work: Objects of Desire in Modern Narrative* (Cambridge: Harvard University Press, 1993) 89–106. Brooks interprets the novel through the lens of fetishism; my own analysis diverges from Brooks's in that I focus more on the courtroom rhetoric, rather than exclusively on the novel itself.

67 Freud, 'Fetishism' (1927), *Standard Edition* XXI, 149–57 at 151.

68 Freud, 'Medusa's Head' (1922), *Standard Edition* XVIII, 273–75 at 273) (my italics).

69 Ibid. 274.

70 Ibid. 273.

which gives form to an otherwise unrepresentable absence. The symbol of the Medusa's head is reassuring precisely because it functions as a symbol.[71]

In this light, Pinard's deployment of the rhetoric of visuality in the courtroom can be interpreted as the law's attempt to arrest fetishistically the free play of gender which constitutes *Madame Bovary*'s androgyny, and hence the novel's political or ideological crime.[72] The legal rhetoric which discursively produced the image of Emma Bovary as an adulteress consciously drew on the denunciation of the representation of women in realist art which circulated within the wider cultural discourse of mid-nineteenth-century France. The art historian Linda Nochlin takes Courbet as the epitome of the male artist's depiction of femininity during this period, and argues that female figures were rarely presented as more than 'objects of (male) artistic desire – and manipulation' in his work.[73]

The women in the paintings are often half-clothed or entirely naked, and their representations as seductive, inviting or simply unresisting figures often created and perpetuated the discourse of female sexual availability. Although he was a defender of Courbet, the writings of the critic and philosopher Pierre-Joseph Proudhon are still exemplary of the language used in the discussion of realist art in this period, and Pinard's rhetoric often echoes the diction and tropes of Proudhon's criticism: the prosecution's condemnation of the author's excessive focus on Emma's voluptuousness and her 'beauty of provocation' parallels Proudhon's argument that realist art functions as an *agent pornocratique* through its frequent depictions of women in various states of 'erotic reverie' and 'satanic seductions'.[74] Indeed, the trope of the 'lascivious image' is one which underpins Proudhon's writings on art.[75] His accusation that 'these days artists . . . look for nothing in their subjects but the occasion to paint them in the nude, to show women in a more or less provocative attitude' also reads like a condemnation from Pinard's prosecution speech in the courtroom.[76]

71 See Neil Hertz, *The End of the Line: Essays on Psychoanalysis and the Sublime* (New York: Columbia University Press, 1985) 165–68.

72 For further discussions of the question of fetishism in nineteenth-century French literary discourse, see Emily Apter, *Feminizing the Fetish: Psychoanalysis and Narrative Obsession in Turn-of-the-Century France* (Ithaca: Cornell University Press, 1991); Rae Beth Gordon, *Ornament, Fantasy, and Desire in Nineteenth-Century French Literature* (Princeton: Princeton University Press, 1992); Naomi Schor, 'Fetishism and its ironies' in Emily Apter and William Pietz (eds), *Fetishism as Cultural Discourse* (Ithaca: Cornell University Press, 1993) 92–100. For a useful discussion of fetishism in a cinematic context, see Laura Mulvey, *Visual and Other Pleasures* (Bloomington: Indiana University Press, 1989).

73 Linda Nochlin, *Representing Women* (London: Thames & Hudson, 1999) 130. See also Thomas B. Hess and Linda Nochlin (eds), *Woman as Sex Object: Studies in Erotic Art, 1730–1970* (London: Allen Lane, 1973).

74 P.J. Proudhon, *Du principe de l'art et de sa destination sociale* (Paris: Garnier Frères, 1865) 245. All translations of this text are my own.

75 Ibid. 250.

76 Ibid. 253.

Pinard's rhetoric drew on the discourse of writers such as Proudhon performatively to displace the radically mobile and indeterminate gender construction within the novel onto a recognisable, and hence reassuring, representation of femininity. In other words, the law's visual metaphors converted the novel's alternative gender construction into a conventional notion of femininity by casting Emma and the narrative as a whole as a lascivious painting. As LaCapra has argued, the crime of the novel was to threaten to explode the frame of the trial itself. The law's response to this threat was to confine the novel's modernity within a picture frame through its performative rhetoric of realist art.

Legal intertextuality, or the case for the defence

Faced with the prosecution's attack, Sénard, Flaubert's lawyer, relied on a number of arguments to defend the novel's publication. First, he dismissed Pinard's portrayal of Emma as an adulteress as inaccurate, arguing that the alleged lascivious colour was the result of an incomplete understanding of the text and only existed 'under the condition of cuts and commentaries'.[77] He claimed that, rather than seeking to paint a beauty of provocation, what Flaubert hoped to do was to 'take a subject of study from real life, to create, to make up real middle class types and arrive at a useful result'.[78]

Flaubert's realism is thus didactic; it aims to expose the problems confronting innocent young girls and to warn them against falling into temptation. Sénard also relied on his personal acquaintance with the Flaubert family when making his argument: according to him, the son of the chief surgeon in Rouen could not possibly have committed an outrage against public morals and religion.[79] Flaubert's father was not the only figure whom Sénard mentioned to defend his client: he told the court that the poet Alphonse de Lamartine thanked Flaubert for writing such a marvellous work, and purported to have spoken to mothers who approved of the story's moral and 'thought they should thank the author' for writing the novel.[80]

However, the most sophisticated strategy that Sénard devised against Pinard, and which formed the most sustained defence of the novel in his speech, is what I will call the 'intertextuality argument'. The notion of intertextuality underpins his defence to both the charge of outrage against public morals and the charge of outrage against religious morals. Sénard in effect argued that *Madame Bovary* was not a bounded or autotelic text, but spilled over into other forms of writing. He then used the novel's inscription in other textual networks to colour the court's interpretation. Flaubert vividly described the effect of the argument on the opposition in a letter to his brother: 'Maître Sénard's speech was splendid.

77 Flaubert, *Madame Bovary* (n 14) 339.
78 Ibid. 338.
79 Ibid. 337.
80 Ibid. 344.

He crushed the attorney from the Ministry of Justice, who writhed in his seat and made no rebuttal'.[81]

The crux of his strategy lies in the way it repeated, on the level of form, an aspect of the novel's content: just as the content of *Madame Bovary* depicts a radical mobility of gender identifications, the form of the novel was shown to be capable of an equally radical textual mobility. In other words, just as the gender positions slip, slide and conflate within the text, so the novel itself constantly merges and spills over into other forms of writing. To counter the charge of 'outrage to public morals', Sénard argued that *Madame Bovary* was not in fact purely a product of Flaubert's imagination, but was a discursive terrain on which other texts intersected and overlapped. Some of these texts are literary in nature: early on in his speech, he asserted that beneath the episode of Rodolphe's seduction was another story, that of Samuel Richardson's *Clarissa*: 'Mr. Flaubert has substituted Rodolphe for Lovelace and Emma for Clarissa. Compare the two authors and the two works and assess'.[82]

The relationship between Emma and Rodolphe turned out to be the same as that between Clarissa and Lovelace, to the extent that one set of relations could be 'substituted' for the other, so that the protagonist's purported licentiousness was reinterpreted as the actions of a young woman who fell victim to a far more worldly seducer. The slippage of gender is here re-enacted on a textual level through the slippage of narratives. Sénard's strategy of presenting the novel as a multi-layered text is strikingly modern, echoing Julia Kristeva's idea that 'each word (text) is an intersection of words (texts) where at least one other word (text) can be read'.[83] His demonstration that there are multiple, hitherto undiscovered layers to the novel seems to present Flaubert's work as a model for Kristeva's poetic language since, in his reading, the novel 'no longer involves lines or surfaces, but rather, *space* and *infinity*'.[84]

This expansion of the 'space and infinity' of the text was especially evident in Sénard's discussion of Emma's affair with Léon, for the novel here expanded to encompass not only other literary texts but also religious tracts, which were seemingly remote from the novel's own genre or plot. He argued that the chapters concerning the affair were but 'imitations of Bossuet', the seventeenth-century theologian and bishop. As such, any accusation of immorality would be tantamount to an accusation directed at the Church. The intertextual relations between the novel and the religious texts were carefully established. He began by describing Flaubert as an avid reader of these texts:

81 Letter to Achille dated 30 January 1857, *Letters 1830–1857* (n 4) 226.

82 Flaubert, *Madame Bovary* (n 14) 359.

83 Julia Kristeva, 'Word, dialogue, and novel' in Toril Moi (ed), *The Kristeva Reader* (Oxford: Basil Blackwell, 1986) 34–62 at 37.

84 Ibid. 58.

> Mr. Flaubert of the lascivious colours, who after so many years of work, so many studies, so many travels, so many notes collected from authors that he has read – My God! You will see from what he has drawn . . . You will see him . . . completely imbued with Bossuet and Massillon.[85]

Having established for the jury that Flaubert's thinking was heavily influenced by Bossuet and Massillon, Sénard then drew an equation between Flaubert's own writing and the religious figures: since the writer 'only lets himself take up the pen after having drawn from the thoughts of Bossuet and Massillon', the ideas expressed in *Madame Bovary*, far from lascivious, were in fact identical to those of religious instruction.[86]

As Flaubert himself noted, 'we flattened him [Pinard] with quotations from Bossuet and Massillon, smutty passages from Montesquieu, etc . . . It was marvellous, and I was in fine form'.[87] Sénard concluded that Flaubert's writings were in fact not original creations, but reproductions of these predecessor texts: what Flaubert sought to do was to 'reproduce in his descriptions their thoughts and the colour used by them'.[88] Cleverly juxtaposing the sections on the illicit affair with excerpts from religious tracts, Sénard then read the lovers' mutual boredom and Emma's disillusionment as a textbook illustration of the sermons against succumbing to sensual pleasures. Flaubert's poignant comment that Emma 'rediscovered in adultery all the platitudes of marriage', a phrase that Pinard singled out as an unacceptable conflation of the transgressive and the institutional, was suddenly echoed in the bishop's warning to 'women of sin':

> But punished for our fault without being freed from its illusions we seek in change a remedy for our error. We wander from object to object. And if there finally is someone that makes us settle down, we are not content with our choice, but are praised for our infidelities.[89]

Sénard's recourse to Bossuet was especially ingenious, for it posited naivety and inexperience in place of loose morals as the reasons for Emma's behaviour. The source of the passage that Sénard quoted has been lost, but Bossuet expresses similar ideas in his writings elsewhere, especially in sections of the *Traité de la concupiscence*. He notes that concupiscence of the flesh is 'the most oppressive yoke that the soul can bear and the most manifest cause of its servitude and its weaknesses'.[90] The superimposition of this text onto Flaubert's novel turned Emma's

85 Flaubert, *Madame Bovary* (n 14) 343.
86 Ibid. 369–70.
87 Letter to Achille dated 30 January 1857, *Letters 1830–1857* (n 4) 226.
88 Flaubert, *Madame Bovary* (n 14) 343.
89 Ibid. 369.
90 Jacques-Bénigne Bossuet, *Traité de la concupiscence* (1691–93) (Paris: Éditions Fernand Roches, 1930) 5. All translations of this text are my own.

desire into a universal human condition rather than a manifestation of her own licentiousness.

Later in the treatise, Bossuet notes that those who are seduced by the temptations of the flesh 'see everything with eyes of sickness'.[91] Emma became portrayed as someone who was ill, someone who needed help, rather than someone who ought to be punished. Finally, Bossuet's treatise, like the words of St John, is aimed at three groups of people: fathers, young people and children.[92] Emma obviously could not fall into the first group, so Sénard's use of Bossuet enabled her to occupy the position of either an inexperienced young person or a child, both of whom fell into the hands of 'Evil, who tempts you', due to weakness and naivety rather than lust.[93] According to the defence lawyer, Bossuet teaches its readers how to behave and Flaubert shows its readers the fatal consequences of ignoring the teachings.

Sénard deployed a similar strategy in countering the charge of the offence to religion. During the discussion of the passage on Emma's death, Pinard had argued that by describing the way in which the sheets covering her body 'sank in from her breast to her knees, and then rose at the tips of her toes', the defendant eroticised Emma's dead body, with the result that the sacred and the voluptuous become conflated.[94] By focusing solely on the representation of Emma's dead body, the prosecution bypassed the detailed description of Emma's slow, agonising death after she consumes arsenic towards the end of the novel, and hence pre-empted the argument that the depiction of her death should be interpreted as the writer's own condemnation of his heroine's behaviour.

However, by setting the description of Emma's corpse in intertextual relation with writings by Sainte-Beuve and the Abbot Ambrose Guillois, Sénard counter-argued that the emphasis on the body was an integral part of the novel's representation of an unction ceremony. The abbot's book, entitled *Explication Historique, Dogmatique, Morale, Liturgique, et Canonique du Catechism*, carried particular weight in this part of the argument. Sénard insisted that his client had 'created the scene of the extreme unction with a book lent to him by a venerable clergyman', and proceeded to demonstrate that Guillois's book gave detailed instruction on the anointment of each part of the body: the eyes, the ears, the nostrils, the lips, the hands, the chest, the buttocks.[95]

Each description of Emma's body parts found its exact parallel in Guillois's text on the religious ritual. Far from constituting a lascivious tableau, Sénard argued, the focal emphasis on the different parts of the body was meant to connote the requests for forgiveness for the sins committed by each limb or organ. In a *coup de grâce*, Sénard made his most radical intertextual claim: the death scene was less a

91 Ibid. 79.
92 Ibid. 98.
93 Ibid. 99.
94 Ibid. 331.
95 Ibid. 377.

product of Flaubert's imagination than the transplantation of the words of the religious documents into the novel. He argued his client 'purely and simply *copied*' the documents, and that the scene did not blur the boundary between the sacred and the profane because it was composed of 'the language of the Church'.[96] Guillois's writing appeared in the novel as 'quotations without inverted commas'; they suffused the novel and hence any attempt to separate the story of Emma Bovary from religious virtue became impossible.[97] The death scene was not a mere interpretation or rewriting of the religious documents: the two turned out to be identical, and the reader of *Madame Bovary* was in fact listening to the voice of the Church.

Sénard's argument that *Madame Bovary* was not so much Flaubert's original artistic product, but the collage of other texts, including works by Richardson, Massillon, Bossuet, Sainte-Beuve and Guillois, amongst others, lends new meaning to Flaubert's own advice on how to read his narrative: following the *Revue de Paris*'s decision to suppress passages in the serialised version of the novel, Flaubert angrily declared that he denied all responsibility for the words of the final instalment appearing in the *Revue*, and instructed his readers 'merely to see them as fragments, and not as a whole'.[98] Fragments of other narratives are transported into Flaubert's novel, which in turn further spills out into other texts, and the mobility and multiplicity of gender we find in the novel's content is repeated in the courtroom at the level of form. This point is worth underscoring: the legal argument, in the form of the defence speech, that *Madame Bovary* constitutes a site of radical textual mobility can be said to repeat the radical mobility which the novel presents in gender terms through its narrative style.

While Pinard's strategy was founded on suppressing the most innovative aspect of Flaubert's work through the dynamic of fetishism, Sénard's argument ultimately succeeded by capitalising on precisely this innovation and turning it into a defence strategy. Flaubert's own observations again give us a sense of the strategy's effectiveness: Pinard 'was completely discomforted when Maître Sénard took a missal from under his seat and read from it. The passage from my novel is nothing but a softened reproduction of what is in the missal: we certainly stuffed them with a famous bit of literature'.[99]

The defence lawyer's strategy in effect constituted a legal repetition of a literary mode of representation: by arguing that *Madame Bovary* was the site of intersection between diverse texts, he not only intuited the importance of the novel's distinctively modern narrative style, but explicitly adopted it as an interpretative strategy in his legal argument. In other words, at least part of the trial transcript, which is a document usually regarded as a purely 'legal' text in so far as it records doctrinal

96 Ibid. 378–80 (my italics).
97 Barthes 160.
98 Flaubert, *Madame Bovary* (n 14) 329.
99 Letter to Achille dated 30 January 1857, *Letters 1830–1857* (n 4) 227.

arguments, lawyerly modes of reasoning and judicial rulings, draws upon and re-enacts the novel's textual mobility. The trial can be read as positing a vision of literary-legal relations; the legal text here repeats the textual mobility characteristic of the novel. The courtroom becomes the site of a scene of reading, throwing into question the epistemological distinctiveness between law and literature by revealing the discursive similarities between them.

The subsequent chapters will further explore the complex intertwining of structures, tropes and rhetorical figures between the two discourses. This textual intertwining or repetition is arguably significant beyond the immediate context of Flaubert's acquittal, for the following reason: viewed as a dispute between censors and writers, law and literature are assumed to be opposed to each other in most literary trials. The law stands on the side of morality, whilst literature, as the object allegedly causing an outrage against public morality, decency and religion, constitutes a form of moral transgression. Moreover, the language of the law parades itself as unambiguous, authoritative and direct, whilst the language of literature becomes regarded as suspicious, seductive and corrupting. The adversarial relationship between them seems to presuppose an absolute epistemological distinction.

Such an assumption is often made by both the people directly involved in the trial and by commentators in our own time. However, by thinking about the trial transcript as a text in addition to a dispute, by focusing on the trial's discursive dimension, it is possible to see that at least Sénard's part of the legal narrative is marked by the radical multiplicity which underpins Flaubert's modernist style. Textual mobility is not distinctive to literature, and can in fact be reinterpreted by the law as a powerful argument in the courtroom.

The confrontation between Flaubert's novel and the law reveals the textual mobility on both sides of the law/literature divide and suggests that the two discourses are not as epistemologically distinct as they may seem initially. To posit a relationship of repetition or implication is of course not to deny the power imbalance which slants in favour of the law: within the courtroom, literature is inevitably at the mercy of the legal institution, in the very real sense that books can be banned and penalties can be imposed by the latter. Yet on the level of textual relations, the law can be said to repeat, unwittingly and unexpectedly, an aspect of the literary text which it finds objectionable.

Chapter 2

The *Charlot s'amuse* trial: onanism and the scandal of naturalist fiction

Paul Bonnetain's *Charlot s'amuse* (*Charlot plays with himself*), a novel about a compulsive masturbator, may be an obscure novel today, but when it was published in 1883 it quickly became the centre of a literary and legal controversy, sparking an obscenity trial the following year. Masturbation, or to use the nineteenth-century medical term, onanism, was widely regarded as a cause of degeneracy, illness and national decline in late nineteenth-century France, and a work of fiction which deliberately took as its subject the life of an onanist was regarded as nothing short of perverse. Its author, who was given the nickname of 'Bonnemain', or 'good hand', after the novel's appearance, was prosecuted for having committed an 'outrage to public decency' (*outrage aux bonnes moeurs*), under the law of 29 July 1881.

The President of the *Cour d'assises* believed the novel's subject matter to be so offensive that he ordered the proceedings to take place *à huis clos*, or as a closed trial, so that journalists would be forbidden from relaying information to the general public. Indeed, the relative obscurity of the novel in our own time can be regarded as a continuation of the work of censorship: even though Bonnetain was eventually acquitted in the trial of 1884, the accusation of obscenity arguably left its mark on the novel so that, even today, it is sidelined in the French literary curriculum.

The eponymous protagonist of *Charlot s'amuse* is the offspring of a degenerate family that includes an epileptic grandmother, a nymphomaniac mother and an alcoholic father. His compulsive masturbation is portrayed as a hereditary trait, and much of the narrative's tragedy lies in the futility of his attempts to fight his innate urges. The novel is intensely anti-clerical; the Catholic institutions to which Charlot is sent, such as the Brotherhood of the rue des Récollets and the school in Saint Dié, are depicted as hotbeds of deviant sexual activity. As an adult, Charlot spends some time in the army and then moves to Paris, where his sexual obsessions worsen. He eventually marries a woman called Fanny Méjean who, like him, suffers from an inherited condition. His attempt at family life ends in disaster: Fanny runs away and leaves him with their newborn son. Charlot is driven to despair and commits suicide by jumping into the Seine, taking the baby with him. However, the child survives, and his re-emergence from the waters on the last page of the novel foreshadows the re-emergence of the degenerative traits in the next generation.

Bonnetain's narrative of sexual perversity and death raised questions about the legitimate ambit of the naturalist literary project. Naturalist writers often took the more sordid, gritty and even pathological facets of life as the subject of their works, including alcoholism, prostitution, nymphomania and incest, and justified their choice in the name of the spirit of scientific investigation. Zola drew an explicit parallel between the work of the scientist and the work of the writer: in science, the return to nature meant the systematic study of 'bodies and physical phenomena' that was 'based on experience' and that proceeded 'by analysis'; in literature, naturalism was 'equally the return to nature and to man' and was similarly based on the 'direct observation, exact anatomy, and the acceptance and portrayal of things' as they were.[1]

Zola was widely regarded as the grand master of naturalism and the next chapter will show that his novels had their own share of legal controversy, but the problem of censorship and obscenity was compounded for a writer like Bonnetain because the younger naturalist writers took the project of representing reality in a scientific manner more literally than their predecessors, and often to its extreme. As Catherine Dousteyssier-Khoze has pointed out, they aimed to 'go further' than first-generation writers such as Zola, to 'paint what was potentially "shocking"' and to 'transgress the limits of what was "sexually correct" and acceptable'.[2]

The naturalist writers regarded sex as a key motivating force of human behaviour, and one of the recurrent themes of their work is the pleasures of the flesh and the consequences of sexual excess on the body. Not surprisingly, their novels were often regarded as pornographic in their time. The metaphor of a 'rising tide' of pornography was often used in calls to stem the spread of naturalist fiction in the writings of the Church, the sciences and the literary establishment in the late nineteenth century, and the government took a deep interest in the circulation of such fiction out of concern for the moral health of the Third Republic.[3]

In the final decades of the nineteenth century, French law construed explicit references to sex as indicative of 'the guilty intent of the author', and those years were marked by a preponderance of obscenity trials on naturalist fiction: in addition to *Charlot s'amuse*, novels which gave rise to legal proceedings included Louis Desprez's *Autour d'un clocher* (*Around a Clock Tower*) in 1884, Paul Adam's *Chair*

1 Émile Zola, 'Le naturalisme au théâtre' (1881) in François-Marie Mourad (ed), *Le roman experimental* (Paris: GF Flammarion, 2006) 129–66 at 133.

2 Catherine Dousteyssier-Khoze, *Zola et la littérature naturaliste en parodies* (Paris: Eurédit, 2004) 187. All translations from French texts in this chapter are my own unless otherwise indicated.

3 Marc Angenot, *Le Cru et le faisandé: sexe, discours social et littérature à la Belle Époque* (Brussels: Labor, 1986) 53.

molle (*Limp Flesh*) in 1885, Jean-Louis Dubut de Laforest's in *La gaga* in 1886 and Lucien Descaves's *Sous-Offs* (*The Under-Officers*) in 1890.[4]

The younger writers understood the term 'naturalism' in different ways; some of them, like Desprez, closely adhered to Zola's teachings until the end of their lives, whilst others, such as Bonnetain, publicly broke ranks with the master as their careers developed. The value and function of naturalist fiction was a subject of intense debate in France, and led to sharp and often acrimonious exchanges not only between writers and critics but also between the *cadet naturalistes*, and the trials can be regarded as the legal manifestation of the controversy which naturalism generated. However, despite their differences, the language through which the younger naturalists defended their works was similar and often rehearsed the scientific approach to the representation of reality.

For example, in the *Autour d'un Clocher* trial, which took place a week before Bonnetain's prosecution, Desprez passionately argued that, as novelists, 'we give a detailed list of the causes and we analyze the effects, just like a doctor who gives the diagnosis of an illness'.[5] Amongst the many naturalist texts which generated legal censure in this period, *Charlot s'amuse* is both exemplary and unique, in that it deliberately represented a sexual taboo – onanism – and drew on the language of science in its representation of this practice, but, as I will demonstrate in this chapter, it also threw into question the assumptions about the relationship between literature and science which forms the basis of the naturalist project.

Since the *Charlot s'amuse* trial took place *à huis clos*, there is a dearth of primary material on the proceedings. Fortunately, some of the material has been preserved in the judicial archive of the *Archives de Paris*, and from the documents it is possible to reconstruct the sequence of events. Part of these documents has been reproduced in the appendix to Yvan Leclerc's *Crimes écrits*.[6]

The story begins with an anonymous letter sent to the Director of Public Prosecutions in Paris. The letter warned that 'a rising tide of mire' was invading France which, if allowed to continue, would 'make French literature the most shameful of all'. It claimed that the second-generation naturalist writers would 'surpass Zola, the Master' in their level of indecency, and singled out Bonnetain's novel as 'not only ignoble' but also 'a most unmistakable attack on morality'. The letter concluded by urging its addressee to take action against the spread of immoral literature. Under Article 23 of the 1881 law, it was the publisher, Henry Kistemaekers, who should have been prosecuted as the main culprit, and Bonnetain, as the author, would have appeared in court as an accomplice to the crime.[7]

4 Annie Stora-Lamarre, *L'Enfer de la Troisième République: censeurs et pornographes, 1881–1914* (Paris: Imago, 1990) 201.

5 Louis Desprez, 'Pour la liberté d'écrire', reprinted in René-Pierre Colin and Jean-François Nivet, *Louis Desprez, 1861–1885* (Charente: Du Lérot, 1992) 213 (my italics).

6 Yvan Leclerc, *Crimes écrits: la littérature en procès au dix-neuvième siècle* (Paris: Plon, 1991) 395–401.

7 Article 23, *Bulletin des lois de la République Française*, 12th series, Deuxième semestre de 1881.

However, since Kistemaekers was a Belgian publisher and hence outside the jurisdiction of the court, Bonnetain was prosecuted as the main culprit, and he was summoned to appear before the Court of First Instance. Henry Céard, who wrote the preface to Bonnetain's novel, was prosecuted as an accomplice to the crime, and in his submissions Céard repeatedly tried to distance himself from his friend.[8] To complicate matters further, Bonnetain was based in Vietnam as the overseas correspondent for *Le Figaro* when the proceedings began. It appears that Bonnetain did not return to France in time to appear before the magistrate in the court of first instance, for a *supplément d'information* was ordered upon his return.[9] The trial at the Assize Court (*Cour d'assises*) took place on 27 December 1884. Bonnetain was acquitted, although the precise reasons for the acquittal were not recorded.

In this chapter, I will situate the trial within the wider discursive constructions of onanism in late nineteenth-century France, and will analyse the ways in which the prosecution and the defence interpreted Bonnetain's novel in the courtroom. In the first section, I will examine the ways in which onanism was represented in the medical discourse of the period, and will ask how the social anxieties it generated were related to configurations of masculinity. In the second section, I will revisit the passages the prosecution presented as instances of obscenity to the court to determine what, specifically, the government lawyer considered offensive or obscene about the text, and how his assumptions are tied to the wider cultural concerns as reflected in the medical discourse. I will discuss the justification of naturalism put forward by the defence in the third section, and will explore its relationship to the literary discourse of the naturalist writers themselves. In the final section, I will focus on the question of what constitutes the literary quality of Bonnetain's novel. I will evaluate the interpretative assumptions made by Bonnetain's lawyer in the course of his defence speech, and ask whether his argument was based on a faithful reading of the literary text.

(I) Onanism, masculinity and late nineteenth-century French medical discourse

Charlot s'amuse appeared at a time when traditional conceptions of masculinity were coming under considerable stress in France, in part because of the country's declining population and falling birth rate. The demographer and statistician Jacques Bertillon, who authored the influential *The Depopulation Problem* (*Problème de la dépopulation*), was so concerned about the health of the nation that he founded a national alliance (*Alliance nationale pour l'accroissement de la population française*) to lobby for policies to save the French population.

8 See, for example, Céard's letter to the *juge d'instruction* dated 7 February 1883.

9 Letter from the Prosecution of the Court of Appeal of Paris dated 22 July 1884. Dossier D2U8 174.

In *The Demography of France* (*La statistique humaine de la France*), published four years before the trial, he argued that France was 'under the threat of becoming a tiny nation'.[10] He pinpointed the cause of decline in no uncertain terms: 'French power is diminishing because of fewer births'.[11] He noted that, back in 1700, France had been one of the largest European monarchies. However, throughout the nineteenth century its population 'grew at a miserable rate', whilst its neighbours 'grew and multiplied, spread out across continents, expanding their commercial activities and covering the entire universe with their language, their ships and their armies'.[12]

In the aftermath of France's humiliating defeat in the Franco–Prussian War, Germany's increasing influence became a particularly contentious point in the national consciousness, and comparisons between the two countries became commonplace: Bertillon pointed out that in 1880 there were 45.6 million inhabitants in the German Empire, compared with a meagre 37.2 million inhabitants in the French nation.[13]

Bertillon further noted that the depopulation had multiple repercussions. First, it led to a weakened military because the healthy young men needed to create a stronger army were in short supply; population growth was 'a part of military force' and hence 'a part of power'. There were also economic consequences, as a smaller population translated into a shortage of able-bodied workers, especially for agriculture and industry. Finally, depopulation posed a threat to France's literary heritage: Bertillon lamented that whereas a French literary classic would only be read by around 45 million people who spoke French as their mother tongue (including the Belgians, the Canadians, the Swiss and the creoles), a comparable work of German literature would be read by 80 million native German speakers, including those in Austria and Switzerland.[14] France's cultural influence would dwindle along with its population size.

France's depopulation problem in the *fin de siècle* was inextricably tied to conceptions of masculinity and sparked concerns about virility. As Robert Nye points out, the problem had two facets. First, the country's falling birth rate was believed to be caused by low marital fertility, and the low fertility rate gave rise to anxieties about masculinity because 'the general physical vigor of the father was usually regarded as the decisive factor in cases of infertility or stillbirth'.[15] In other words, the male sperm was regarded as the 'active' element in the fertilisation process, and 'the male's generative material could thus be held responsible for a couple's failure to produce viable offspring'.

10 Jacques Bertillon, *La statistique humaine de la France (naissance, mariage, mort)* (Paris: Germer Baillière, 1880) 23.

11 Ibid. 73.

12 Ibid. 28.

13 Ibid. 29.

14 Ibid. 33.

15 Robert A. Nye, *Masculinity and Male Codes of Honor in Modern France* (Berkeley: University of California Press, 1998) 86.

Secondly, there were concerns about the imbalance between male and female children, with the number of boys lagging behind the number of girls born every year. Nye notes that 'male responsibility for the sex of the offspring was clearer still, because of the direct relationship that was held to exist between the masculinity and vigor of the father and the production of male offspring'. Men in their prime were more likely to produce male children, whilst men beyond a certain age are believed to be more likely to father female children. The relatively low number of boys being born was regarded as indicative of the declining potency of French men.

In the wider cultural context of declining birth rates and diminishing national grandeur, onanism, considered to be a highly addictive and dangerously debilitating depletion of male essence, came to be regarded as the cause of much that was harmful to the French nation. Some of the medical texts of the period dealt with this supposedly noxious practice, either exclusively or as part of a wider spectrum of sexual perversities, and adumbrated its dangers with all the self-proclaimed authority and objectivity of scientific discourse. However, as Thomas Laqueur has demonstrated, the epistemological certainty of this 'scientific' discourse is problematic at best.

In his magisterial study of the cultural history of masturbation, Laqueur demonstrates that the rhetoric of danger, self-pollution and death associated with masturbation has remained remarkably consistent for much of Western history. He traces this rhetoric to a single text published in England in the early eighteenth century, not by a doctor or public hygienist, but by a quack surgeon and writer of soft-core pornography whom he identifies as John Marten. Laqueur argues that Marten instilled the belief in onanism's disastrous effects in his readers as part of a scam, to make money from the sale of his pamphlet and his bogus medicines. His depiction of masturbation was given the stamp of scientific approval when it was picked up by physicians on the European Continent, including Samuel-Auguste Tissot, author of *A Treatise on Diseases Produced by Onanism* (*L'Onanisme; ou, Dissertation physique sur les malades produites par la masturbation*).

Despite Tissot's insistence on the differences between his own text and Marten's pamphlet, it is indisputable that his treatise was the key text inciting and sustaining fears of this new found illness. Laqueur concludes that, remarkably, the 'shameless effort to invent a new disease and at the same time offer its cure at a steep price became a founding text for a medical tradition that would draw in the pillars of high-Enlightenment medicine and help create modern sexuality'.[16]

The understanding of onanism derived from the eighteenth century remained influential in *fin-de-siècle* France. Tissot's influence was especially strong in the years leading up to the trial: between 1875 and 1885, *L'Onanisme* was reissued five times, and Bonnetain's lawyer cited him as part of his defence. Whilst some physicians

16 Thomas W. Laqueur, *Solitary Sex: A Cultural History of Masturbation* (New York: Zone Books, 2003) 16.

defined onanism broadly as encompassing all non-procreative sexual activities, including masturbation (either on one's own or with another person), sodomy, oral stimulation, and many other acts, most people defined it more narrowly as manual masturbation alone.

The term 'Onanism' is derived from the biblical story of Onan: after his brother dies, Onan's father tells him to fulfil his family duty through coitus with his sister-in-law, hence giving her a child and continuing the family line. Onan does not complete the act, instead withdrawing at the last moment and spilling his seed on the ground. There are different views of what constituted Onan's exact sin, but given the concerns about diminishing virility in late nineteenth-century France, medical practitioners of the time became fixated on one interpretation: as Pierre Garnier, the most prolific practitioner writing on onanism, succinctly put it, 'the act of Onan was specifically the frustration of procreation', and he believed that God struck down Onan for being unwilling to further the bloodline.[17]

Garnier's discursive construction of onanism is underpinned by his veneration for the procreative act. He began by noting that the ability to procreate was at once the most superior and the most pre-eminent of all human faculties, but also the most delicate and most in need of protection, such that non-sanctioned sexual acts could 'negatively affect this precious and delicate faculty, trouble it, alter it, diminish it, and could often go so far as to annihilate it'. He pointed out that onanism was of particular concern not only to the medical establishment but to all French people because it constituted 'an agent acting directly and actively against procreation'; it was both the most common and 'the most fatal' of the possible obstacles to the continuation of humanity. He singled out men who initiated their wives into onanistic practices and indulged in them with their partners as 'debauched, corrupted and perverse' because they were deliberately replacing the procreative act with a secondary act which precluded the begetting of offspring.

Garnier's views were by no means unique and were echoed by other practitioners, including Doctor André Lebel, who penned a widely-circulated essay on the dangers of onanism. Lebel argued that semen was produced from blood, and that an excessive depletion of semen would have disastrous consequences on the body's blood supply and hence its overall constitution. He explained that blood flowed from the two large arteries to the testicles, where they would 'divide into numerous small arteries and undergo a new transformation which gives rise to spermatic fluid'.[18] Excessive masturbation thus meant that the onanist was not only draining his body of seminal fluid but of blood: 'most onanists let themselves get carried away by this fatal act before sperm can form in the body . . . the blood will

17 Pierre Garnier, *Onanisme seul et à deux sous toutes ses formes et leurs conséquences* (9th edn, Paris: Garnier Frères, 1895) 3.

18 Doctor André Lebel, *Vade-Mecum des jeunes gens, ou guide pratique des maladies syphilitiques vénériennes à l'usage des gens du monde, précédé d'un essai sur l'onanisme et contenant l'exposition d'une méthode certaine de préservation* (5th edn, Paris: Morris et Comp., 1858) 4.

be consistently impoverished, and all parts of the body will weaken and fall into disorder.[19]

Modifying Tissot's formula, he pointed to a supposed medical consensus that 'the loss of thirty grams of spermatic fluid weakens the body more than the loss of a kilogram of blood'.[20] Like Garnier, he believed onanism to be harmful to the nation because it led to the wastage of the main ingredient for reproduction: he pointed out that seminal fluid was 'the most vital, the most fortifying fluid' in our body because it contained within it 'all that belongs to the essence of human nature'.[21] He hyperbolically describes spermatic fluid as 'an aromatic liqueur', a few drops of which would 'suffice to give life to a new being'.[22] Onanism not only undermined but destroyed a man's desire and ability to procreate because it was, literally, draining.

As the understanding of onanism as a perverse practice with fatal consequences intensified in the late nineteenth century, the onanist emerged as a figure upon which fears about diminishing masculine virility centred, and as a threatening sexual identity in need of medical surveillance. Nye argues that, in light of such anxieties, there developed in French society 'an "ideal" or "typical" male sexual identity'. This identity embodied qualities thought to 'contribute best to national welfare: strength, vigor, decisiveness, courage, a manly appearance and comportment, and of course, fertility'.[23] Since procreative ability was key to the conception of masculinity at this time, to be considered a real man one had to contribute towards the nation by fathering strong, healthy male children, and moral and physical attributes such as strength and courage were read as signs or proof of this procreative ability. The onanist, as the figure indulging in a practice depleting his very male essence, came to represent the antithesis of this idealised, virile, manly Frenchman. In the medical discourse, the figure was defined by symptoms which marked him as the embodiment of multiple negative qualities.

Doctor Pouillet's *Étude médico-psychologique sur l'onanisme chez l'homme*, published in the same year as *Charlot s'amuse*, gives a detailed description of the physical symptoms arising from onanism. This text provides an especially interesting instance in the discursive construction of the onanist in that it is entirely free of the moralistic, judgmental language characteristic of the medical discourse of this period, yet it is nonetheless exemplary of the way medicine discursively constructed an identity that was the pale, sickly other of the ideal male. There are no overt condemnations or accusations of immorality, but the disapproval is implicit in the representation itself.

19 Ibid. 5–6.
20 Ibid. 4.
21 Ibid. 2.
22 Ibid. 4.
23 Ibid. 96.

Pouillet noted that, overall, the onanist was in 'a weakened state, a state of general exhaustion'.[24] He was too frail to hold his body upright: his back was bent, and he let his head 'hang in front and swing slightly from the left and to the right' as if he did not have the strength to keep it in place. He legs were 'frail and trembling', so that he walked with 'an unsure step'. His sexual organ, whilst enlarged due to over stimulation, nevertheless remained 'wrinkled and decrepit when in a state of rest', and his testicles hung loosely in sacks that were 'limp, flaccid, loose'.[25] His face was a picture of exhaustion: his eyelids, 'red around the edges', were 'thick' and 'swollen'; his gaze was 'languid, dull, unfocused'; his glance 'worn, cloudy, dim'; his pupils overly dilated; his lips 'discoloured'; his complexion 'pale, livid, poorly' and at times 'ashen or leaden'.[26]

Pouillet thus presented the onanist's physique as a sign of ill-health, passivity and overall degeneracy; the depletion of essence taking place in private became publicly legible on his body. In short, the onanist was a particularly vilified figure in this period because, as the opposite of the ideal, virile and reproductive man, he represented sterility, feebleness and general unproductiveness when the country needed strength for its army, economic productivity to maintain its international competitiveness and, above all, procreative energies to reverse its population decline.

The 'scientific' discourse on onanism shows that the term 'science' needs to be placed in quotation marks in the late nineteenth century; the medical texts can be more productively read as a reflection and reinforcement of cultural anxieties about gender than as an objective, ideologically-untainted diagnosis of a malady. Onanism became regarded as a problem because it was continuously imagined, discursively constructed and textually represented to be so. In this light, it is no surprise that in Bonnetain's novel Charlot's suicide takes place amidst the fanfare, the laughter and the bright tricoloured flags of the 14th of July celebrations: despondent, drunk and helpless, he looks on at the National Day celebrations in solitude, in a moment of painful exclusion from French nationhood, before plunging to his death. The ending of the novel reflects the status of the onanist as an outcast in the cultural imagination, to be excluded from a citizenry reserved for his more virile, reproductive counterparts.

(II) On (not) becoming a man, or the case for the prosecution

Bonnetain was brought to trial in the *Cour d'assises* on 27 December 1884. The exact contours of the offence, *outrage aux bonnes moeurs*, are difficult to

24 T. Pouillet, *Étude médico-psychologique sur l'onanisme chez l'homme, précédé d'une introduction sur les autres abus génitaux* (Paris: Adrian Delahaye et Émile Lecrosier, 1883) 182.

25 Ibid. 181–82.

26 Ibid. 182–83.

delineate: which dimension of public decency was the novel allegedly offending, and how far from accepted notions of decency did it have to stray before it could be considered as an 'outrage'? Was Bonnetain brought to the dock merely because he wrote a novel on a sexual topic, or was there something particularly offensive about the specific sexual activity he chose to write about?

Situated within the context of the broader cultural anxieties about manliness and nationhood, the specific reasons why *Charlot s'amuse* came under the scrutiny of the censors start to become clear: whilst the immediate impetus of the prosecution was the anonymous letter sent to the Director of Public Prosecutions, the novel gave rise to an obscenity trial at least in part because it took as its subject a topic that constituted the focal point for much of the social angst about masculinity in late nineteenth-century France.

In many ways, Charlot is a faithful portrayal of the onanist as imagined and described within the medical discourse of the time, a resemblance that formed the core of the argument of the defence lawyer and of Bonnetain himself, and one to which we shall return. The novel places great emphasis on Charlot's body, and the corporeal descriptions could have been lifted from any one of the medical treatises of the period. Like Garnier's subjects, who are 'pale, skinny, underdeveloped', Charlot is thin and worn.[27] His gaze is 'apathetic', his pupils are always dilated and unfocused, and his eyelids are heavy. As he grows older, Charlot starts to carry himself with 'a sagging upper body'. With his 'dangling arms' and his 'limp legs', he walks around 'like a madman'.[28] Garnier identifies masturbatory 'excesses' as the 'unique cause of . . . retardation' in his subjects.[29]

The narrator of the novel echoes Garnier, noting that it is Charlot's self-polluting exertions which turn him from 'the charming blond kid who was the envy of mothers' to 'the little sick child who looked drawn, preoccupied and morose', and in whom 'some unidentified harm had mercilessly shriveled the flower of health and made its colors fade'.[30] Furthermore, 'the animation in his face' gives way to 'a pallid, even leaden, complexion'. His eyes are no longer bright and lively, but appear 'dull, languid, as if veiled by something, especially in the morning'.[31] In terms of personal qualities, Garnier's description of the onanist as 'poorly adjusted, poorly developed, timid, easily frightened, cowardly, sad or melancholic, solitary' also applies to Charlot.[32] The novel's descriptions of the body, reproducing the classic symptoms of onanism in the medical literature and charting the decline of a healthy young man into degeneracy and physiological exhaustion, refract and amplify the social apprehension about gender and virility of the time.

27 Garnier (n 17) 253.
28 Paul Bonnetain, *Charlot s'amuse* (1883) (Geneva: Slatkine Reprints, 1979) 164–65.
29 Garnier (n 17) 253.
30 Bonnetain (n 28)124.
31 Ibid. 123.
32 Garnier (n 17) 253.

The exact argument of the prosecution has now been lost; the trial transcript contained in the dossier at the *Archives de Paris* does not contain any details of how the lawyer presented his case to the jury. However, what is known about the prosecution's argument is that it presented 12 passages from *Charlot s'amuse* which it considered particularly offensive to public decency. These passages were included in the original summons to Bonnetain, and are reprinted in the 1885 edition of the novel. It is possible to attempt at least a partial reconstruction of the logic of the prosecution in the trial from these passages, and to discern the interpretative assumptions underlying its decision to excerpt the novel in the way it did.

Many of those excerpts singled out as being particularly offensive were the ones which most directly challenged the ideal masculine type imagined to sustain the French *patrie*, either because they threw into question some of the assumptions underpinning the cultural conception of this ideal or because they represented non-reproductive sexuality in a sympathetic way. The question of what constituted an outrage or an offence against public decency was therefore determined by an unspoken belief in the need, or at least the desirability, for the court to uphold the ideal masculine type. In other words, the law resisted literary depictions of masculinity where they challenged most intensely the construction of the heterosexual, reproductive, virile male in the national consciousness.

A discussion of four of these passages will suffice to make clear the interpretative assumptions in the law, and the reconfiguration of masculinity at work in the episodes it sought to proscribe. The first passage comes from Chapter VIII of the novel, in which Charlot ejaculates for the first time. Charlot's new companion, Lucien, has left for another town for a week, leaving Charlot on his own. The narrator notes that Charlot's urges 'came back all the more intensely . . . in the absence of the caresses his friend used to lavish on him'.[33] It is therefore clear that Charlot has been indulging not only in onanism, but in onanism of the worst kind according to the medical literature, with another partner of the same sex. Charlot is initially frightened when it happens; he finds the whole experience 'strange', the 'convulsive emission' terrified him, and he fears that some 'atrocious illness' was responsible for the emission. However, as he gradually realises what has happened, the fear subsides and is replaced by pride and a newfound self-confidence: 'suddenly, with a long, quivering spasm, *he realized that he had become a man*' (my italics).

The reference to manhood here is significant. In a narrower, literal sense, Charlot achieved manhood because his body has reached sexual maturity; the experience marks the end of childhood. However, when read within the wider cultural context of the increasingly destabilised foundations of masculinity and also in the context of the events in the novel immediately preceding this scene, the passage can also be interpreted as positing an alternative, perverse definition of what it means to be a man: Charlot 'had become a man' not, as the circulating

33 Bonnetain (n 28) 181.

cultural ideas would dictate, because he is now able to father a child, but because he has repeatedly engaged in onanistic activity until his seed is wasted on solitary indulgences.

The first ejaculation is here presented as the epitome of maleness, not because it marks the onset of Charlot's procreative ability, but perversely because it is the height of a non-procreative sexual pleasure. It also marks the beginning of a long process of physical exhaustion and degeneration, and Charlot redoubles his masturbatory activity in part because of his newly minted manhood. As such, the novel depicts a deviant masculinity which is markedly non-reproductive, and presents onanism not as antithetical to masculinity, but as constitutive of it.

The culmination of this representation of deviant masculinity can be found in another passage cited by the prosecution, in which Charlot masturbates and ejaculates in the direction of a crucifix: 'a fierce libidinal force was already coursing through him . . . he turned towards the crucifix, positioning himself in the direction of the presbytery. . . . He then abandoned himself to his impulses, gritting his teeth, rolling his eyes, writhing in the heightened intensity of his long-delayed outburst'.[34] This act constitutes a gesture of defiance against the Church, society, and life: shocked by the death of Mademoiselle de Closberry who had cared for him, thrown out of the school run by the Maristes, fed up with the abuse and corruption to which he had been subjected at the hands of the brothers at the rue des Récollets, and frustrated at his own inability to control his sexual urges, Charlot yearned to 'avenge himself of the nuns, the priests, the injustice of fate, and the whole of society'.

However, it is ironically in this scandalous and blasphemous episode that Charlot exhibits some of the best qualities of the ideal masculine type: roused from his usual state of passivity by his anger, his act constitutes a determined, active mode of defiance and is by far the most decisive action he undertakes in the novel. The 'seed of man' produced here cannot be further from its procreative purposes, and Charlot's masculine qualities of action, decisiveness and determination manifest themselves perversely, in the sacrilegious act of achieving a sexual climax in front of the crucifix.[35] The passage was construed as evidence of an *outrage aux bonnes moeurs*, arguably because it decouples the positive qualities of manhood from procreation and aligns them with an act of blasphemy.

A passage on Charlot's encounter with a prostitute chosen by the prosecution as evidence against Bonnetain further interrogates the seemingly unquestionable supremacy of the ideal masculine type. This passage comes from Chapter XI of the novel. Charlot joins the army but appears morose, listless and physically weak. In an attempt to revive his spirits, the other soldiers in the regiment take him to a brothel, where he is introduced to a prostitute named Camélia. As Peter Gay has pointed out, the brothel was often the sexual initiation ground for young,

34 Ibid. 204–205.
35 Lebel (n 18) 3.

heterosexual bourgeois men, a 'school for the inexperienced'.[36] More than a few male youths were 'pushed into initiation by a genial father or shameless classmate'.[37] Visiting a brothel, at least for the sexual novice, was considered part of nineteenth-century normative masculinity, such that Charlot's non-consummation, his failure and even refusal at initiation, underscores his deviancy.

At first glance, the passage seems to establish an opposition between the normativity of heterosexual intercourse and the abnormality of onanism. The narrator notes that Charlot is unresponsive to Camélia's charms: 'he no longer wanted to see . . . this despicable bedroom, these sickening clichés, this naked woman'.[38] Significantly, even though he is uninterested in coitus with her, he becomes aroused when she masturbates him: 'his face turned white with joy' at the point where Camélia caresses him with her hands, but he longs to go home when she pushes him towards a fuller sexual union.[39] Charlot's preference for manual masturbation over intercourse exemplifies one of the problems with onanism which the medical literature identified: onanists risked displacing their natural desires with 'false images' and 'phantoms' of their fantasies, and their 'dreadful habits' prevented them from 'developing even the smallest grain of attraction towards the other sex'.[40]

The medical literature depicted onanism as a disruption of the relationship between copy and original in the sexual domain: solitary sex was a pale imitation of real, heterosexual union, and the onanist's penchant for imaginary pleasures rather than actual sex constituted the core of his perversity. To a great extent, Charlot internalises these sexual norms: he is 'angry and ashamed at his own impotence' when he fails to have full intercourse with her, and he is so humiliated that he 'hurried towards the stairs and fled'.[41]

Even though the novel adopts some of the assumptions and language of the medical discourse of the period, it also challenges this discourse by positing an alternative definition of masculinity. Despite his frustration, Charlot realises that his solitary pleasures offer him the comfort of self-sufficiency and a certain sexual independence which the men in his regiment lack. Whilst the medical texts define the inability to engage in a full heterosexual union as a problem, the novel subtly throws into question the distinction between normality and pathology. The narrator notes that when Charlot reflects upon the 'the ridiculous things his comrades did for such creatures, the pain they went through to gather the money

36 Peter Gay, *The Bourgeois Experience: Victoria to Freud. Vol 2: The Tender Passion* (New York: Oxford University Press, 1986) 355.

37 Ibid. 353.

38 Bonnetain (n 28) 241.

39 Ibid. 242.

40 H. Fournier, *De l'Onanisme: causes, dangers et inconvénients pour les individus, la famille et la société. Remèdes* (2nd edn, Paris: Librairie J.B. Baillière et Fils, 1876) 116.

41 Bonnetain (n 28) 242.

to come wallowing at their feet', he does so with 'a smile of pity' for them.[42] He prefers to be on his own, because 'at least his solitary pleasure had something sublime about it!'

The medical literature insists that the onanist is a sexual deviant who cannot control his own desires and succumbs to excesses, but this passage suggests that heterosexual men are not necessarily in better control of their desires. In fact, Charlot's ability to stand aloof from 'the influence which women have over so many millions of men' makes him feel 'vaguely superior to humanity'. The narrator notes that Charlot 'became a man again' when the prostitute manually caresses him, even though he cannot proceed to full intercourse.[43] Manhood, at least in the episode of the brothel, seems to be defined by precisely the ability to maintain one's preference for the imitation over the real sex act; it is this preference which shields Charlot from demands of the flesh that bring his companions grovelling back to the whorehouse.

The fourth passage concerns an accident which happens to Origène, one of the brothers at the seminary at the rue des Récollets. The single or celibate man was an intensely problematic figure in the second half of the nineteenth century, the period which represents the heyday of the nuclear family and in which the *paterfamilias* became the hegemonic cultural figure, and this was especially so in the case of the clergyman. On the one hand, his influence on married women was suspect; the great moral and spiritual influence he had over them through the confession meant that he was a potential threat to the husband. Jules Michelet calls him the 'invisible man' whose presence at the family dinner table was always felt, but not always welcomed.[44] On the other hand, the clergyman who voluntarily excluded himself from family life was often assumed to harbour some deviant sexual interest, and 'around this strange figure all manner of abominable suspicions gathered all too easily, and indeed all too correctly'.[45]

This view is expressed in the novel by Perrin, an anti-clerical doctor, who noted that 'they were all the same, these cassock-wearing men. Rotten from childhood, and physically jaded (*blasés physiquement*) at age thirty!'[46] The passage from Bonnetain's novel concerns the non-procreative sexual activity that was imagined to take place amongst the clergy. Charlot quickly becomes the object of attention amongst the men at the seminary. Brother Hilarion, an older, lecherous clergyman, attempts to rape him, and another clergyman, Brother Eusèbe, turns Charlot into the object of his sexual fantasies, making him lick the ground and flagellating him as a punishment when he fails to recite his catechism.

42 Ibid. 241.
43 Ibid. 243.
44 Jules Michelet, *Le prêtre, la femme et la famille* (Paris: Calmann Lévy, 1881) 2.
45 Jean Borie, *Le célibataire français* (Paris: Le Sagittaire, 1976) 142.
46 Bonnetain (n 28) 131.

It is the experience of Brother Origène, however, on which the prosecution focused in the trial. With his pale complexion, languid gaze and limp body, his exclusive sexual interest in men and his indulgence in masturbatory practices, it is possible to interpret Origène as combining the attributes of the onanist, the erotomaniac and the homosexual. Initially hesitant to make any sexual advances towards Charlot, Origène is eventually consumed by 'the unhealthy and obscene desires of an onanist' at the sight of his naked body, and cannot help succumbing to his desire for the young man.[47] The scene which came under legal scrutiny concerns an injury which Origène has sustained. The clergy's own doctor is unable to resolve the crisis and summons Perrin for help, despite the tensions between the Church and the secular, anti-clerical doctor.

It is at first unclear how Origène injured himself; the scene is filtered through Charlot's consciousness, and the reader only understands and overhears as much as Charlot does. It gradually transpires that the young clergyman has fainted from pain because the penholder which he inserted into his posterior punctured his prostate; Perrin exclaims 'whoever told you to stick the wick of the penholder in there first?'[48] This episode can be read as offensive to public decency in multiple ways. First, the way it is framed means that the reader is co-opted into the same perverse practice of voyeurism as Charlot: in an attempt to find out what happens to Origène, Charlot hides inside a cupboard, and then could not resist peeking inside the room: 'he wanted to see. . . . There was stained glass on the door separating the office from the bedroom, and he went up and looked through the part of the glass that was not completely covered by the cotton curtain'.[49]

Since the scene is filtered through Charlot's consciousness, the reader is placed in the same voyeuristic position as the character in the novel, which means that it becomes difficult for him to distance himself morally from this supposedly perverse voyeuristic act. Moreover, this episode can be read as a literal reversal of the scene of normative, heterosexual coitus: instead of being the virile man who adopts an 'active' sexual position and fathers strong children for the nation, Origène here becomes the 'passive' partner in the act, and the artificiality of such a change in sexual position is highlighted by the fact that the substitute object for the phallus is ill-suited for the purpose.

It is also possible to read the passage in a psychoanalytic frame, to articulate the deeper anxieties about masculinity which the episode triggered. Reading the episode in light of Lee Edelman's psychoanalytic notion of '(be)hindsight' enables us to think through what is at stake in this 'preposterous' scene of the punctured prostate. Edelman's essay is concerned with the near-universal aversion to sodomy. He asks: 'What, after all, can the scene of sodomy inflict to make its staging, if only in the space of the imagination, so dangerous to effect, and what within that scene

47 Ibid. 98.
48 Ibid. 133.
49 Ibid. 128.

has such power to implicate—and, by implicating, to sully—that such a scene, or even the possibility of such a scene, ought properly to be disavowed?'[50]

Edelman argues that this aversion arises in part because of a disturbance of spatio-temporal logic which is central to one's identity. Edelman points out that the Latin root of the adjective 'preposterous' refers to a problematic rearrangement between 'pre-' and 'post-'; a preposterous situation is one 'that disturbs the relationship of early and late, or before and behind'.[51] Whilst heterosexual, reproductive sex prioritises the frontal part of the body, the sex act of sodomy privileges the posterior part of the body; by turning the 'back' of the body into the 'front' it problematises normative dimensions of coitus and can be said to constitute a disruption of its 'spatio-temporal positioning'.[52] In other words, for Edelman the scene of sodomy may seem offensive or perverse to the reader in part because it problematises the logic of 'prior' and 'after', of 'front' and 'back', on which identity is premised, and the reader's feelings of unease or discomfort become condensed onto this corporeal representation of the disruption.

In light of Edelman's analysis, it is possible to argue that the horrific physical trauma arising from Origène's passive sexual position and his use of an artificial phallus to mimic coitus can be interpreted as the bodily representation of a disturbance to a certain spatio-temporal logic of identity, and the reader's sense of discomfort or unease arising from such disturbance is both condensed and displaced onto the discomfort or disgust about the injury. The fact that the injury came about because the victim inserted 'the wick of the penholder in there first', or the wrong side up, with the proper order inverted, underscores the significance of the disturbance of positioning.

Origène's accident causes the reader to cringe not only because of the more literal reason of the character's pain, but also because the specific way in which the injury was brought about – a man adopting a 'passive' sexual position vis-à-vis a flawed phallic object – and can be read as a bodily representation or a staging of a deeper disturbance in the axes along which reader identity is constructed. Since normative, procreative sexual intercourse dictates a linear, frontal logic, a sodomitical sex act is deemed offensive at least in part because it disrupts this linear logic on which heterosexual coitus, and indeed male heterosexual identity, is premised.

50 Lee Edelman, 'Seeing things: representation, the scene of surveillance, and the spectacle of gay male sex' in Diana Fuss (ed), *Inside/out: Lesbian Theories, Gay Theories* (New York: Routledge, 1991) 93–119 at 94. For further discussions of gay anality, see Leo Bersani, 'Is the rectum a grave?' in Leo Bersani (ed), *'Is the Rectum a Grave?' and Other Essays* (Chicago: University of Chicago Press, 2009) 3–31 and Eve Kosofsky Sedgwick, 'Anality: news from the front' in Jonathan Goldberg (ed), *The Weather in Proust* (Durham: Duke University Press, 2011) 166–83.

51 Ibid. 96

52 Ibid. 104.

(III) Literature as science, or the case for the defence

Léon Cléry's defence speech was recognised in its time as the decisive factor in securing Bonnetain's victory. Desprez, who had lost the obscenity trial over his own novel the week before, professed to be delighted at Bonnetain's acquittal, and observed that Cléry 'had gotten his hand on the pulse' (*pincé les cordes sensibles*) of the court in the *Charlot s'amuse* trial.[53] Bonnetain himself decided to publish the 1885 edition of the novel with a note of thanks to his lawyer and wrote: 'I owe to your admirable defence speech my acquittal by the Jury of the Seine'. This section examines the defence speech in detail. It highlights its main arguments, and examines the relationship between the lawyer's own legal narrative and the literary narrative which he defended.

Cléry made several arguments in his closing speech. Like Sénard in the *Madame Bovary* trial, he established comparisons between Bonnetain's novels and other works of literary merit, including those by such revered writers as Voltaire and Denis Diderot, in an attempt to portray the text as serious literature. As we shall see in the next chapter, Zola was prosecuted for obscenity in England but not in France, and Cléry contended that it was absurd for the French court to prosecute Bonnetain, a mere disciple of the school of naturalism, when it allowed the grand master himself to publish novels which he argued were more immoral.

Cléry was also attuned to concerns about the impact of fiction reading in the late nineteenth century, and explicitly addressed the worry that the novelistic representation of vice could engender vice in the reader, that 'if you present debauchery and drunkenness in a positive way, you could lead me into drunkenness or debauchery'.[54] He parried such concerns by pointing out that the danger would only arise if onanism was depicted favourably in the novel, and that no reader would wish to imitate a practice that was depicted as leading to mental anguish, physical degeneration and death. He further argued that, in Bonnetain's case, 'it takes almost as much courage as writing the book to read it till the end'.[55] Thus, far from aiming to instil a love of vice, he contended that *Charlot s'amuse* sought to create a distance between its protagonist's practices and the reader: in the novel onanism 'became an object of horror for those unfortunate enough to be plagued by this vice, and something to stay away from for those who may succumb to its temptations'.[56] To hammer home his rebuttal, Cléry posited that, whilst the public may have the right not to purchase Bonnetain's novel if it deemed it offensive, it did not have the right to stop Bonnetain from writing it.

Cléry's most significant line of defence could be described as a justification of *Charlot s'amuse* in the name of science. The rhetoric of his legal defence of the

53 Cited in *Desprez* (n 5) 144.
54 Léon Cléry, *Souvenirs du Palais* (Paris: A. Lemerre, 1890) 201.
55 Ibid. 201.
56 Ibid. 199.

novel in the courtroom overlapped almost completely with the rhetoric in the pronouncements by many naturalist writers themselves in the wider cultural sphere. He characterised the naturalist literary project as inherently scientific in nature, such that Bonnetain's text should be regarded as a serious, dispassionate and well researched study of a particular medical condition which, by implication, could not be construed as pornography.

He began by noting that the naturalist school was underpinned by its 'love of what is true'.[57] It was dedicated to representing reality as accurately as possible; it refused to embellish or sanitise and presented this reality in all its grittiness and harshness. The language here approximates the language of realism, but with a scientific element. The irony, of course, is that, as we have seen, no easy correspondence to reality or truth in the 'scientific' discourse on onanism can be taken for granted. Cléry, however, insisted that Bonnetain's choice of onansim as his subject stemmed from a real-life engagement with its devastating effects. He argued that when Bonnetain was a soldier, he witnessed at first hand the harm this illness inflicted on French soldiers: he was 'moved by seeing this sickness, which was more widespread than we had imagined' and 'he had witnessed the havoc that this malady produced in organisms' in military hospitals.[58] Furthermore, he had lost friends in the army 'to this horrible illness', and the loss affected him deeply.[59]

The lawyer further underscored that the character of Charlot was based on a real person, 'an unfortunate young man from a well-to-do family in Brittany, who had joined the force out of his own volition' but who ended up not only deserting the troops but also stealing their ammunition and supplies. He noted that, having witnessed the noxious effects of onanism, Bonnetain decided to take action, and wrote a study of the 'genesis' and the 'diverse evolutions' of the illness. Far from aiming to titillate or arouse, then, Bonnetain wrote his novel in an attempt to further our understanding of onanism and to curb its spread; the author himself considered the novel as a text which could 'contribute towards the treatment of onanists' and emphatically 'not as one which could propagate onanism'.[60]

After establishing the truth value of the novel, Cléry expounded on its 'scientific' method of representing reality: he noted that Bonnetain 'aimed to take seriously a scientific theory', and that his novel was based on information gathered from numerous 'specialized works, medical theses' and 'courses given by professors'.[61] He went on to claim that a doctor actually praised the novel as 'the first novel dealing with a scientific subject in which he saw a respectable engagement with science'. Cléry contended that naturalism's scientific turn constituted its modernity: unlike previous writers who based their work on imagination and fantasy, Bonnetain

57 Ibid. 203.
58 Ibid. 198.
59 Ibid. 210.
60 Bonnetain's statement to the court dated 12 August 1884. Dossier D2U8 174.
61 Cléry (n 54) 211.

and other naturalist writers had 'opened up a new path' to literature through their methodical approach and their rigorous research on their subject.[62]

He concluded that Bonnetain's scientific approach to sex, including 'the long period of deliberation which gave rise to and determined the choice of subject, the particular care he took when writing' and 'the search for a scrupulous truth which compels one to such hard work', all constituted evidence that *Charlot s'amuse* was of substantial literary value, so that the court should refrain from construing it as one of those obscene books written 'for the satisfaction of old perverts and loose women'.[63] Despite its insistence on the absolute equivalence between literature and science, the argument about the scientific nature of Bonnetain's text perhaps did not so much establish the novel as a medical treatise per se, but drew on the signification of authority, objectivity and seriousness in the concept of 'science' to establish the literary merit of fiction. The references to science thus had the effect of creating a generic divide between the novel, which Cléry maintained was literary because of its purportedly medical premise, and pornography, which was non-literary because it was produced for the sole purpose of eliciting the reader's sexual pleasure.

Significantly, Cléry's argument is articulated in the language of the writers of naturalist fiction. As David Baguley points out, the manifestos of naturalism should not be read literally as formulas for the application of a scientific method to literature, but as deliberately 'polemical' texts designed to carve out a space for naturalism within the 'continuous battle of prefaces, manifestos and journal articles . . . which was the reality of literary life (and survival)' in the late nineteenth century.[64] The need to carve out a space for naturalism was equally strong in the courtroom, and Cléry adopted the same discursive strategy as the writers in his attempt to parry the accusations of obscenity by the prosecution.

The repetition of the rhetoric of science from the literary discourse within the legal discourse is evident when the lawyer's speech is juxtaposed with Bonnetain's own statement to the court. In unequivocal terms, the writer insisted that his novel was a moral book, that it represented not only 'a work of art' but also 'the elaboration of a very precise scientific theory'.[65] He added that he had received 'the congratulations of a number of doctors and prominent men of letters'. His publisher, Kistemaekers, also emphasised that the novel was 'a work of art conceived in an essentially scientific spirit'.[66] As evidence of his firm conviction of the work's literary merit, he said he would be willing to appear before the French court should Bonnetain not be able to return to France from Vietnam in time to defend it. Desprez defended his artistic method in similar terms in the

62 Ibid. 203.
63 Ibid. 212.
64 David Baguley, *Naturalist Fiction* (Cambridge: Cambridge University Press, 1990) 61.
65 Bonnetain, Statement dated 12 August 1884.
66 Henry Kistemaekers's deposition at the Court of First Instance (20 February 1884).

Autour d'un clocher trial in the same year: he stood by his belief that one must not choose to write only on socially acceptable subjects, that 'every detail must be reproduced' to avoid distortion and that the only crime for which he was brought to the dock was the refusal 'to deface truth with an eclecticism at once arbitrary and anti-scientific'.[67]

Naturalism's reliance on the rhetoric of science as a means of establishing its literary merit has been attacked by its critics. The most famous instance of this attack came from Louis Ulbach who, writing under the pseudonym of Ferragus, penned an article entitled 'Putrid Literature' in *Le Figaro* denouncing the publication of Zola's *Thérèse Raquin*. Ulbach claimed that 'a monstrous school of novelists' had gained currency on the literary scene. Ulbach was attuned to naturalism's rhetorical strategies: parodying its scientific jargon, Ulbach claimed that this school honed in on 'the most surgical curiosities', that it gave detailed descriptions of 'plague victims so as to make us admire their blotches', and that it produced works 'directly inspired by cholera'.[68] He argued that a literature which was obsessed with sex, sickness and death spoke to the human instinct which was at once 'the most universal', but also 'the lowest', 'the least respectable' and 'the most bestial'.[69]

In response, Zola redoubled his deployment of scientific language. He angrily chided his critic for hiding behind a pen name, and retorted that his novels were not about the charnel house, pus or cholera, but engaged with 'human realities, the most terrible lessons of life'.[70] In the preface to the second edition of *Thérèse Raquin*, which was written as a response to its critics, Zola explicitly stated that he had 'above all a scientific objective'. Zola's language in his response to Ulbach parallels that of Cléry in his argument before the court. He claimed to have written 'each scene, even the most feverish (*fiévreuses*) ones, solely with the interest of a scientist', and Bonnetain reproduced the passage containing this justification from Zola's novel as the epigraph to his own.[71]

Writing in defence of his narrative about an adulterous couple who conspired to murder the woman's husband, Zola argued that he wanted to study the behaviour of individuals dominated by 'their nerves and their blood', whose actions are determined by 'the inevitability of their flesh', 'the drive of their instinct', their 'neurotic crises' and their 'cerebral disorders'.[72] Words such as 'nerves', 'blood', 'instinct', 'flesh', 'cerebral' and 'neurotic' were used in such a way that their wider linguistic resonances gave way to specific, medical, even clinical significations carried over from scientific discourse. Each chapter, he said, was no more than 'a curious physiological case'. The blurring of the common sense of 'case' as a

67 Desprez (n 5) 212.

68 Ferragus (Louis Ulbach), 'La littérature putride' (1868), reprinted in Émile Zola, *Thérèse Raquin* (Henri Mitterand (ed), Paris: GF Flammarion, 1970) 39–44 at 39.

69 Ulbach, 'La littérature putride' (n 68) 40.

70 Émile Zola, 'Réponse à Ferragus' (1868), reprinted in Zola, *Thérèse Raquin* (n 68) 44–48 at 44.

71 Zola, *Thérèse Raquin* (n 68) 61.

72 Ibid. 60.

specific instance of a novel and the more medically precise 'case' as a subject requiring close examination and diagnosis was part of a rhetorical move to give *Thérèse Raquin* a stamp of literary merit. He concluded that he has 'simply performed on living bodies the analytical work which surgeons perform on dead ones'.

This rhetoric of science not only gave naturalist fiction form and value, but also provided it with a defence against accusations of immorality: Zola argued that accusations of immorality had 'absolutely no meaning in scientific matters'.[73] Naturalist fiction drew on the authority of scientific discourse so that nothing, not even murder or onanism, could be considered off-limits to the novelist: fiction was aligned with scientific advancement; the novelist wrote about the aspects of life which critics would rather disavow not for licentious or morbid reasons, but in order to further our understanding of humanity in all its complexity and contribute to human progress. The adoption of scientific rhetoric went beyond the adoption of vocabulary to the adoption of entire argumentative structures: just as a scientist like Garnier would justify writing about onanism because 'it is by placing squarely before each male or female reader the pain or the wound devouring them that it is possible to achieve a better understanding of its dangers and its remedies', so the naturalist writer would justify his choice of subject with the purported aim of contributing to a better understanding of all aspects of life.[74]

When Cléry's defence and the statement of naturalist writers such as Bonnetain, Zola and Desprez are placed side by side, we can see that the defence of both the lawyer and the writers drew on the same linguistic resources to justify the merit and value of naturalist fiction. In the *Charlot s'amuse* trial, both law, in the form of Cléry's defence speech, and literature, in the form of the novelists' multiple manifestos of the naturalist aesthetic, were suffused with a rhetoric of science: both discourses drew on the technical or clinical significations of scientific jargon and structures to give a sense of seriousness and authority to naturalist fiction that in turn established its status as literature.

The 'scientific' language can be said to have flowed from the manifestos and fictive texts of the naturalist writers and to have entered the linguistic fabric of the courtroom, such that the structure, tropes and rhetorical moves between law and literature became indistinguishable. The language of the law and the language of literature emerge as overlapping and intertwined. The similarity between the two discourses was such that it is at times difficult to distinguish who was speaking – the lawyer or the writer of fiction; the language of the law and the language of literature echoed, blurred into, and imitated each other.

The discursive entanglements between law and literature become even more visible when we consider not only the scientific terminology underpinning Cléry's legal language, but the legal metaphors which formed an integral part of

73 Ibid. 61.
74 Garnier (n 17) 13.

naturalism's response to its critics. Zola's preface to *Thérèse Raquin* can be said to take the form of a narrative of defence or an *apologia*, for the novel specifically and for the naturalist approach to literature more generally. In fact, the word 'défense' was one Zola deliberately used, and in the preface it had a specifically legal ring to it.[75] He imagined himself 'before a court', and he addressed his readers as 'my judges'.[76]

Lamenting that his critics have not appreciated his intentions and his art, he felt obligated to 'present my work to my judges myself'.[77] Furthermore, he justified his literary output in the language of rights, arguing for 'the right, in our time of artistic liberty, to choose my subjects as I see fit'.[78] Naturalism's entanglements with the law, both in the form of obscenity trials and in the metaphors which underpinned its manifestos, created affinities between legal and literary narratives, which meant that at times it became virtually impossible to distinguish, linguistically, the legal defence of literature in the courtroom and literature's defence of itself in the wider cultural sphere.

(IV) Moral judgment and the question of literature

Cléry's argument that *Charlot s'amuse* should be construed as a work with a scientific basis, a study of a particular medical condition known as onanism, seemed effective: Bonnetain was acquitted. Cléry's interpretation of the novel is an influential one, and is echoed in the work of many critics of our own time. In his introduction to the Slatkine edition of *Charlot s'amuse*, Hubert Juin, like Cléry, underscored its scientific accuracy by noting that it is 'wholly in keeping with' (*s'inscrit dans le droit fil*) the entry on 'solitary vice' in the *Pierre Larousse Dictionary*.[79] In a similar vein, Lawrence Schehr argued that the medical discourse was the only language available to Bonnetain to give voice to masturbation, so that 'to write about it, he must buy into the discourse of disapproval'.[80]

However, despite the verdict, Cléry's argument that *Charlot s'amuse* is *literary* because it is *scientific* raises more questions than it resolves. What does it mean to say that a work of fiction is scientific, and what assumptions about science are made here? In particular, his argument raises important questions about the definition and status of literature, and the remainder of the chapter will consider this aspect of the trial. To what extent can the vocabulary and models of science function as a mark of a novel's literary quality? By arguing that *Charlot s'amuse*

75 Zola, *Thérèse Raquin* (n 68) 63.
76 Ibid. 63 and 59.
77 Ibid. 59.
78 Ibid. 62.
79 Hubert Juin, 'Présentation' in Bonnetain, *Charlot s'amuse*, introduction unpaginated.
80 Lawrence R. Schehr, *Parts of an Andrology: On Representations of Men's Bodies* (Stanford: Stanford University Press, 1997) 126.

is literature because it is actually another scientific text, does Cléry not subsume literature under name of science?

If Bonnetain's novel is to be considered a work of literature, then it is necessary to probe more deeply into what constitutes its literariness, beyond the justification proffered in the defence's reading. Even though the question of how literature should be defined, or what constitutes the literary dimension of Bonnetain's novel, did not explicitly arise in the courtroom, it is nonetheless important to bring it to the forefront because it is a question which hovers just beneath the surface not only of the *Charlot s'amuse* trial, but of all literary trials, never fully emerging but always alluded to or obliquely invoked when a novel is contrasted to other, non-literary categories such as pornography, or when its literary dimension is argued to be premised on other disciplines such as science.[81]

Since both Cléry and the naturalist writers argued that there was an alignment between literature and science, it may be fruitful to return to the 'scientific' or medical texts on onanism in late-nineteenth-century France with which this chapter began. A survey of this corpus quickly shows that medicine and morality were closely intertwined in the late nineteenth century, as evidenced by the co-presence of a technical, medical vocabulary and a judgmental, moral language in the construction of the 'vice' of onanism. There was also a preponderance of religious vocabulary, as religion functioned as the presumed basis of morality. Garnier described onanism as 'the universal evil, the illness that brings no pain, the odious and deathly vice that ruins the body and the spirit'.[82] Here, onanism is given form by way of a medical vocabulary ('the illness that brings no pain') and a moral and religious one ('evil', 'vice'). Moreover, its effects were presumed to have both physical and spiritual dimensions, and Garnier posited that onanism had 'physical and moral' consequences.[83]

In a similar vein, Lebel noted that masturbation degraded 'the soul' and was 'no less harmful to the body'.[84] In his *Étude médico-psychologique sur l'onanisme chez l'homme*, Pouillet more systematically divided the effect of onanism into three categories: intellectual, moral and physical. In addition to the physical symptoms such as paleness, emaciation and languidness, the illness stunted intellectual development: in a typical case the subject's 'memory is halting, unreliable, weak, such that it is more or less lost; the ability to relate ideas to one another is lessened or nullified . . . it becomes difficult, and at times impossible, to pay attention to things'.[85] On a moral level, he became 'devoid of frankness, shifty, deceitful'. He was 'without

81 For further discussions of the 'literary', see Shoshana Felman, *Writing and Madness* (Martha Noel Evans, Shoshana Felman and Brian Massumi (trans), Ithaca: Cornell University Press, 1985); Derek Attridge, *The Singularity of Literature* (London: Routledge, 2004); and Jonathan D. Culler, *The Literary in Theory* (Palo Alto: Stanford University Press, 2007).

82 Garnier (n 17) 198.

83 Ibid. 51.

84 Lebel (n 18) 2.

85 Pouillet (n 24) 180.

affection' and full of 'aversion towards others, disdain for women' and 'indifference to the family'. Onanism was imagined to create a distance between its subject and the community, such that the onanist eventually became 'a perfect egoist'.

The use of moral terms as part of medicine's attempt to conceptualise the physical act of onanism raises interesting questions. On what basis did moral considerations enter the picture? Why was a sexual identity supposedly most readily recognised by physical symptoms also imagined to exhibit a set of moral attributes? What justified the somatisation of moral ideas, such that physical signs become read as indicators of immoral behaviour? Laqueur traces the merging of the medical and the moral to the Enlightenment, a time when science was 'reclaiming the authority that had for so long belonged to religion'.[86] As the questioning of religious authority deepened, it became evident that 'norms were to be grounded not in divine revelation but in an understanding of what nature demanded', so that 'violations of such norms became evident through pathology' rather than through scripture.[87] In this intellectual climate, doctors became 'both guides to what was right and diagnosticians of what was wrong', and this dual emphasis meant that scientific discourse came to express itself in a 'medico-moral' vocabulary, a mode of expression that continued throughout the nineteenth century.

One especially pertinent medico-moral question in the scientific discourse on onanism in the *fin de siècle* seemed to be that of agency. Garnier defined onanism as 'all voluntary practices or actions which have, as their goal or effect, the emission or production of seminal fluid outside of the natural pathways of human reproduction'.[88] For Garnier, the problem with onanism was not only that it did not lead to procreation, but that the subject had *voluntarily* chosen to engage in a sexual act which does not lead to procreation. He had in mind, as an explicit 'goal' or as a reasonably foreseeable 'effect', the procuration of a non-reproductive pleasure. The issue of agency can therefore be regarded as pivotal to the understanding of the moral dimension of onanism. It was because the subject had consciously decided to engage in it that moral considerations arose; a deliberate choice implied responsibility for one's own actions and it was this responsibility for a non-procreative act which, in a time of depopulation and growing concerns about virility, led to moral opprobrium.

Garnier went on to argue that, whilst some people may be more prone to succumb to onanistic practices because of hereditary reasons, in most cases this view was 'without possible proof', and most onanists wallowed in their perversion out of their own free will. He concluded that in these cases, which were 'quite numerous', they were 'entirely conscious of their acts' and hence 'completely

86 Laqueur (n 16) 40.
87 Ibid. 41.
88 Garnier (n 17) 19.

responsible for them'.[89] The premise of agency, free will and choice entailed responsibility for one's decision to engage in onanistic practices, and this agency could be regarded as one reason for the widespread moral vocabulary used in the discursive construction of the onanist.

Questions of agency and free will are central to *Charlot s'amuse.* Like the medical experts of the late nineteenth century, the narrator adopts a morally disapproving tone when describing Charlot's indulgences. However, the novel also repeatedly problematises Charlot's agency; the narrative urges the reader to reconsider what constitutes a deliberate choice in any episode involving Charlot's onanism, and to reflect upon whether it is possible to say for certain whether the protagonist 'voluntarily' – to use Garnier's term – chooses. Given that moral judgment is premised on agency, the novel also invites readers to question the possibility of moral judgment. One of the passages selected by the prosecution, in which Origène initiates Charlot into mutual same-sex onanistic practices, illustrates the dynamic of the text.

In this passage, the narrator adopts the moral vocabulary of the medical treatises: the experience is at once a physical, 'manual sullying' and a spiritual, 'moral sullying', and what Charlot learns is described as the 'monstrous mysteries of unisexual practices'.[90] However, despite its moral vocabulary, the passage refuses to provide any easy answer to the question of Charlot's agency. First, the possibility of choice, a free decision to engage in onanism, is undermined by the reference to the degenerative heredity from his mother, a nymphomaniac and a hysteric. One determining factor of Charlot's behaviour is thus the 'neurotic impressionability which heredity instilled in his entire being'.[91] This 'hereditary neurosis' not only 'predisposed him to the fall into temptation', but is repeatedly described as 'fatal', here used both in the sense of being associated with death and the sense of being associated with an inevitable fate.[92] Moreover, in this episode the language of the narrator implicitly places the moral responsibility on Origène. In contrast to Charlot's inexperience and passivity, Origène is characterised by his energy and activity: he is 'febrile' and grows 'restless' at the sight of Charlot.[93] The narrator also underscores the power imbalance between them: Origène is the 'master', whilst Charlot is his 'victim'; Charlot is the 'student' and Origène the 'ignoble cassock-wearing sex maniac' who 'instructed' him. The scene is one in which an innocent child is corrupted by a seasoned deviant, which again raises questions about Charlot's responsibility. The two factors reinforce one another; Charlot succumbs to Origène's advances so readily in part because of the hereditary influence of his nymphomaniac mother.

89 Ibid. 63.
90 Bonnetain (n 28) 102.
91 Ibid. 101.
92 Ibid. 102.
93 Ibid. 101.

There are also less immediate factors at work: the narrator notes that Charlot responds also because of 'a child's inevitable curiosity', a curiosity natural to every human being of Charlot's age and which by implication precludes blame on this one particular child for wanting to know more. Finally, the reader is told that Charlot loves Origène as someone who has 'never known a mother's tenderness and whose heart overflowed with affection'.[94] Charlot's response is implicitly portrayed as a natural one; the lack of maternal love from an early age is imagined to orientate him towards anyone showing him affection. Between the influence of heredity, the seduction by a determined and seasoned pederast, and the various psychological factors at work, Charlot's agency is thrown into question, and it becomes difficult to argue that he knowingly and deliberately chose his course of action.

If, as argued above, moral condemnation is premised on the assumption of agency, the problematisation of Charlot's agency in the novel also necessitates the suspension of moral judgment on the part of the reader. Furthermore, if, as the medical texts seem to indicate, moral culpability arises from agency, then the basis for the moral condemnation of a subject whose agency is lacking, or at least indeterminate or troubled, would also need to be reconsidered.

Another episode presented as evidence in court further illustrates this dynamic. The incident occurs early on in the novel. Charlot witnesses his mother's coitus with a man and later has a dream in which he takes the man's place in the scene. Far from being an oedipal fantasy, this scene takes on the dimension of a 'nightmare'.[95] The portrayal of the mother seems to have come straight out of a textbook on hysteria, and in fact Charlot encounters his mother again later in the novel, in a lecture by Jean-Martin Charcot at the Salpêtrière hospital. Charlot sees his mother 'howling, writhing in a sort of hysterical crisis, her body twisted and stiffened, banging her head against the frame of the bed with rapidity'.[96] That night, in his dream, he feels 'something quivering', and then he feels 'something born deep within him'. The narrator's description of the onset of Charlot's condition is significant: it is described as a thing being born, something that is subsequently described, through repeated use of active verbs such as 'awaken',[97] 'grab',[98] 'seize'[99] and 'invade',[100] as an agent physically taking hold of Charlot. The hereditary traits are therefore represented as a living force which determines Charlot's actions; the language of the text not only describes Charlot's condition but also places pressure on the possibility of a non-hereditarily predetermined course of action.

94 Ibid. 103.
95 Ibid. 71.
96 Ibid. 70.
97 Ibid. 267.
98 Ibid. 102.
99 Ibid. 123.
100 Ibid. 124.

The significance of this episode is amplified when it is read alongside structurally similar situations in other naturalist novels. In Zola's *La Terre*, the murder of Fouan by Buteau and Lise is witnessed by the couple's children, and their presence can be read as implying that such violence is likely to be repeated in the next generation. Similarly, in *L'Assommoir*, Gervaise's adultery is witnessed by her daughter, the 10-year old Nana; the presence of the child presages Nana's future promiscuity and her fate as a prostitute in the next novel of *Les Rougon-Macquart*. The presence of children at a scene of sex or violence in naturalist fiction often underscores the deterministic influence of heredity. In this episode, Charlot's nightmare implies that his own inability to control his sexual urges is already predetermined through his lineage, thus again undermining the view that he chose to indulge in onanistic practices of his own free will.

It is possible to probe the question of agency further. Heredity plays a major role in the novel's interrogation of agency, but it would be a mistake to see heredity as the ultimate structuring principle or the final answer in naturalist fiction. In one of the most intriguing passages on responsibility and free will in *Charlot s'amuse*, the narrator notes:

> To account for his decline, he reminded himself of his father and his grandfather's alcoholism, his mother's hysteria, and the epileptic madness of her mother. It would never have occurred to him to suppose that he took from them merely morbid predispositions, which were surmountable through his will and without medication. That would have affected his mental self-defence, and he preferred to be able to cry over his fate than to have to despise himself – to have to concede defeat. . . . With the help of his terrifying readings, perhaps he himself also felt that there was no hope for him.[101]

This passage could be read in multiple ways. Baguley argues that it represents the novel's 'criticism of the very fatalism which characterizes the naturalist novel'.[102] In other words, for Baguley it highlights the possibility of Charlot's agency, and suggests that it is Charlot himself who has allowed such agency to become eclipsed by choosing to believe that the hereditary influence would overpower his free will. Baguley concludes that 'Bonnetain is both employing and indicating the limits of naturalist physiology'.

However, it is also possible to argue that, whilst this passage makes reference to the presence of agency, it also indicates the difficulty of establishing or locating it: the idea that the hereditary influence may be surmountable through the

101 Ibid. 162: '*Pour excuser sa déchéance, il se rappelait l'alcoolisme de son père et de son grand-père, l'hystérie de sa mère et l'épileptique folie de la mère de celle-ci. Il ne lui serait jamais venue à l'idée de supposer qu'il tenait d'eux seulement des prédispositions morbides surmontables par le vouloir et sans médication. Cela aurait entamé son système de défense, et il préférait pouvoir pleurer sur lui-même que d'avoir à se mépriser, – à se vaincre. . . . Ses terrifiants lectures aidant, peut-être lui aussi se sentait-il perdu*'.

102 Baguley (n 64) 111.

protagonist's will and 'without medication' is expressed in the curiously chosen phrase: 'It would never have occurred to him to suppose that . . .'. The possibility of overcoming the hereditary influence is doubly hedged: it is but a supposition, and one which is all the more distant because it has never taken place and so has never been tested. The passage therefore should not be read as an unequivocal affirmation of the existence of a free will stronger than the hereditary force. Moreover, the idea has never occurred to Charlot in part because of the medical establishment: the 'terrifying readings' of medical texts robbed him of his independent thinking and planted in his mind the idea of his own fatality, and it is his reading of 'Tissot and the fanciful vulgarizations of the same genre' which made him expect endless 'suffering' and 'aggravation'.[103]

This passage shows that there exists in fact an acute awareness of the ideological dimensions of the scientific literature that constructed the onanist in a language of fatalism, in part to sustain traditional masculinity, and of the role this language played in developing Charlot's overwhelming sense of futility. Finally, it is from the mouth of the doctors of the Saint-Mandrier hospital that he hears that 'it was an early death, if he did not recover' (*c'était la mort à brève échéance, s'il ne se guérissait pas*).[104] The undermining of agency in the novel occurs in part because of the medical discourse.

To return to Cléry's defence in the courtroom: despite its many overt proclamations of affinities with or faithfulness to the scientific method, and despite Bonnetain's own pretensions, the defence's reading of *Charlot s'amuse* as a text which is underpinned by a scientific method represents a problematic interpretation, for it overlooks the interrogation of the assumptions of science at work in the literary text.[105] In fact, by taking literally the statements by people such as Zola of the alignment of science and literature, Cléry misses the specifically literary quality of Bonnetain's novel and, in his reading, the text becomes something akin to a medical treatise or what one critic has called a 'sexual pathography'.[106] Far from sharing science's assumptions about the unequivocal agency of the subject and its moral disapproval of the onanist's practices, the novel in fact interrogates the possibility of agency.

In each of the episodes I have examined, the presence of Charlot's free will when choosing to indulge in his masturbatory excesses is either implicitly or explicitly thrown into question. The influence of heredity, the naivety of the protagonist, the advances of older and more experienced agents, the impact of medical literature and other circumstantial factors all play a part in Charlot's behaviour, and between all of these factors one wonders how much room is left for the operation of free, independent decision-making.

103 Bonnetain (n 28) 162.
104 Ibid. 264.
105 Bonnetain, Statement dated 12 August 1884.
106 Michael R. Finn, *Hysteria, Hypnosis, the Spirits and Pornography: Fin-de-siècle Cultural Discourses in the Decadent Rachilde* (Newark: University of Delaware Press, 2009) 165.

In light of this problematisation of agency, the novel implicitly invites the reader to suspend moral judgment; one should not express moral disapproval if one cannot unequivocally determine where responsibility for Charlot's actions lies. The novel thus emerges not as a text parallel to or aligned with science, but as part of a discourse that precisely problematises the moral assumptions which are taken for granted in the scientific discourse of the period. The novel can be interpreted as a forum in which the reader's moral judgment has to be suspended or withheld, a forum in which one is invited to understand or appreciate another's experience without disapproval, criticism or judgment. *Contra* Cléry's argument that the novel is literary because it is scientific, it would perhaps be possible to regard this quality as precisely what constitutes the literary dimension of the novel, the quality which sets it apart from other discourses: the interrogation of agency, the suspension of moral considerations and the invitation to appreciate the experience of another human being without moral condemnation.

Chapter 3

The Henry Vizetelly trials: Émile Zola's obscene patricide

Vizetelly and Company was a large and influential publishing house in late nineteenth-century London.[1] It specialised in the translation and publication of French novels, and played a major role in introducing English readers to such writers as Gustave Flaubert and Guy de Maupassant, as well as figures less well known in our own time such as Fortuné du Boisgobey and Émile Gaboriau. The most lucrative publications for Vizetelly were undoubtedly Émile Zola's novels: the company boasted that it would 'reckon it a bad week' if the sale of its Zola translations fell below a thousand volumes.[2]

Even though Zola's works did not lead to formal legal censure in his native country, they were not uncontroversial amongst French readers. French critics accused the author of championing subjects unfit for respectable fiction, and described his work as 'garbage', 'decay' and 'pornography'.[3] Popular caricatures of Zola in the French magazines of the period depicted him as a giant pig, a visualisation encapsulating the double senses of sexual smuttiness and lack of physical hygiene in the French word *cochonnerie.* Louis Ulbach's critique of *Thérèse Raquin* in 'la littérature putride' discussed in the previous chapter not only parodied the rhetoric of science in the text, but also made use of these popular metaphors to inveigh against the purported filthiness of the novel, describing it as 'mud' that was not fit for the reader's consumption.[4]

French novels, especially those by Zola, were also coming under increasing moral scrutiny in England in the final decades of the century.[5] The metaphors in

1 For a discussion of the company's history, see Marie Elena Korey and Richard Landon (eds), *Vizetelly and Compan(ies): A Complex Tale of Victorian Printing and Publishing* (Toronto: University of Toronto, 2003) 108–124.

2 Edward Vizetelly, 'My life and publications' *Pall Mall Gazette* (24 March 1888) 2–3 at 2.

3 Catherine Dousteyssier-Khoze, *Zola et la littérature naturaliste en parodies* (Paris: Eurédit, 2004) 22.

4 Ferragus (Louis Ulbach), 'La littérature putride' (1868) in Émile Zola, *Thérèse Raquin* (Henri Mitterand (ed), Paris: GF Flammarion, 1970) 39–44 at 41.

5 For further discussions of the reception of Zola in England, see Clarence R. Decker, 'Zola's literary reputation in England' (1934) 49 *PMLA* 1140–53; Colin Burns, 'Zola et l'Angleterre' (1959) 12 *Cahiers naturalistes* 495–504; Mary Elizabeth Leighton and Kirsten Macleod, 'The trials of

the French reception of Zola migrated across the English Channel, and even the more positive reviews in England shared this vocabulary of disgust. Zola became the focal point of a more general concern about the influence of French fiction on English readers. One of Zola's harshest English critics was W.S. Lilly. In his review of *Nana*, he contended that Zola would never rise 'above the mud', because it was 'his native element'.[6] He concluded that the French writer did no more than reduce his characters to 'the bestial, or something lower'.[7]

In a similar vein, George Saintsbury accused Zola of being a 'dirt compeller'.[8] Even H. Schultz Wilson, who was one of Zola's more favourable reviewers and who praised him for his accurate depiction of working-class life, could not help but regard Zola's 'unvarnished allusions' to things which were 'outside the pale of modesty and decency' as revolting.[9] As concerns about the spread of corrupt foreign literature, and of Zola's fiction in particular, became more prevalent, it found a powerful voice in the National Vigilance Association, an organisation founded by the Protestant fanatical reformer John Kensit and which counted W.T. Stead, the editor of the *Pall Mall Gazette*, among its supporters.[10]

The National Vigilance Association believed there was a pressing need to curb the circulation of French novels. At its request, the legislator Samuel Smith initiated a debate on the issue in the House of Commons. Smith's speech in Parliament epitomised fears about the impact of novel reading in nineteenth-century England. He warned that 'a class of low booksellers in London' was offering 'indecent literature to young girls' for a small deposit of six dimes, and reminded his fellow legislators that Parliament had a responsibility to 'rescue the young from their snares'.[11] He castigated Zola's novels as the worst instance of the immoral French fiction invading the English reading nation, describing them as reading material 'only fit for swine', the constant perusal of which 'must turn the mind into something akin to a sty.'[12] As voices calling for government intervention became louder, Henry Vizetelly became targeted as 'the chief culprit in the spread of pernicious literature' in the country.[13]

On 10 August 1888, Vizetelly was summoned before the Bow Street Magistrates' Court for translating and publishing three novels by Zola: *Nana*, *Pot-Bouille* (translated as *Piping Hot!*) and *La Terre* (first published by Vizetelly as *The Soil*;

naturalism: Zola in the British literary and cultural imagination of the *Fin de Siècle*' (2001) 15 *Excavatio* 322–36; Denise Merkle, 'Horizons d'attente victoriens et réécriture de Zola: 1880–1890' (1997) 9 *Excavatio* 103–110.

6 W.S. Lilly, 'The new naturalism' *Fortnightly Review* (August 1885) 240–57 at 248.

7 Ibid. 251.

8 George Saintsbury, 'The present state of the novel' *Fortnightly Review* (January 1888) 112–24 at 112.

9 H. Schultz Wilson, '*L'Assommoir*' *Gentleman's Magazine* (December 1878) 737–50 at 742.

10 For a further discussion of the National Vigilance Association, see Donald Thomas, *A Long Time Burning: the History of Literary Censorship in England* (London: Routledge & Kegan Paul, 1969) 258–60.

11 *Hansard's Parliamentary Debates* (20 April 1888–10 May 1888), vol 325, col 1712.

12 Ibid. col 1709.

13 Ibid. col 1708.

subsequently translated by Douglas Parmée as *The Earth*). The proceedings focused on *La Terre*, which was singled out as the worst of the three books, and the magistrate, John Bridge, committed Vizetelly for trial in the Central Criminal Court. The case was heard on 31 October 1888. Edward Clarke, who was Solicitor-General at the time, represented the government, and Francis B. Williams headed the defence team.

Vizetelly pleaded guilty to the charge, but was summoned before the magistrate a second time in 1889 as a result of a misunderstanding of his undertaking arising from the first trial: Vizetelly wrongly believed that he had the right to continue publishing French novels as long as he excised potentially objectionable or offensive passages, when the court had in fact imposed a complete ban on any further publication of such novels. Clarke remained the chief prosecutor in the second trial, and Vizetelly changed his lead counsel from Francis Williams to Alfred Cock, hoping that a Queen's Counsel would bolster his chances of winning the case.

However, the change of counsel did little to affect the outcome: Vizetelly lost and was sentenced to three months in prison in Pentonville. He was eventually lodged in Holloway owing to his ill health. No fine was imposed because Vizetelly clearly had insufficient means to pay.[14] In the aftermath of the prosecution, the National Vigilance Association reproduced the transcript of the parliamentary debate initiated by Smith, together with press reactions to the Vizetelly trials, in a pamphlet entitled *Pernicious Literature* in order to alert the public to 'the enormous amount of evil' brought about by the circulation of French novels.[15]

In this chapter, I examine the ways in which Zola's novels were interpreted in the English courts by approaching the legal arguments through the concept of intertextuality. I use the term 'intertextuality' to refer to the complex, inexhaustible and, at times, surprising ways in which a text can be read in relation to other texts. The question of intertextual relations was at the heart of the Henry Vizetelly trials: the prosecution and the defence both presented arguments situating Zola's novels within a wider network of writings. Two forms of intertextuality were at work in the courtroom.

The defence relied on what I term a 'literary' intertextuality. As we saw in Chapter 1, in the *Madame Bovary* trial Sénard displaced Pinard's depiction of Flaubert's novel as a lascivious painting by inserting the novel into a discursive network of moral tales and religious writings. Such a strategy enabled him to argue that *Madame Bovary* did not offend public morality or religion, and that it was in fact in line with Christian teachings. Even though Zola was regarded as the head

14 The best record of the Vizetelly trials remains the first-hand account by Henry Vizetelly's son, Ernest Alfred Vizetelly in *Émile Zola: Novelist and Reformer* (London: John Lane, 1904) 242–300. See also Graham King, *Garden of Zola: Émile Zola and his Novels for English Readers* (London: Barrie and Jenkins, 1978) 228–55.

15 'Pernicious literature. Debate in the House of Commons. Trial and conviction for the sale of Zola's novels. With opinions of the press' in George Joseph Becker (ed), *Documents of Modern Literary Realism* (Princeton: Princeton University Press, 1963) 350–83.

of the naturalist movement and wrote prolifically about naturalist aesthetics, the defence of Zola's writings by Vizetelly's lawyers (and by Vizetelly himself) bore a closer resemblance to Sénard's defence of Flaubert's *Madame Bovary* than it did to Cléry's defence of Bonnetain's naturalist novel *Charlot s'amuse*. The defence's argument was based on the juxtaposition of Zola's novels with canonical artistic works, rather than on their supposedly 'scientific' nature. This form of intertextuality is 'literary' in that established comparisons between Zola's novels with texts conventionally defined as literature – novels, plays and poems – in order to highlight their literary merit.

The prosecution's argument was premised on what I would call a 'legal' intertextuality, whereby the novels were read not in relation to literary works but to another genre of writing: the legal case. As Alan Durant has pointed out, the legal case constitutes a distinctive narrative form which can be identified by its unique 'genre features' such as headings naming the parties to a legal dispute, sections corresponding to the legal judgments making up the case itself, and a narrative progression applying principles to a set of facts and culminating in a verdict or ruling.[16] As we shall see, the prosecution's approach relied on the use of a precedent case it argued was binding. Reconceiving the doctrine of precedent as a form of intertextuality allows us to approach the legal discourse from a different angle: the prosecution in effect forged an intertextual lineage between the novels examined in the courtroom and a previous legal decision. The outcome of the Vizetelly trials was, to a great extent, determined by the confrontation between Vizetelly's own 'literary' intertextual argument and the prosecution's 'legal' intertextual argument.

As is well known, precedent cases play a central role in English law. Michael Zander has observed that precedents have 'a greater potency' in the English common law than in civil law systems such as the one in France.[17] Crucially for the purposes of our discussion, in the Vizetelly trials the translation of Zola's novels represented more than a linguistic translation. There was also a translation of legal frameworks: the publication of his works in England meant that adjudication took place in an English legal setting rather than a French one, which in turn meant that precedent legal cases exerted a determinative influence on the court's interpretation of Zola's work, an influence far greater than would have been likely under the French system. As Rupert Cross and James Harris have stressed in their classic study, 'the peculiar feature of the English doctrine of precedent' was 'its strongly *coercive* nature'.[18]

16 On the legal case as genre, see Alan Durant, 'Reading cases in interdisciplinary studies of law and literature' in Marco Wan (ed), *Reading the Legal Case: Cross-Currents between Law and the Humanities* (Abingdon: Routledge, 2012) 11–29 at 22.

17 Michael Zander, *The Law-Making Process* (6th edn, Cambridge: Cambridge University Press, 2004) 214.

18 Rupert Cross and James W. Harris, *Precedent in English Law* (4th edn, Oxford: Clarendon Press, 1991) 3 (my italics).

The formidable and, at times, unchallengeable authority of precedent cases is a unique feature of the common law, as encapsulated in the principle of *stare decisis* (literally meaning 'do not disturb that which has been decided'), whereby each court is bound by decisions from the courts above them. As we shall see, the prosecution formulated its argument against Vizetelly at a particular moment in the history of *stare decisis* when the coercive force of precedent was at its height. The precedent cases addressing the issue of obscenity not only informed, but actively directed, the court's reading of the novels.

My analysis of the Vizetelly trials will proceed in four stages. I will first examine Vizetelly's own strategy of defence, and will then focus on Clarke's argument for the prosecution. The first two sections will situate the two forms of intertextuality in their legal-historical context, to give a fuller sense of the traditions the lawyers were drawing on and the ways in which their arguments were received at the time of the trials. In the third part of the chapter, I will further the discussion of Clarke's 'legal' intertextuality by examining its jurisprudential dimension through the lens of Jacques Derrida's seminal essay, 'Force of Law: the "Mystical Foundation of Authority"'. Bringing Derrida's account of the foundation, self-perpetuation and violence of the law to bear on the historical material in the Vizetelly case will give greater theoretical precision to the operation of judicial precedent in late-Victorian England.

In the final part of the chapter, I will compare the structure of the common law, as it manifested itself in the Vizetelly trials, with the narrative structure of Zola's *La Terre*, and will draw on Freud's writings on censorship to argue that the legal discourse bears an unexpected, and unacknowledged, resemblance to the very novel that it condemns.

(I) 'Literary' intertextuality

Vizetelly was prosecuted under the Obscene Publications Act 1857, commonly known as Lord Campbell's Act, which gave magistrates the power to seize and destroy material deemed offensive.[19] It is necessary to look briefly at the background to the passage of the statute in order to gain a fuller understanding of the way the publisher defended himself against accusations of obscenity. Lord Campbell was first alerted to the extent of the problem of pornography in London through two cases which appeared before him in court. In May 1857, a man called William Strange was charged with the publication of two obscene texts, entitled *Paul Pry* and *Women of London*. Lord Campbell sentenced Strange to three months'

19 For an overview of the cases brought within the ambit of the statute, see Colin Manchester, 'Lord Campbell's Act: England's first obscenity statute' (1988) 9 *Journal of Legal History* 223–41. For further discussions of the background to the Obscene Publications Act, see Donald Thomas (n 10) 258–72 and Alison Smith, *The Victorian Nude: Sexuality, Morality, and Art* (Manchester: Manchester University Press, 1996) 62–67.

imprisonment, taking into account the fact that this was his first offence. Another man charged with the publication of obscene material on the same day was the repeat offender William Dugdale. Lord Campbell found it 'shocking to see a man of the prisoner's years abandoning honest living and trying to procure a scandalous livelihood by the sale of such infamous publications' and sentenced him to hard labour for a further year.[20]

Cases such as those of Strange and Dugdale made Lord Campbell realise, with 'alarm and horror', that a range of sexually explicit material, including erotic prints, catalogues of prostitutes, and guidebooks for finding homosexual encounters, was unabashedly put on display and sold on London's Holywell Street, popularly known as Bookseller's Row. Not only was such material publicly available, but it could be procured at such a low price – one penny – that it had 'a far greater tendency to demoralize the public than the others which were sold at a higher price'. Lord Campbell introduced a bill in Parliament aimed at preventing the sale of such material; he argued vehemently that the police should be able to apply for search warrants to uncover such obscene publications, and that magistrates should be given the power to grant destruction orders.

The background to the 1857 Act shows that literary intertextuality has been a problem for those seeking to regulate literary or artistic production from the time the legislation was first introduced. During the debate on the 1857 Act, Lord Lyndhurst noted that even though concern over the spread of immoral and obscene texts was a valid reason for more stringent controls, Parliament should be wary of intervening because many items of artistic merit would potentially be brought within the scope of Lord Campbell's proposed Act. He noted that such items included prints of artwork which drew on Greek mythology as their subject, statues of 'nymphs, fauns and satyrs, all perfect naked', and much of English poetry.

Lord Lyndhurst singled out the particular vulnerability of booksellers in possession of Ovid and Rochester's writings, and added that 'there was not a page in any one of' the dramatists of the Restoration – 'Wycherley, Congreve, and the rest of them' – which 'might not be seized under this Bill'. He urged the Law Lords to rely on the existing law on misdemeanour to control the dissemination of indecent writings rather than to introduce new legislation. His comments were echoed by Lord Wensleydale, who warned that:

> There was not a library in which books could not be found containing passages which a strict dealing magistrate might consider to bring them within the operation of this bill. The classic authors might be held to be obscene, and the possession of *Lucian, Lucullus, or Juvenal,* might expose the owners to the penalties which the Bill prescribed.[21]

20 'The Queen v. William Strange', *The Times* (11 May 1857) 8.
21 *Hansard* (13 April 1857–18 June 1857), vol 145, cols 331–32.

The debate over the bill led to a bitter, amusing and, at times, childish squabble between Lord Campbell and Lord Lyndhurst in the House of Lords. Despite the opposition, the bill was eventually passed after the insertion of four amendments narrowing its scope.

The debate on the 1857 Act did not resolve the question of the exculpating potential of literary intertextuality, which persisted after the legislation came into effect. In the *Hicklin* case, which was the first case to be considered under the new statute and which will be examined in more detail below owing to its centrality in the Vizetelly trials, the defendant's lawyer inscribed the pamphlet under consideration in a network of intertexts as his defence strategy. How could it be possible, he asked, for this text to be more obscene than the 'many pictures publicly exhibited, as the Venus in the Dulwich gallery? What can be more obscene than Bayle's Dictionary, or many of the works of the standard authors in English poetry, from Chaucer to Byron?'[22] A conviction would problematise the sustainability of the entire canon of literature.

When Vizetelly argued that Zola's works should be considered as literature – and therefore not as obscene material – by juxtaposing them with classics of the literary canon, he was drawing on a long tradition of intertextual reasoning. He presented an open letter to Sir A.K. Stephenson, Solicitor to the Treasury and the official in charge of the prosecution, with a series of extracts from great works of English literature, ranging from William Shakespeare's plays to John Dryden's poetry to Henry Fielding's novels. Vizetelly pointed out that the chosen passages were all 'far more objectionable than any that can be picked out from the Zola translations'.[23] He then questioned whether canonical works such as '*Tom Jones* and *Roderick Random*, *Moll Flanders* and *The Country Wife*, *The Maid's Tragedy* and *The Relapse*, in all of which the grossest passages are to be met with', would 'still be allowed to circulate without risk of legal proceedings' should Zola's novels be interdicted.

In particular, given that one of the objections to Zola's works was the depiction of bestial impulses in his characters, he included passages from Shakespearean plays, which included references to sex between animals, such as Touchstone's reference to the copulation of cattle in *As You Like It*.[24] Having established the similarities between Zola's novels and these works, he argued that the depictions of sex and violence did not diminish Zola's standing as 'a great writer' who exercised 'a wide influence on contemporary literature', and prophetically noted that he would in the future occupy the same place which Daniel Defoe, Laurence Sterne and Tobias Smollett occupied in the nineteenth century.[25]

22 *R v Hicklin* (1868) LR 3 QB 360, 365.

23 Henry Vizetelly, *Extracts Principally from English Classics: Showing that the Legal Suppression of M. Zola's Novels would Logically Involve the Bowdlerizing of Some of the Greatest Works in English Literature* (London: H. Vizetelly, 1888) 1.

24 Ibid. 14.

25 Ibid. 3.

Zola himself was aware of the exculpating potential of placing his works alongside literary intertexts: when asked about his reaction to his English publisher's conviction, he boldly admitted 'I completely and radically do not give a damn' (*Je m'en fiche complètement et radicalement*), and added:

> We have recently honoured the Englishman Shakespeare with a statue in our city. Let those who presume to condemn my writings read what he has written; let them also read Ben Johnson, and Smollett, and Byron, and say whether in the whole range of French literature they can find anything more coarse and indelicate. If you walk along the rue de Rivoli you will find vile books in abundance. It is a significant fact that they are written in English.[26]

Zola's response is worth highlighting because it can be regarded as more radical than that of Vizetelly. The publisher's objective in gathering the extracts from canonical works was to establish Zola's literary status; the premise of Vizetelly's argument was that, like the authors of these other works to which Zola was being compared, the man who penned the allegedly obscene novels of *La Terre*, *Nana* and *Pot-Bouille* was also 'a great writer'. His defence therefore kept intact the literary status of the other writers, and sought to place Zola's writings on the same pedestal.

Zola's own defence, however, did the opposite. Rather than seek to assert the literary qualities of his own novels, he challenged the literary status of the English works: Johnson, Smollett and Byron were all 'coarse and indelicate', and the 'vile books' on the rue de Rivoli in Paris were all 'written in English'. He invoked the Bard not to praise him, but to question whether it was worth having a statue of him in France. Implicit in his retort is the view that the distinction between his own 'filthy' novels and the 'literary' works of figures such as Shakespeare, Johnson, Smollett and Byron made little sense: they were all equally filthy, and all equally literary. The English courts were in no position to condemn his novels, because the English 'literature' which the judges and jury condoned was every bit as debased as his own writings were alleged to be.

(II) 'Legal' intertextuality

Literary intertextuality formed the premise of the mode of reading advocated by Vizetelly and his lawyers. To understand why this argument, which had secured Flaubert's acquittal in the *Madame Bovary* trial, was unsuccessful here, it is necessary to examine the strategy of the opposing side in some detail. Clarke's argument was premised on a firm reliance on legal precedent. His key authority was the mid-century case of *R v Hicklin*, which concerned whether someone who distributed material of an allegedly sexual nature without the intention of making a financial gain could be convicted of selling or distributing obscene material.

26 'M. Zola on his English critics', *Pall Mall Gazette* (14 November 1888) 11.

The prosecution's reliance on *Hicklin* framed the legal analysis differently and displaced the question of whether Zola's novels had literary merit. Vizetelly's defence, as shown above, had been to argue that the translations of Zola's novels should be considered as literature, and that they would therefore not be in danger of adversely influencing their readers. Clarke sidestepped this argument about literary merit by citing a key passage from *Hicklin*. He introduced the case early on in his opening speech to the court, and argued that Zola's novels had to be read in the shadow of precedent:

> It is perfectly true . . . that there are a great many publications of high repute in the literary productions of this country the tendency of which is immodest, and, if you please, immoral, and possibly there might have been subject-matter for indictment in many of the works which you have referred to. But it is not to be said, because there are in many standard and established works objectionable passages, that therefore the law is not as alleged on the part of the prosecution, namely, that obscene works are the subject-matter of indictment.[27]

By reading Vizetelly's translations and the facts of the current case in relation to this passage from *Hicklin*, Clarke was able to show that the question of the novels' literary quality was simply irrelevant; a work could be of 'high repute' and could form an integral part of the nation's 'literary productions', but under the *Hicklin* principle those qualities did not pre-empt a judicial ruling of obscenity.

It was for this reason that Vizetelly's literary intertextual argument failed: the strategy of inserting Zola's novels into a network of texts conventionally defined as literature would do little for the publisher if a precedent case stated that their status as 'literature', even if established, did not serve any exculpating function. 'With these decisions before me,' Clarke triumphantly proclaimed, 'it is not open to me to contend that the work is not obscene.' In other words, legal intertextuality functioned in such a way that *Hicklin* became not only an adequate, but an irrefutable basis upon which to dismiss literary intertexuality as a possible defence. Whilst he admitted that there were works containing 'certain immoral and indecent passages' whose authors were nonetheless 'recognised as kings in the world of letters', recourse to the authority of *Hicklin* enabled him to declare that such a counter-argument was 'entirely out of the question here', and that literary merit was 'in no degree an excuse for the publication of obscene matter'. The court quickly, indeed uncritically, accepted the applicability of the legal authority cited by Clarke.

To the modern-day lawyer, the court's ready acceptance of the prosecution's argument seems peculiar. Common law lawyers are adept at distinguishing cases, but neither the defence nor the judge put much pressure on the applicability of the

27 *R v Hicklin* (n 22) 371.

Hicklin case to the facts at hand. One explanation for the unyielding force of *Hicklin* in the Vizetelly trials may be that the proceedings took place at a moment in legal history when the grip of precedent cases on the English law courts was especially tenacious. This meant that the defence was pitting its argument of literary intertextuality against the prosecution's argument of legal intertextuality at a time when the coercive force of precedent was at its strongest.

As the legal historian Jim Evans has shown, the convention that precedent cases bind a court absolutely is a relatively recent one. He argues that 'the English doctrine of precedent hardened during the nineteenth century', and that much of this process of hardening occurred in the second half of that period.[28] More specifically, it was between 1862 and 1890 that 'the concept of rules of precedent' became 'firmly established'. Prior to that, there had been a judicial practice of following previous decisions, but courts did not regard such decisions as absolutely binding and would depart from them if they believed that there were good reasons to do so. Judges regarded cases not as embodiments of law, but merely as evidence or illustrations of law. The belief that precedent cases constituted binding law, that it was not open to a court to deviate from authority even if the judges did not agree with the result, consolidated from the mid-Victorian period.[29]

Evans argues that by the 1850s the lower courts already regarded the decisions of the House of Lords as strictly binding. They also exhibited an increasing tendency to follow the decisions of coordinate courts and, whilst the practice of abiding by decisions of courts at the same level never approached a formal rule, the adherence was still 'noticeably strict'. Moreover, the Court of Appeal began to regard itself as bound by its own decisions from the 1890s. Finally, the question of whether the House of Lords would bind itself received an affirmative answer in the case of *Beamish v Beamish* (1861) and was finally put beyond doubt in 1898 in the case of *London Tramways*.[30]

The Vizetelly trials, occurring in the late 1880s, therefore took place within a broad judicial climate in which there was little sympathy towards arguments for the courts to deviate from previous decisions. Cases were regarded as laws that bound a court, rather than as mere evidence or illustrations of law that guided it. The moment in the development of the doctrine of precedent in which the proceedings took place meant that it was especially difficult to dislodge precedents such as *R v Hicklin*. Vizetelly's defence counsel himself realised that 'after the dictum of the late Lord Chief Justice, it really would be no defence to say that even standard works in our literature contain passages of great grossness and indelicacy,

28 Jim Evans, 'Change in the doctrine of precedent during the nineteenth century' in Laurence Goldstein (ed), *Precedent in Law* (Oxford: Clarendon Press) 35–72 at 35.

29 Ibid. 57.

30 *Beamish v Beamish* (1861) 9 HL Cas 273; *London Street Tramways Co Ltd v London County Council* [1898] AC 375.

and yet are found in thousands of libraries and households perfectly pure and respectable'.[31]

After a brief consultation with his client, he offered 'at once to withdraw all these translations of M. Zola's works from circulation' and expressed their readiness to accept whatever judgment the court saw fit. The defence's defeatist attitude reflected an unquestioning acceptance that the case cited as authority by the opposing side could not be distinguished or challenged. There was little attempt to set *Hicklin* aside on its facts or to question the scope of its principle. This seemingly strange approach becomes more comprehensible in historical context: it reflected the crystallisation and entrenchment of the understanding that previous cases were absolutely binding in the judicial minds of late nineteenth century England.

(III) The 'Force of Law': obscenity, repetition and legal violence

The argument so far has shown that the defence's literary intertextuality became displaced by the prosecution's legal intertextuality, at a time when the rule that past decisions would bind absolutely was becoming entrenched in the English courts. This section proposes to probe more deeply into the operation of the prosecution's legal intertextuality. I will first examine the facts and reasoning of the *Hicklin* case in greater detail. I will then analyse the relationship between *Hicklin* and *Vizetelly* which Clarke forged in the trials in light of Jacques Derrida's argument about legal repetition in his influential essay, 'Force of Law'.

The facts of the Hicklin *case*

The proceedings concerned a metal broker named Henry Scott who purchased, and then resold at cost price, several thousand copies of a pamphlet entitled *The Confessional Unmasked: Shewing the Depravity of the Roman Priesthood, the Iniquity of the Confessional and the Questions put to Females in Confession.* According to the pamphlet, the Roman Catholic Church was an institution promoting ideas and practices which would 'put the most profligate to the blush and would not be endured in the veriest den of infamy.'[32]

The text consisted of extracts from instruction manuals written for Catholic priests on the proper ways of conducting a confession, including the rules involved in discussing matters of a sexual nature; the passages were translated from Latin into English for the comprehension of the general reader, and over half of them contained lengthy descriptions of sexual behaviour. *The Confessional Unmasked* was

31 'Zola's novels', *Daily Telegraph* (1 November 1888) 8.

32 *The Confessional Unmasked: Showing the Depravity of the Romish Priesthood, and the Iniquity of the Confessional, and the Questions put to Females in Confession* (Protestant Electoral Union, 1867) iv.

published and distributed with the immediate aim of persuading Parliament to discontinue its financial support of £30,000 a year to a Catholic educational institution, and with the more general aim of exposing the purported indecency and immorality inherent in the practice of the confession.

The question before the court in *Hicklin* was whether Scott should be convicted of selling and distributing obscene material in light of the fact that his intention was to expose the 'fearful reality' behind the doors of the Catholic Church rather than to sell sexually explicit material for monetary gain per se.[33] Scott had appealed against an order to destroy the pamphlets at the quarter sessions in the borough of Wolverhampton, where the recorder, Benjamin Hicklin, revoked the order of destruction. The authorities then appealed *Hicklin*'s reversal and brought the case to the Queen's Bench, where Scott was found guilty. The case is now mostly remembered for the legal test for obscenity that Chief Justice Cockburn propounded, a test which continues to resonate in obscenity cases in our own time. Cockburn CJ opined that:

> The test of obscenity is this, whether the tendency of the matter charged as obscenity is to deprave and corrupt those whose minds are open to such immoral influences, and into whose hands a publication of this sort may fall'.[34]

It is important to note that this test relegated to secondary importance the question of whether the seller or distributor actually *intended* to deprave or corrupt the unsuspecting reader who was likely to come across the publication; evidence of the relevant *tendency* or *effect* was sufficient to convict.

The reasoning in the Hicklin *case*

The *Hicklin* case was determinative of the outcome of the Vizetelly trials, yet its reasoning is problematic at best. The test for obscenity posited by the Queen's Bench in *Hicklin* is based on a fundamental act of misinterpretation. It is a cornerstone of criminal law that, in addition to showing criminal conduct, the prosecution needs to show that the conduct is accompanied by an intent to carry out that conduct, or *mens rea*, in order to convict. Scott should therefore only have been found guilty if the prosecution could prove that, in addition to the act of selling obscene material for gain, he had the requisite intention to do so: the 1857 Act stated very clearly that only material sold, distributed, exhibited, lent, or otherwise published 'for purposes of gain' would be confiscated. Such an intention could not have been simply assumed or inferred; it had to be proven.

33 Ibid. iv.
34 *R v Hicklin* (n 22) 371.

The need to show a clear intention to obtain financial gain from the publication of such material was also reflected in the preamble of the Act, which stated that the legislation sought to prevent 'the *sale* of obscene books, pictures, prints and other articles' rather than their circulation more generally. Scott's defence lawyer made this point very firmly when he noted that 'criminal intention must be shewn before the justices have jurisdiction', and added that it was the jury that had the power to determine whether such intention existed or not.[35] As such, 'the mere use of obscene words, or the occurrence of obscene passages, does not make the work obscene' without *mens rea*.[36]

Before the case reached the Queen's Bench, the recorder had found for the appellants precisely because of the lack of *mens rea*: since Scott distributed the pamphlet not for the purpose of circulating obscene material for gain but did so 'as a member of the Protestant Electoral Union, to promote the objects of that society, and to expose what he deems to be errors of the Church of Rome, and particularly the immorality of the Confessional', he could not be said to have had the intention to publish obscene material.[37] The fact that he 'did not keep or sell the pamphlets for gain, nor to prejudice good morals' meant that the mental element required for conviction was lacking.

When the case reached the Queen's Bench, however, the judges not only reversed the recorder's decision, but in doing so they changed the requirements for conviction and so in effect created a new law of obscenity. Cockburn CJ's test, based on a text's tendency to deprave and corrupt the reader likely to come across the publication, in one stroke turned the definition of obscenity from one based on *intention* to one based on *effect*: the question of whether a person should be found guilty of publishing obscene material for gain now turned on what kind of impact the material would have on the reader, rather than on the psychological state of the appellant when he published the material. Cockburn CJ went on to state that if the necessary negative impact on the mind of the reader was found, then the court would infer an intention to publish the material.

As noted in the Introduction to this book, the reader exposed to the published material was in the Victorian period imagined to be a peculiarly susceptible young person who did not have the mental fortitude to withstand the influence of fiction, a being who 'lived only in the nervous imagination of men inhabiting a particular class and historical moment', the kind of reader Charles Dickens ridiculed in the term 'Podsnappery'.[38] The widespread belief that such readers needed to be protected perhaps explains the shift in *Hicklin* from the intention to publish for gain to the effect a publication would have on the people likely to come across it; its

35 *R v Hicklin* (n 22) 364.

36 Ibid. 365.

37 Ibid. 363.

38 Walter Kendrick, *The Secret Museum: Pornography in Modern Culture* (Berkeley: University of California Press, 1987) 123.

reasoning both reflected, and amplified, the fears over the deleterious impact of reading at a time of ever increasing literacy.

The *Hicklin* test for obscenity was thus based on a misreading of the 1857 Act: the wording of the statute made clear that it was paramount to demonstrate the requisite *mens rea* in order to convict, but the test introduced in the judgment relegated the mental element of the crime to the margin by focusing on the effect of the published work and then inferring a mental state from it afterwards. The slippage is reflected in the number of times the word 'effect' appeared in the judge's reasoning; it appeared four times in the remaining page and a half after the new test was posited. Based on this new definition of obscenity, and brushing aside the question of *mens rea*, Cockburn CJ concluded that *The Confessional Unmasked* was 'mischievous and against the law'; he opined that it was 'not to be justified' simply because the immediate object of the publication was 'not to deprave the public mind, but, it may be, to destroy and extirpate Roman Catholicism'. The defence's reminder of the criminal law's insistence that 'the animus must be looked at' fell on deaf ears.[39]

Hicklin, Vizetelly, Derrida

To put my argument slightly differently, the modern English law of obscenity is *founded* on an act of misinterpretation. This foundational act was then repeated, perpetuated and amplified to both construct and sustain legal discourse through legal intertextuality. The initial misreading took on legal force and legal status through subsequent citation in the courts. Derrida's argument helps to bring the operation of the law into focus. In 'Force of Law', Derrida argues that violence lies at the heart of the law; it underpins both law's inception and its continuation. He notes that 'the very emergence of justice and law, the founding and justifying moment that institutes law implies a *performative force*, which is always an *interpretive force*'.[40] This characterisation arguably reflects the dynamic at work in the founding of the modern law of obscenity.

Three points can be made about Derrida's argument. First, the emergence of the law is based on an 'interpretive force'. The definition of obscenity in *Hicklin* was founded on an act of interpretation; Cockburn CJ misread the intention requirement in the 1857 Act and in his act of misreading posited a new law of obscenity based on a text's tendency to deprave and corrupt the minds of the readers into whose hands the text was likely to fall. The significance of the misinterpretation is highlighted when one juxtaposes the *Hicklin* test on obscenity with the original discussion about the need to limit the circulation of obscene material in Parliament. When Lord Campbell introduced the original bill in 1857,

39 *R v Hicklin* (n 22) 367.

40 Jacques Derrida, 'Force of law: the "mystical foundation of authority"' (1990) 11 *Cardozo Law Review* 920–1046 at 941 (my italics).

he envisaged that intervention would only be necessary if 'there were people who *designedly* and industriously manufactured books and prints with the *intention* of corrupting the public morals'.[41] In order words, the need to show the requisite intention was paramount. Yet, as we have seen, the *Hicklin* judgment defined obscenity in relation to a text's effect and relegated intention to the margins, as something that could be simply inferred or assumed.

Secondly, Derrida notes that the 'interpretive force' of this founding moment also has a 'performative force'. Here, the performative dimension of *Hicklin* is precisely not only the inauguration of a whole new domain of law, the modern law of obscenity, but also its perpetuation. The operation of the 'performative' aspect of this founding moment is complex. On one level, *Hicklin* inaugurated a new doctrine of law not because of superior reasoning, but because the law was formulated within the legal machinery – the Queen's Bench – and acquired its status as law because it was always law. As such, 'its ultimate foundation is by definition unfounded': the modern law of obscenity can be said to find itself because its epistemological underpinning rested on the fact that it was always already law.[42]

On another level, *Hicklin* remained the founding moment of the modern law of obscenity only because it was treated as positing a new doctrine by the courts in subsequent cases. In other words, cases subsequent to *Hicklin* – such as *R v Vizetelly* – made *Hicklin* an integral part of the law of obscenity by continuously citing it, using it as authority and keeping it alive as law through the very process of citation. The operation of binding precedent meant that it must be cited and followed in subsequent cases. In Derrida's words, the 'foundation or position of law' (law's originary moment) is indissociable from the 'conservation of law' (the process by which the law sustains and perpetuates itself).

Derrida's observation about the indissociability of the foundation of law and the perpetuation or conservation of law sheds light on the English law of obscenity: *Hicklin* was law because it was repeated as legal authority in subsequent cases; the founding or originary moment of the modern law of obscenity only gained its status as such because of its repetition or recitation in the cases that followed it.[43] As Kendrick has pointed out in his study of the history of pornography, *Hicklin* was 'continuously cited, paraphrased, and quibbled with' well into the twentieth century and 'still haunts discussions of pornography today.'[44]

Cockburn CJ's obscenity test continued to be law and continued to be known as the originary moment of this area of law because it has been endlessly cited well into the twentieth century: in the Vizetelly trials, and again in the *Well of Loneliness* trial, and again, in statute form, in section 1 of the Obscene Publications Act 1959

41 *Hansard*, vol 145, col 865 (my italics).

42 Derrida, 'Force of law' (n 40) 943.

43 Ibid. 997.

44 Kendrick (n 38) 123.

and beyond. The recitation or repetition of this founding moment – the 'iteration' of the founding moment of the modern law of obscenity – was precisely what gave it its status as the founding moment. The 'origin' of law and the 'conservation' of law are therefore inextricably linked; the law conserved *Hicklin* as origin by re-emphasising it as such in subsequent cases. It is for this reason that 'iterability inscribes conservation in the essential structure of foundation'.[45]

Thirdly, when Derrida notes that the originary moment of law implies a 'performative force' and an 'interpretive force', he uses the word 'force' interchangeably with the terms 'power' and 'violence'.[46] Ayelet Ben-Yishai has compellingly demonstrated the prevalence of precedential thinking in Victorian law and literature, but her analysis arguably overlooks the violence inherent in the use of precedent that Derrida underscores.[47] At the moment the *Hicklin* judgment was laid down, the 'force' of law consisted of the obfuscation of previous traditions or pronouncements on obscenity and its power to forge a whole new legal doctrine. This 'force' of law gained traction as the case came to be recited or repeated as legal authority, to such an extent that one could speak of a 'co-implication of violence and law'.[48] Derrida notes that the English expression 'enforcing the law' more accurately describes the nature of legal discourse than the French equivalent (*appliquer la loi*) because the English verb 'to en*force*' captures the centrality of 'force' or violence in the law. That law is associated with violence is undeniable.

The statute under which Vizetelly was prosecuted gave police officers a warrant to enter into any 'house, shop, room or other place . . . and, if necessary, to use force, by breaking open doors or otherwise' to seize any allegedly offending material.[49] The material would then be impounded and the legal authorities would retain the power to destroy it should it be found to be obscene. Vizetelly and his family felt the force of law particularly acutely; the trials did great damage to the reputation of the company and financially ruined the publisher. Henry Vizetelly's son, Ernest Vizetelly, noted that as a result of the prosecution 'the trade became afraid to handle any books he [Henry Vizetelly] published, and thus his sales rapidly decreased'.[50] After he was summoned to Bow Street a second time, the publisher 'assigned everything he possessed for the benefit of his creditors . . . It was impossible to carry it on any longer. The wreckers had resolved to ruin him, and had succeeded to their heart's desire'.[51]

45 Derrida, 'Force of law' (n 40) 1007–1009.
46 Ibid. 941.
47 Ayelet Ben-Yishai, *Common Precedents: The Presentness of the Past in Victorian Law and Fiction* (Oxford: Oxford University Press, 2013).
48 Derrida, 'Force of law' (n 40) 1003.
49 *R v Hicklin* (n 22) 361.
50 Ernest Vizetelly, *Émile Zola* (n 14) 275.
51 Ibid. 286.

The burden of being prosecuted also significantly worsened the health of the already old and frail publisher; Ernest noted that his father was 'in very bad health indeed' by the time of the trial for his appeal took place in 1889.[52] The effect on the defendant was especially pronounced given the vigilance with which Vizetelly was prosecuted. Ernest could not help lashing out at the prosecution towards the end of the second trial: 'You have made the defendant a pauper! What more do you want?'[53] Robert Cover has famously noted that 'legal interpretation takes place in a field of pain and death', because often 'somebody loses his freedom, his property, his children, even his life' as a result of a court decision, and legal institutions 'frequently leave behind victims whose lives have been torn apart by these organized, social practices of violence'. Vizetelly's fate serves as an illustration of the violence inherent in the law which both Derrida and Cover underscore.

The 'very moment of foundation or institution' of the modern law of obscenity in *Hicklin* therefore consisted of a *coup de force*, whereby previous traditions and discussions about the permissibility of material of a sexual nature were obliterated and became replaced by a new doctrine, and the repetition of this foundational moment gave traction to this force of violence as the courts' unswerving reliance on it in the late nineteenth and early-twentieth centuries inflicted suffering on writers and publishers in England. One conclusion that can be drawn, then, is that the law of obscenity in the final decades of the nineteenth century constituted itself through the repetition of violence; the recitation or iteration of *Hicklin* in the law courts meant that the violence of legal foundation became merged and sustained by the violence of legal conservation.

In the aftermath of the Vizetelly trials, one newspaper wrote approvingly of the court's decision, noting that there could be 'little difference of opinion as to the justice of the judgment'.[54] Thinking about the trials in relation to Derrida's essay leads one to reconsider the justness of the decision; the argument that the ruling was based on an act of misreading, which was then reiterated as a legal force suggests that its justness is questionable at best. The operation of binding precedent in the Vizetelly trials epitomised the repetition of violence in the law. However, this repetition, as we shall see below, has important implications for the study of the relationship between law and literature, because the legal violence bears a curious resemblance to the violence depicted in the very novels which the court condemned.

(IV) Zola, Freud, repetition and violence

The intertextual relations between *R v Hicklin* and *R v Vizetelly* show that in the late nineteenth century the law of obscenity was characterised by a repetition of

52 Ibid. 291.
53 Ibid. 293.
54 *The Morning Advertiser*, reprinted in 'Pernicious literature' in Becker (n 15) 378.

violence. This underlying dynamic means that, unexpectedly, the law shares the same structural characteristics as the literature which it condemns, for the repetition of violence forms the narrative structure of some of the novels for which Vizetelly was brought to the dock. This resemblance between the law and fiction is closest in *La Terre*, and it is not a coincidence that this novel received the most intense legal scrutiny: in the 1888 trial, Clarke's argument centred almost solely on *La Terre* after he was directed by the magistrate to concentrate on the worst instances of the alleged obscenity. Clarke had prepared 21 passages as evidence, but the jury requested him to refrain from reading all of them in court owing to their offensive nature. As the *Daily Telegraph* reported, *La Terre* occupied such a prominent place in the trial that 'the Court did not find it necessary to go into the question of the other translations published by Mr. Vizetelly from the same author, nor was the Solicitor-General obliged even to complete his evidence in support of the indictment, so far as it related to *La Terre* alone'.[55]

The Times' reportage of the trial attributed Vizetelly's conviction solely to 'the sale of an English translation of Zola's novel, *La Terre*', even though the defendant also pleaded guilty to translating *Nana* and *Pot-Bouille*.[56] The paper labelled it as 'the worst of Zola's novels' and regarded its publication as 'a grave offence against public morals'. In addition to the English court's condemnation of it as the most objectionable of Zola's translated novels, *La Terre* sparked the publication of *The Manifesto of Five* in France, which signalled the defection of such writers as Paul Bonnetain and Paul Margueritte from the naturalist movement.[57] The prominent place *La Terre* occupied in the trial and in wider debates about the literary value of Zola's works calls for a closer examination of the novel.

The narrative of *La Terre* takes place in the rural community of Rognes, in La Beauce. It centres on the family of an elderly farmer named Fouan, and one of the main strands of the narrative tells of the events leading to Fouan's death at the hands of one of his children, Buteau, and Buteau's wife, Lise. The patricide has often been read as the inevitable outcome of a system of inheritance, known as the *donation entre vifs*, in which the farmer divides his property amongst his children in exchange for a pension which is payable until the day he dies. As a result, Fouan is increasingly seen by the next generation as a financial burden that had to be disposed of.[58] The interaction between Fouan and Buteau can be said to be marked

55 'London, Thursday, November 1', *Daily Telegraph* (1 November 1888) 7.

56 'The sale of M. Zola's works – sentence', *The Times* (1 November 1888) 9.

57 For a detailed discussion of the genesis and reception of the novel, see Guy Robert, *La Terre d'Émile Zola* (Société d'édition les Belle Lettres, 1952).

58 See, for example, Sylvie Lapalus, *La Mort du Vieux* (Paris: Tallandier Éditions, 2004). For a reading that dissociates the patricide from the discourses on the system of inheritance, see Andrew Counter, *Inheritance in Nineteenth-Century French Culture: Wealth, Knowledge and the Family* (Oxford: Legenda, 2010) 158–86.

by 'Oedipal strife', and the aggression the son shows towards the father implies that violence is inscribed into their relationship.[59]

The centrality of familial violence is indicated early in the narrative, when Fouan and his family gather in the office of the solicitor M. Baillehache to determine how Fouan's property would be distributed amongst his three children Buteau, Hyacinthe (or Jésus-Christ) and Fanny. Fouan's violent temperament has long maintained his authority in the family. When Buteau confronts him about a hidden hoard of money, Fouan quickly loses his temper and asserts his authority as the *paterfamilias*, as '*le maître, le père*'. The effect of this violence on the family is worth quoting in full:

> In this sudden access of authority, he seemed all at once to have grown taller. For years, all of them, wife and children, had trembled under his rule, the harsh and tyrannical rule of a peasant father over his family. If anyone thought he was finished with, they were mistaken.
>
> He stood there, dominating and threatening. His wife sat trembling, afraid that one of his blows might miss its target. Their children sat quite still, holding their breath, cowed.[60]
>
> The violence of the father strikes fear into the hearts of his children. As Fouan continues to age, however, he becomes physically weaker and his authority is undermined by his own next of kin, and by Buteau in particular. Towards the end of the novel, Fouan is reduced to 'complete silence'.[61]

As the father ages, however, he finds this violence repeated in the next generation, as reflected in the following exchange between Buteau and Fouan:

> – That's your fault. But now I'm here and it's my turn. I take after you, I don't like people mucking me about. And once again, shut your trap or there'll be trouble.
> – Trouble for you. I would never have dared to speak to my father like that.
> – Oh, I like that. You'd've done him in, if he hadn't died first.[62]

The reversal of power between father and son stems from Buteau's inheritance of Fouan's violent temper: as Buteau himself points out, it is Fouan's 'fault' that Buteau develops a violent temperament because it is passed on to him through

59 Nicholas White, *The Family in Crisis in Late Nineteenth-Century French Fiction* (Cambridge: Cambridge University Press, 1999) 119.

60 Émile Zola, *The Earth* (Douglas Parmée (trans), London: Penguin Books, 1980) 45.

61 Ibid. 419.

62 Ibid. 309.

heredity. The son repeats the violent nature of the previous generation. His statement that 'I take after you' underscores this dynamic: just as Fouan desired the death of his father, so Buteau desires Fouan's death. In his classic study of *La Terre*, Guy Robert highlights the myths which structure the novel, and points out that the notion of eternal return constitutes one of the novel's structural myths. He notes: 'Zola's vision of the universe is too profoundly epic for it not to suggest, more or less clearly in the poet's mind, the need to see both trivial and important situations and acts [in the text] as repeating themselves until the end of time'. He goes on to ask: 'to a certain extent . . ., isn't heredity one of the manifestations of this return?'[63]

The passing on of the violent traits as a form of patrilineal inheritance means that the father himself ensures the continuation of violence by creating the murderer in his own image. This repetition of violence is expressed in the metaphor of the son devouring the father: 'He was forgetting that he had devoured his own father in the same way' (*Il oubliait qu'il avait mangé son père ainsi*)'.[64] As we have seen, the maintenance of paternal authority, or 'father rule', was essential to the conception of masculinity as social status in Victorian England. A true man had to maintain patriarchal power in his home. By portraying violence as a force internal to the family, and by defining the inevitable, and reluctant, loss of patriarchal power as an integral part of fatherhood, Zola's novel struck at the very heart of Victorian masculinity. It intimates that, far from being natural or unquestionable, paternal authority is destined to be subverted by the next of kin.

The nature of violence as an inherited trait that repeats itself is further highlighted by the parallel between the inheritance of violent propensities and the transfer of physical property in the novel. In his old age, Fouan realises:

> He had adored his land like a woman who will kill you and for whom you will commit murder . . . And now he had grown old and, like his father before him, would have to hand over this mistress to his sons, furious at being so powerless.[65]

Like the land, the murderous impulse – what the narrator calls 'the brutal authority which the father had bequeathed to his son' (*La brutale authorité que le père avait léguée au fils*) – is perpetuated in an endless cycle of reproduction.[66] Violence is the

63 Robert (n 57) 385–86 (*la vision de l'univers qui s'impose à Zola est trop profondément épique pour qu'elle m'implique pas, plus ou moins claire dans la conscience du poète, la nécessité de voir se répéter jusqu'aux confins du temps des situations et des actes simples et signifiants. Dans une certaine mesure, l'hérédité . . . n'est-elle pas une manifestation de ce retour?*).

64 Zola, *The Earth* (n 60) 44.

65 Zola, *The Earth* (n 60) 38.

66 Émile Zola, *La Terre* (1887) (Henri Mitterand (ed), Paris: Gallimard, 1980) 341 (my translation).

property that the son inherits from his father. The elderly farmer eventually comes to realise that this impulse is passed on from generation to generation:

> An old man is useless and he costs money to feed. He himself had longed to see his father die. That his children in their turn might want him to die, too, caused him neither surprise nor resentment. *Such things had to be.*[67]

The final line ends the passage on a tone of inevitability; since violence is inherited, the undermining of paternal authority is always already built into the structure of the family. If one traces it to the past, a community which, as the reviewer Simmias points out in his review of the novel, is 'without God' (*sans Dieu*) does not have a transcendental or ultimate paternal figure to which one can attach the significance of a primal origin.[68] If one projects it into the future, one does not find a logical stopping point to the dynamic: as noted in the previous chapter, Buteau and Lise's murder of Fouan is witnessed by their children, whose presence at the scene of the crime hints at the repetition of the violence in the next generation.[69]

Family relations in *La Terre* are structured by a self-perpetuating repetition of violence which is always in *medias res*, without beginning and without end. The structural similarity to the law should be clear: both Zola's novel and the trials in which it is read are structured by an endless repetition of violence. In the Vizetelly trials, both the literary narrative, in the form of the novel, and the legal narrative, in the form of the series of cases on obscenity which repeat themselves through the judicial system, are underpinned by a cycle of violence. W.S. Lilly thus correctly identifies the dynamic underlying the legal censure of Zola's novels, although perhaps not in the way he had intended, when he notes that the 'proceedings in the courts of justice . . . are merely an experimental novel unfolding itself, chapter after chapter, before the public'.[70]

One question remains to be asked: why was the law so eager to condemn the novels whose traits it in fact repeated? Could the resemblance between law and literature that this chapter has identified shed light on an unacknowledged or unconscious dimension to literary–legal relations in late nineteenth-century England? Whilst the alleged obscenity in Zola's fiction goes some way towards explaining the vigilance with which Vizetelly was prosecuted, it does not entirely account for the intensity of the law's reaction. As Kendrick has observed, 'the ferocity of the Vizetelly prosecution is difficult to explain. It was far from typical; no other case in the history of Anglo-American obscenity trials offers a comparable example of determined hostility and ruthlessness towards an individual'. He speculated that the publisher's 'foreign sounding name . . ., combined with high

67 Zola, *The Earth* (n 60) 418 (my italics).
68 Simmias, 'Sans Dieu', *La Gazette de France* (5 September 1887) 1.
69 Zola, *The Earth* (n 60) 481.
70 See Lilly (n 6) 242.

intellectual pretensions and a record of sailing close to the wind in matters of obscenity', may have sparked animosities.[71]

It is also possible that Vizetelly simply became the scapegoat for the wider social problem of the importation of obscene works; the impossibility for the English courts to prosecute Zola himself across the English Channel meant that the full force of the law fell on his English translator, ruining his health, his business and his reputation. Anthony Cummins has returned to the context of the rising literacy rate and expanding readership of the period to argue that the ire against the publisher represented 'an extreme reaction to the emergence of a new, and therefore unpredictable, mass audience for fiction in English'.[72] Cummins noted that the 1870 Education Act led to the emergence of a new reading class that had the ability, although not necessarily the breeding or the self-control, to purchase and read the low-priced translations of Zola's novels without being adversely affected, and that the court regarded itself as the bearer of the duty to protect the readers. He concluded that 'the Vizetelly affair was less about Zola's intrinsic merit as a novelist . . . and more about the perceived consequences of releasing his fiction to a new, post-1870 readership'.[73]

More recently, Katherine Mullin has argued that Vizetelly's sales tactics suggest that he was 'a canny businessman willing to exploit Zola's reputation' for titillation and immorality, and that he was therefore partly responsible for bringing the force of law upon himself.[74] The work of Kendrick, Cummins and Mullin is helpful for understanding the forces behind the trials, but does not exhaust the discussion. Could there be further reasons for the tenacity of the prosecution, beyond the immediate historical and social contexts of the efforts of the National Vigilance Association to censor French novels?

A psychoanalytic reading of the trials could perhaps give us some insight. In her analysis of historic trials, Shoshana Felman has argued that repetition in legal discourse could be interpreted as a response to an unperceived traumatic occurrence. She posits that it is: 'because of what the law cannot and does not see that a judicial case becomes a legal trauma in its own right and is therefore bound to repeat itself through a traumatic legal repetition'.[75] Felman's discussion, although specific to the relationship between law and trauma, points towards the possibility of thinking about legal repetition in a psychoanalytic frame. The adoption of a psychoanalytic framework to analyse the politics of legal censure is also justified

71 Kendrick (n 38) 166.

72 Anthony Cummins, 'Émile Zola's cheap English dress: the Vizetelly translations, late-Victorian print culture, and the crisis of literary value' (2009) 60 *The Review of English Studies* 108–133 at 117.

73 Ibid. 109.

74 Katherine Mullin, 'Pernicious literature: vigilance in the age of Zola (1886–1889)' in David Bradshaw and Rachel Potter (eds), *Prudes on the Prowl: Fiction and Obscenity in England, 1850 to the Present Day* (Oxford: Oxford University Press, 2013) 30–52 at 35.

75 Shoshana Felman, *The Juridical Unconscious: Trials and Traumas of the Twentieth Century* (Cambridge: Harvard University Press, 2002) 57.

by Freud's own use of the metaphor of political censorship to represent psychical censorship.

In *The Interpretation of Dreams*, Freud compares dream-censorship to the censorship of a writer in an authoritarian regime:

> A similar difficulty confronts the political writer who has disagreeable truths to tell to those in authority. If he presents them undisguised, the authorities will suppress his words – after they have been spoken, if his pronouncement was an oral one, but beforehand, if he had intended to make it in print. A writer must beware of the censorship, and on its account he must soften and distort the expression of his opinion.[76]

A number of critics have pointed out that Freud's metaphors of censorship are at times inconsistent.[77] In the present instance, it hovers between the assumption that the material to be repressed is already formed and is subject to cuts or amendments before it can appear in a dream, and the assumption that it remains amorphous and does not take on a definite shape until after censorship. However, regardless of these inconsistencies, the parallel to real-life suppression is clear. Freud reproduces this metaphor in 'The Censorship of Dreams', in which he notes that dream-censorship finds parallels in the excision of objectionable passages in political newspapers, and in the 'circumlocutions and obscurities of expression' in the works of writers undergoing self-censorship.[78]

Nicholas Harrison underscores the indissociability of the political and psychical mechanisms within the Freudian *schema* when he argues that there exists 'two-directional connections between . . . that which is ("metaphorically") censored in the psyche and that which is literally eliminated by censors in the outside world', so that 'to look for a point at which the switch from the literal [legal/political] to the metaphorical [psychical] is made . . . is to misunderstand the status of the metaphorical usages of "censorship" in Freud's work'.[79]

Freud's use of the term 'censorship' first appears in *Studies on Hysteria*, in which he invokes the concepts of 'defence', 'resistance' and 'repression' to explain its operation. He notes that when the ego is confronted with 'an idea which proved to be incompatible', it produces 'a repelling force' which aims to act as a 'defence against this incompatible idea'.[80] If the defence is successful, the idea becomes

76 Sigmund Freud, 'The Interpretation of Dreams' (1900) in James Strachey (ed and trans) *The Standard Edition of the Complete Psychological Works of Sigmund Freud, 24 vols* (London: Vintage, 2001) IV, 141–42.

77 See, for example, Alexander Welsh, *Freud's Wishful Dream Book* (Princeton: Princeton University Press, 1994) 79–109.

78 Freud, 'The Censorship of Dreams' (1916) XV, 136–49 at 139.

79 Nicholas Harrison, *Circles of Censorship: Censorship and its Metaphors in French History, Literature, and Theory* (Oxford: Clarendon Press, 1995) 99.

80 Freud, Studies on Hysteria' (1893–1895) II, 269.

subject to 'repression'; it is 'forced out of consciousness and out of memory' but its 'psychical trace' remains. The analyst who tries to recover this repressed idea will be met with resistance, which is indicated by the fact that 'connections are broken, solutions fail to appear', and 'pictures are recalled indistinctly and incompletely' by the patient during the course of analysis.[81] Freud's model of censorship, encompassing defence, repression and resistance, operates in such a way that the repressed material can only be extracted in a 'mutilated manner'.

Freud further develops the metaphor of censorship in *The Interpretation of Dreams* to argue that there are two psychical forces at work in the formation of a dream: one of these forces constructs the wish which tries to enter consciousness, whilst the other 'exercises a censorship upon a dream-wish' and brings about the distortion.[82] He concludes that the passage of ideas or desires from the unconscious into the conscious is a 'specific psychical act'.[83]

The analyst is met with the same force of resistance when attempting to interpret the dream: 'the resistance to interpretation is only a putting into effect of the dream-censorship'.[84] This resistance to analysis testifies to the strength of the censorship which is in operation to bring about dream distortion: 'the censorship persists as a permanent institution which has as its aim the maintenance of the distortion'. Psychical censorship, like legal or political censorship, prevents an 'incompatible idea' from finding full expression, either through full expurgation or through modification. Freud concludes that the two forms of censorship are 'similarly determined' because they 'correspond down to their smallest details'.[85]

Thinking about the Vizetelly trials in light of the parallel between political or legal censorship and censorship in dreams posited by Freud leads one to ask: what was the 'incompatible idea' that the law seeks to repress in Zola's novels? Zola's description of the fornication and the violence in a rural society no doubt offended the sensitivities of many of his late-Victorian readers, yet it is possible to push the analysis beyond the doctrinal question of obscenity. Freud notes that ideas or wishes which are repressed are 'all of a distressing nature, calculated to arouse effects of shame, of self-reproach and of psychical pain, and the feeling of being harmed; *they were all of a kind that one would prefer not to have experienced, that one would rather forget*'.[86]

Similarly, in 'The Censorship of Dreams' he characterises them as matters of which 'one does not venture to think at all'.[87] In other words, the censoring mechanism represses those wishes or ideas which the subject is unwilling to confront, which he would rather erase from his memory. The Freudian model thus

81 Ibid. 281.
82 Freud, 'The Interpretation of Dreams' (n 76) IV, 143.
83 Ibid. 144.
84 Freud, 'The Censorship of Dreams' (n 78) XV, 141.
85 Freud, 'The Interpretation of Dreams' (n 76) IV, 143.
86 Freud, 'Studies on Hysteria' (n 80) II, 269 (my italics).
87 Freud, 'The Censorship of Dreams' (n 78) XV, 142.

raises the question of what the specific aspects of Zola's novels which the law 'would prefer not to have experienced' could have been, and which dimension of naturalism it would 'rather forget' or, rather, not have directly acknowledged. What was it about Zola's writings which made them so unsettling to the law that it would seek to censor them with such tenacity?

From the foregoing discussion of the way in which the nineteenth-century English law of obscenity exhibits the compulsion to repeat the violence which it condemns in Zola's novels, it is possible to argue that one answer to this question is that Zola's novels exposed the law's unacknowledged similarity to literature: what the encounter between literary and legal discourses in the Vizetelly trials revealed was that the two discourses were intertwined and uncannily resembled each other; the underlying structure of Zola's fiction was more similar to the structure of the law than the law would have liked to admit.

Just as Zola's novels are underpinned by an endless cycle of repeated violence, the operation of the law on obscenity during this period can be said to be premised on a similar dynamic of iterative violence. Moreover, just as Zola's characters inherit the murderous impulses of their forefathers, so each legal case recites rulings from previous cases and perpetuates the legal violence which Derrida highlights and which Vizetelly's fate exemplified. Lilly's remarks about the parallels between the experimental novel and the legal proceedings can be read as alluding to the questionable basis upon which the law claims authority over the regulation of literature, for it points out that the law shared some of the key structural characteristics with the literary text which it condemned. The law's power over literary production is premised on the assumption that it stands in opposition to it: Zola's novels represented transgression while the law represented order; Zola's novels represented perversion while the law represented moral righteousness; Zola's novels are premised on inherited violence while the law is premised on justice.

It is therefore problematic for the law to acknowledge that it is caught in the same compulsion to repeat violence which it condemns in Zola's novels; to do so would be tantamount to undermining its self-conception as the guardian of 'public morals' and 'public decency' and hence to challenging the very justification of its power over literary production.[88] To maintain the illusion of absolute opposition, it became necessary to obliterate any similarity between the two discourses by purging Zola's literary discourse. In light of the Freudian dynamic of censorship, it could be argued that this unexpected resemblance between law and literature constituted an important reason for which Vizetelly was prosecuted with such vigilance in the late nineteenth century.

88 *The Times* (1 November 1888) 9.

Chapter 4

The Oscar Wilde trials: reading sodomitical texts in court

Oscar Wilde is most often remembered for three things: his plays, his sex life and his conviction for acts of gross indecency – not necessarily in that order. The narrative of the Wilde trials is well known: the Marquess of Queensberry, incensed by the open displays of intimacy between Wilde and Lord Alfred Douglas, or Bosie, left a card at Wilde's club with the words 'For Oscar Wilde posing [as a] somdomite [sic]'.[1] Wilde reacted by suing the Marquess for libel, but agreed to break off the trial at the final moment when it became apparent that the Marquess had in fact acquired evidence against Wilde in the form of testimonies from rent boys who had had sexual relations with him. This evidence was passed to the Director of Public Prosecutions, and led to two further trials in which Wilde was accused of engaging in 'acts of gross indecency' with other men contrary to the Labouchère Amendment of the Criminal Law Amendment Act 1885. As Sos Eltis has noted, 'Wilde's life was an affront to the Victorian establishment and the Victorian public', and Victorian society punished him for this affront by convicting him and sentencing him to two years' hard labour at Pentonville Prison.[2]

This chapter approaches the Wilde trials from two perspectives. Section (I) examines the use of the word 'pose' in the proceedings by placing the trials in the context of the history of sexuality. The subsequent sections explore the ways in which Wilde's 'literary' works were interpreted as 'legal' evidence in the courtroom, and the implications of such interpretative acts for our understanding of law and literature. Edward Carson, the lawyer for the Marquess, attempted to use Wilde's writings as a way of ascertaining the writer's lifestyle and conduct: if he could convince the court that their allusions to same-sex desire were based on, or inspired by, the author's own experience, then he would win his case.

Wilde, in turn, challenged the correlation the lawyer attempted to draw between his works and his life. Section (II) places the question of interpretation in the trials

1 Merlin Holland (ed), *Irish Peacock and Scarlet Marquess* (London: Fourth Estate, 2003) xix.

2 Sos Eltis, *Revising Wilde: Society and Subversion in the Plays of Oscar Wilde* (Oxford: Clarendon Press, 1996) 7.

in a broader historical framework by locating Wilde's 'aesthetic' vision of literature in the context of debates about the relationship between literature and reality in Victorian England. Sections (III) and (IV) explore, in detail, the legal interpretations of Wilde's writings in the trials. They argue against existing discussions of the legal case to show that the courtroom exchanges between the lawyer and the playwright represented a conflict not only between a 'legal' mode of reading and a 'literary' mode of reading, but between two competing literary conceptions of the relationship between text and reality in the second half of the nineteenth century.

(I) Homosexuality and theatricality: Wilde's 'pose' in the courtroom

Scholars of gay and lesbian history have long argued that the Wilde trials occupy a central place, if not *the* central place, in the history of sexuality. These scholars regard the 1880s and 1890s as the turning point at which modern gay identity came into being, and that the trials stood at the cusp of a messy, entangled and gradual transition from the nineteenth-century 'sodomite' who engaged in specific sexual acts to the modern figure of the 'homosexual' with an innate desire for the same sex. The conception of sexual identity both oscillated between and conflated these two categories, until the trials offered a recognisable image of the homosexual in the form of Wilde himself.

It was Jeffrey Weeks who first posited that the Wilde trials 'created a public image for the homosexual'.[3] Alan Sinfield's 1994 study furthered Week's claim by demonstrating that they presented to English society a figure in which effeminacy and same-sex desire were brought together to form a recognisable homosexual 'type', and that this figure continues to exert its influence on conceptions of gay identity in our own time. For Sinfield, the trials were the point at which the 'vaguely disconcerting nexus of effeminacy, leisure, idleness, immorality, luxury, insouciance, decadence and aestheticism, which Wilde was perceived, variously, as instantiating, was transformed into a brilliantly precise image'.[4]

Ed Cohen also argued that Wilde became a recognisable homosexual type as a result of the trials, and showed that the news reportage played a major role in the construction of this type by shifting the emphasis from specific acts of gross indecency to Wilde's body and character, so that there 'crystallized a new constellation of sexual meanings predicated upon "personality" and not practices'.[5] For Weeks, Sinfield and Cohen, the Wilde trials constituted the pivotal moment in the formation of modern homosexual selfhood in English culture. Moe Meyer

3 Jeffrey Weeks, *Coming Out: Homosexual Politics in Britain from the Nineteenth Century to the Present* (London: Quartet Books, 1977) 21.

4 Alan Sinfield, *The Wilde Century: Effeminacy, Oscar Wilde and the Queer Moment* (New York: Columbia University Press, 1994) 3.

5 Ed Cohen, *Talk on the Wilde Side: Towards a Genealogy of a Discourse on Male Sexualities* (New York: Routledge, 1993) 131.

captured this position succinctly when he noted that: 'Wilde entered the court as a run-of-the-mill sodomite, but exited as the first homosexual'.[6]

The word 'pose' appeared multiple times in the Wilde trials, and constituted the focal point of a set of connections between theatricality, deviancy, sodomy, homosexuality and impropriety in the proceedings which merits further analysis.. It forms part of Wilde's aesthetic vocabulary, but was also a keyword through which Carson attempted to cast doubt on the playwright's sexual propriety. The word 'pose' has a dual connotation. It connotes both a specific sense of theatricality – as in an actor who 'strikes a pose' on stage – as well as a more general sense of pretence and dishonesty. What is the link between theatricality and sexuality, and how did this link become relevant in the courtroom?

One point of entry into the question is the figure of the sodomite discussed above, which arguably also carried this dual connotation. In terms of the first, more specific theatrical connotation, Matt Cook has pointed out that 'the theatre had long-standing associations with homosexuality', for it 'offered an additional space for men to cruise and socialise with each other'.[7] This association deepened in the Victorian period, as the theatre district expanded in central London and more men in search of sexual encounters congregated in the area. Cook also noted that the theatre often constituted a forum in which gender norms were inter-rogated or ridiculed, and that the crossdressing in music-hall performances further undermined gender conventions. The theatre was thus a site of illicit desires and destabilised gender conventions, and male spectators had to be careful not to visit it with undue frequency to avoid suspicion of questionable behaviour and associations.

In terms of the second, more general connotation, the sodomite's need to hide his willingness to engage in this specific sexual act in order to avoid legal persecution, as well as some men's more overt penchant for cross-dressing, meant that the sodomite became regarded as an actor in the broadest sense in the cultural imagination. As the historian H.G. Cocks points out, he was often described in 'the language of concealment, disguise and impersonation'.[8] Cocks further notes that he was a particularly troubling figure in nineteenth-century England: 'the Victorian sodomite became modern . . . as a figure of equivocation, both reported and unseen, flagrantly visible and at the same time invisible and mysterious'. It was difficult to ascertain whether someone who engaged in sodomy did so out of true sexual desire, or whether he did it only for financial reward. The sodomite's desire could be genuine, feigned or perhaps even somewhere in between, and the blurred distinction between real and simulated attraction reinforced the association of this figure with play-acting and pretence.

6 Moe Meyer (ed), 'Under the sign of Wilde: an archaeology of posing' in Moe Meyer (ed), *The Politics and Poetics of Camp* (London: Routledge, 1994) 75–110 at 96.

7 Matt Cook, *London and the Culture of Homosexuality, 1885–1914* (Cambridge: Cambridge University Press, 2003) 28.

8 H.G. Cocks, *Nameless Offences: Homosexual Desire in the Nineteenth Century* (London: I.B. Tauris, 2010) 78.

The Ernest Boulton and Frederick Park trial of 1870–1871 illustrates the dual connotations of posing, and the links between theatricality and sexuality. This was a widely-reported case in which two men were arrested at the Strand Theatre for cross-dressing as 'Stella' and 'Fanny' in a public place. During the proceedings, the prosecution argued that by donning women's clothing, the defendants were engaging in a gender-defying performance, and it urged the jury to construe such a performance as evidence of unnatural desire. The defence, on the other hand, argued that the two men's impersonation and their fondness for extravagant costumes testified solely to a deep, if somewhat excessive, fascination with theatre rather than to any inclination towards sexual abnormality. Boulton and Park were eventually acquitted, but the fact that a full trial was need to maintain the distinction between a fascination with theatre and same-sex desire is indicative of the entanglement of those two traits in the Victorian imagination.

The performance of the sodomite could be so convincing that he may even pass for a respected *paterfamilias* that formed the core of bourgeois masculinity. As it was impossible to identify a person as a sodomite with certainty, it followed that any respectable head of the family could potentially slide away from his seemingly solid masculinity along the spectrum of homosociality. The figure of the sodomite was troubling in part because he could always be lurking in the middle-class home, posing as a father and a husband. As Cook points out, what was striking, and unsettling, about homosexuality was its 'indistinctness'; there was 'neither an entirely discernible figure nor a separate territory' for same-sex desire and the sodomite troubled normative masculinity 'by using the same city spaces and appearing indistinguishable from the "normal", middle-class, "modern man"'.[9]

In the decades before the trials, the news coverage of events such as the arrest of Boulton and Park, the Cleveland Street Affair of 1885 that culminated in the exposure of a male brothel purportedly frequented by prominent members of society, the coming into effect of the Labouchère Amendment in 1886 and the publication of Richard von Krafft-Ebing's *Psychopathia Sexualis* in the same year generated considerable societal interest in same-sex intimacy. As an increasing number of middle-class men became aware of the pervasiveness of such intimacy and desires, there arose a fear that a 'homosexual conspiracy' would strike at the foundations of gender normalcy.[10]

In the aftermath of the Wilde trials, W.T. Stead famously wrote that: 'if all persons guilty of Oscar Wilde's offences were to be clapped into gaol, there would be a very surprising exodus from Eton and Harrow, Rugby and Winchester, to Pentonville and Holloway'.[11] Whilst Stead subscribed to the view of the

9 Cook (n 7) 40.

10 George L. Mosse, *The Image of Man: The Creation of Modern Masculinity* (New York: Oxford University Press, 1996) 87.

11 W.T. Stead, 'The sacro-sanct male' *Review of Reviews* (1 June 1895) 2.

abnormality of same-sex desire, his remarks forced the reader to acknowledge the anxiously disavowed contradiction between the supposed singularity of Wilde's behaviour and the pervasiveness of similar behaviour in educational institutions shaping proper, bourgeois masculine conduct.

Given that the sodomite was thought of as a constant actor, 'an imposter, an impersonator and a figure of gender reversal, whose true purpose was concealed by his dress, his class or his location', Wilde could be read as embodying, on multiple levels, the anxieties about false display, disguise and deception grounding the nineteenth-century understanding of the sodomite.[12] Wilde was a particularly unsettling figure at this historical juncture because, as a married man with children who nonetheless consorted with young men of socially inferior backgrounds, he represented a 'fissured subject' who threw into question the distinction between normative masculinity and sexual deviancy.[13] The association of accusations of illicit sex and Wilde's thespian identity could also have reinforced the suspicion that his persona as a respectable husband and father was an integral part of the act of play-acting and script-writing with which he was so familiar. During the trials, the fact that the theatre 'related closely to the performativity which clung to prevailing conceptions of homosexual behaviour and identity' would have worked against him.[14]

In other words, in light of the Victorian association of the sodomite as an actor and an im-pose-tor, Wilde's reputation as a man of theatre could have coloured the public's understanding of his private life, such that his identity as husband and father could have been interpreted as a pose, his writings could have exposed themselves to being read as the textual concealment of illicit desire, and his professed non-sexual reasons for interacting with the rent boys could have been heard as a set of well rehearsed lines maintaining the gap between appearance and reality which extended from the stage, to the family home, to the courtroom. Wilde's theatrical 'pose' raised troubling questions of how one could know a sodomite, of who might be a sodomite and of how far this figure could challenge gender conventions.

It may be for this reason that Carson brought up the question of the 'pose' in court so relentlessly. The Marquess's lawyer began his cross-examination by accusing Wilde of lying about his age, and Wilde's response was that he had 'no intention of posing for a younger man at all'.[15] The debate over the appropriateness of the term became more heated as the cross-examination continued: Carson said to Wilde that he insisted on seeing 'what position you pose in'.[16] He also pointedly asked Wilde: '"Pose" is a favourite word of yours, I think?'.[17] Of course, the

12 Cocks (n 8) 97.
13 Terry Eagleton, *Heathcliff and the Great Hunger: Studies in Irish Culture* (London: Verso, 1995) 331.
14 Cook (n 7) 29.
15 Holland (n 1) 74.
16 Ibid. 70.
17 Ibid. 74.

lawyer's insistence on the word was in part dictated by the need to justify his client's use of it in the original statement that gave rise to the libel trial in the first place. However, given Wilde's close links with the theatre which were firmly entrenched in the public's – and the jury's – mind, Carson's insistence on Wilde's 'pose' may be further interpreted as a strategy to evoke the prevailing associations between the sodomite and impersonation, acting and theatricality. To bring up the term 'pose' repeatedly in court was arguably a way to reinforce the link between sexuality and theatricality.

Kerry Powell has argued that the link between the two resonates beyond the specific repetition of the word 'pose' during the cross-examination to the court's interpretation of Wilde's works more generally, and posits that in the trials Wilde's writings constituted 'theatrical sites where Wilde became visible as a bad actor, performing or "posing" sodomy and gross indecency in, or through, texts that he wrote or was associated with'.[18] Wilde may have heard the evocations of theatricality in Carson's interrogation and may have realised how such evocations could colour the way he was seen in court, for he was quick to dissociate himself from the term: 'that is not the way to talk to me – "to pose as". I am not posing as anything'.[19] The trials foregrounded the troubling nexus of sexual behaviour, sexual identity and theatricality at the core of Victorian anxieties about deviant desire. The following sections expand the scope of analysis by turning from the interpretation of the specific word 'pose' to the interpretation of Wilde's works in the courtroom more broadly.

(II) Wilde's aesthetic philosophy

What was Wilde's aesthetic philosophy, and to what extent did it form the premise of Wilde's defence and shape the work of interpretation in the courtroom? Wilde's aestheticism represents a reaction against the dominance of realism in England in the second half of the nineteenth century. As the literary critic Lawrence Danson points out, 'the question of realism is not a side issue' but forms the 'contemporary polemical context' in which Wilde's ideas must be understood.[20] 'Realism' was a literary term that came to England from across the English Channel. Chapter 1 of this volume highlighted the inter-connections between realist literature and realist painting in nineteenth-century France. Another important dimension of French realism is its commitment to truth: at its core is the attempt to give a faithful representation of reality. A literary or artistic work sought 'to tell the truth, the whole truth and nothing but the truth', and the demand for transparent representation constituted 'a moral as well as an episte-

18 Kerry Powell, *Acting Wilde: Victorian Sexuality, Theatre, and Oscar Wilde* (Cambridge: Cambridge University Press, 2009) 148–49.

19 Holland (n 1) 70.

20 Lawrence Danson, *Wilde's Intentions: The Artist in his Criticism* (Oxford: Oxford University Press 1997) 47.

mological or aesthetic imperative', such that a fictional narrative which wilfully distorted reality was considered morally problematic, representationally unsound and aesthetically flawed.[21]

Whilst some of the best criticism of the late twentieth century has challenged precisely the correlation between realism and truth – for example, by arguing that realist texts which seemingly give the most faithful account of reality are ultimately the most self-referential – it is important to note that, as Christopher Prendergast has pointed out, such a view of realism is a product of the postmodern ethos of our own *fin de siècle*, and that in the mid-nineteenth century the realist premise was taken quite seriously, if somewhat naively to late-twentieth and early-twenty-first century eyes.[22] When the first instalment of *Madame Bovary* appeared in 1856, the *Nouvelliste de Rouen* praised Flaubert for the 'accuracy' of his portrayal of local customs and habits and described the narrative as a 'conscientious study of provincial mores', although it later suspended serialisation as allegations of immorality proliferated.[23] In a similar vein, the critic Charles Augustin Sainte-Beuve praised the author for his meticulous representation of provincial life when *Madame Bovary* was published; he noted that the question 'is this true?' constituted the author's sole concern, and that in the novel 'stern and implacable truth' had 'entered art as the last word of experience'.[24]

Unsurprisingly, 'Realism' emerged as a literary term in England through the discussions of the French novels, especially those by Honoré de Balzac: although a few scattered uses were made of the term before, the boundaries of 'realism' were first delineated in England in 1853, in a review of Balzac's fiction in the *Westminster Review*. English writers and critics took the French concern with truth in fiction to new heights. In that article, the reviewer described Balzac as a writer who attempted to give his readers an unbiased, unmediated representation of a pre-discursive reality, and regarded this as his best quality: the 'principle characteristic of Balzac's novels' is 'their reality', and his novels differ from their predecessors 'in the truthfulness of the characters'.[25]

21 Linda Nochlin, *Realism* (Harmondsworth: Penguin, 1971) 34.

22 Christopher Prendergast, *The Triangle of Representation* (New York: Columbia University Press, 2000) 119. For a selection of 'post-modern' criticism on realism, see Christopher Prendergast, *The Order of Mimesis: Balzac, Stendhal, Nerval, Flaubert* (Cambridge, Cambridge University Press, 1986); J. Hillis Miller, *The Ethics of Reading: Kant, De Man, Eliot, Trollope, James, and Benjamin* (New York: Columbia University Press, 1989); D.A. Miller, *The Novel and the Police* (Berkeley: University of California Press, 1988); Ann Jefferson, *Reading Realism in Stendhal* (Cambridge: Cambridge University Press, 1988); Roland Barthes, *S/Z* (Richard Miller (trans), Oxford: Basil Blackwell, 1990).

23 Cited in Francis Steegmuller, *Flaubert and Madame Bovary: A Double Portrait* (revised edn, Chicago: University of Chicago Press, 1977) 322.

24 C.A. Sainte-Beuve, 'Madame Bovary par M. Gustave Flaubert' *Causeries du Lundi* (1868–1870) 346–64 at 348. The English translation above is taken from the version reproduced in Gustave Flaubert, *Madame Bovary* (Margaret Cohen (ed), Eleanor Marx Aveling and Paul de Man (trans), first published 1857; New York: W.W. Norton, 2005) 334.

25 'Balzac and his writings' *Westminster Review* (July and October 1853) 199–215 at 209.

Another article in the *Westminster Review* in the same period attested to the centrality of faithful representation in realism: writing in 1858, G.H. Lewes notes that fiction 'must always be real – true,' and that the novelist 'is not at liberty to falsify' because 'every departure from truth in motive, idiom or probability is, to that extent, a defect'.[26] Underpinning the English reviewers' praise of Balzac is the firm belief that fiction functions as a window into real life; literary discourse is presumed to be characterised by a kind of linguistic transparency to a 'true', non-discursive reality.

This conception of the relationship between literature and reality is further expressed in the famous seventeenth chapter of George Eliot's novel *Adam Bede*, which remains the most succinct statement of the realist position in English fiction. Speaking of her own literary endeavour, Eliot notes:

> I aspire to give . . . a faithful account of men and things as they have mirrored themselves in my mind. The mirror is doubtless defective, the outlines will sometimes be disturbed, the reflection faint or confused; but I feel as much bound to tell you as precisely as I can what that reflection is, as if I were in the witness-box, narrating my experience on oath.[27]

It is worth pausing over the metaphor of the mirror in this passage, for it has important implications for understanding the realist conception of the relationship between art and life against which Wilde was reacting. First of all, the premise that art is a 'mirror' of life implies that art has no independent existence: it exists not in and of itself as a distinct entity, but as a recreation or imitation of another entity called life. The role of the artist is to recreate life as 'precisely' as she can, to be as faithful to reality as possible. The legal metaphor of the witness-box underscores the high degree of fidelity to life which is required of literature; the artist must write about this external reality in such a way as if she was narrating her experience 'on oath'. Art has no autonomous existence; its content, value and overall *raison d'être* will always be tied to the facts of life.

Related to this view that art has no autonomous existence is the corollary conception of art as subordinate or secondary to life. Further on in the same chapter Eliot notes that 'falsehood is so easy, truth so difficult', and reiterates that the task of the artist is to strive for this 'truth' of reality as much as she can, even though her final product may be 'defective' or distorted. Since the function of art is to imitate reality, it follows that it will always be inferior to reality, a mere representation of the concrete, material world of 'men and things'.[28] As a reflection or imitation of life, it follows that art will always be at one remove from the real

26 G.H. Lewes, 'Realism in art: recent German fiction' *Westminster Review* (July and October 1858) 488–519 at 495.

27 George Eliot, *Adam Bede* (1859) (London: Penguin Books, 1985) 177.

28 Ibid. 178.

world. In Eliot's realist vision, art is the copy while life is the original, and the colours of the former will never be as vivid as those of the latter.[29]

It is against the realist conception of the relationship between art and life that Wilde's own position should be understood. 'As a method, realism is a complete failure,' he states starkly in 'The Decay of Lying'.[30] For Wilde, an artist who puts reality before art neglects the supremacy and the noble quality of the artistic impulse; and 'if a novelist is base enough to go to life for his personages he should at least pretend that they are creations, and not boast of them as copies'.[31] In reaction against the realist aesthetic, Wilde posits a vision which champions art's supremacy over life. It is based on two fundamental premises: first, art has an autonomous existence and secondly, art does not seek to imitate or reproduce reality. The first premise is encapsulated in one line, which appears repeatedly in 'The Decay of Lying': 'Art never expresses anything but itself'.[32]

In other words, art does not seek to mirror life, for it exists for no other reason than to be beautiful: a painting exists not to show its viewer an external reality on which it is supposedly based, but to allow him to appreciate its own innate artistic qualities, such as its combination of colours, the texture of its material or the spatial contours of its lines. Similarly, a literary work does not refer to any purported reality, but encourages its reader to appreciate its rhetorical and stylistic devices for their own sake. Since art no longer strives to mirror life, it no longer depends on external reality for its *raison d'être*, and it is for this reason that art can be said to develop 'purely on its own lines'.[33]

Like most of Wilde's disarmingly simple adages, the idea that 'Art never expresses anything but itself' contains a profound meditation on the relationship between art and life, in that it insists on a complete dissociation between the two domains, an insistence which, as we shall see, underpins Wilde's responses to the barrister Edward Carson in the trials. Similarly, the seemingly obvious statement 'The artist is the creator of beautiful things', which sounds like mere platitude to modern ears, begins to sound more like a war cry against realism when read in

29 For further discussions of the principles and techniques of nineteenth-century realism, see Peter Brooks, *Realist Vision* (Yale University Press, 2005) and George Levine, *The Realist Imagination: English Fiction from Frankenstein to Lady Chatterley* (University of Chicago Press, 1981). For a more 'post-modern' reading of English realist fiction, see J. Hillis Miller, 'The fiction of realism: *Sketches by Boz, Oliver Twist*, and Cruikshank's illustrations' in Ada Nisbet and Blake Nevius (eds), *Dickens Centennial Essays* (Berkeley: University of California Press, 1971) 85–153. Also illuminating are George Levine, *Realism, Ethics and Secularism: Essays on Victorian Literature and Science* (Cambridge: Cambridge University Press, 2008) 185–210 and Matthew Beaumont (ed), *Adventures in Realism* (Oxford: Blackwell, 2007).

30 Oscar Wilde, 'The Decay of Lying' (1891) in Linda Dowling (ed), *The Soul of Man under Socialism and Selected Critical Prose* (London: Penguin, 2001) 163–93 at 175.

31 Ibid. 169.

32 Ibid. 185.

33 Ibid. 191.

context, for it insists that art is answerable to beauty alone, and never to any facts or events in real life as commonly assumed.[34]

The insistence on the autonomy of art has profound implications not only for art itself, but on the way it is viewed or read. Since art exists independently of life, it follows that any attempt to find in an artwork 'the temper of its age, the spirit of its time', or 'the moral and social conditions' which gave rise to it is misguided.[35] The realist reader who conceives of an artwork as an imitation of reality may seek to find evidence of that reality in it, but Wilde argues that any attempt to recuperate elements of an external reality in an artwork would be futile because there is no external life or reality waiting to be uncovered. The viewer or reader seeking reality in art would find nothing but art itself. It is for this reason that 'All art is at once surface and symbol'; the symbol of art is all surface and no depth because there is no hidden reality within it.[36] Those who go beneath the surface or read the symbol in an attempt to find the external reality which the artwork supposedly reflects thus 'do so at their peril'.

The second premise of Wilde's aesthetic philosophy is a corollary of the first: since art exists as an autonomous entity, independent of the claims of an external life or reality, it follows that art is not subordinate or inferior to life. Art is not a pale imitation of life, nor can life be regarded as the primary source of experience on which art depends. 'Life! Life! Don't let us go to life for our fulfilment or our experience', Gilbert expounds in 'The Critic as Artist', an essay in the form of a dialogue through which Wilde argues for the centrality of the creative faculties in criticism.[37] Unsurprisingly, Wilde was full of scorn not only for the realist writers but also for Zola, whose naturalism combined the basic tenets of realism with a purported scientific rigour. Zola was vocal about his commitment to reality, arguing that the artist should 'simply take from real life the history of a human being or a group of human beings', whose acts he would then reproduce 'faithfully' in writing.[38]

Wilde acknowledges that Zola's fiction 'is perfectly truthful, and describes things exactly as they happen'.[39] He then points out that naturalism's subservience to reality does nothing but turn the novel into a 'record' of the 'dreary vices' and 'drearier virtues' of characters whose lives are 'absolutely without interest' to the reader. He concludes that as a writer, Zola is 'determined to show that, if he has not got genius, he can at least be dull'. The view that art is not inferior to life because it is not a mere reflection of it also manifests itself in the discussion of the distinction between art and ethics in the same essay: since ethics belongs to the

34 Oscar Wilde, *The Picture of Dorian Gray* (1890/91) (London: Penguin Books, 2003) 3.
35 Wilde, 'The Decay of Lying' (n 30) 185.
36 Wilde, *Dorian Gray* (n 34) 4.
37 Oscar Wilde, 'The Critic as Artist' (1891) 213–280 at 251.
38 Émile Zola, 'Le naturalisme au théâtre' (1881) in François-Marie Mourad (ed), *Le roman experimental* (Paris: Flammarion, 2006) 129–67 at 141.
39 Wilde, 'The Decay of Lying' (n 30) 169.

domain of reality, and art to the domain of beauty, it follows that art and ethics belong to different orders. One cannot speak of an ethics of art, because to do so would again be to misunderstand art as an imitation or reproduction of some external reality in which ethics dwells. As Gilbert notes: 'the first condition of criticism is that the critic should be able to recognise the sphere of art and the sphere of ethics are absolutely distinct and separate. When they are confused, Chaos has come again'.[40] The reader who attempts to find ethical issues in art is mistakenly placing life before art.

This second Wildean premise that art is not inferior or subordinate to life leads to what is commonly regarded as one of Wilde's most radical claims: Wilde asserts that not only is art not inferior to life, it is in fact superior to life because, contrary to the realist notion that art imitates life, it is life which imitates art:

> All that I desire to point out is the general principle that Life imitates Art far more than Art imitates Life, and I feel sure that if you think seriously about it you will find that it is true. Life holds the mirror up to Art, and either reproduces some strange type imagined by painter or sculptor, or realises in fact what has been dreamed in fiction.[41]

Wilde therefore turns the epistemological assumptions of realism on its head: it is life that imitates art, not the other way around. He uses the example of fog as evidence of his argument:

> At present, people see fogs, not because there are fogs, but because poets and painters have taught them the mysterious loveliness of such effects. There may have been fogs for centuries in London. I dare say there were. But no one saw them, and so we do not know anything about them. They did not exist till Art had invented them.

Wilde's claim is in fact less outrageous than it seems: art is superior to life because the way we perceive life is conditioned by art, by those literary works which we read and by those paintings which we see. The only effects which life or reality can show us 'are effects that we have already seen through poetry, or in paintings'.[42] In other words, life imitates art because our notion of what is beautiful, of what is worth noticing in reality, is always mediated by art. This idea that art is superior to life reappears in *The Picture of Dorian Gray* and underpins the episodes concerning the actress Sybil Vane. Dorian falls in love with Sybil precisely when he sees her in the realm of art, as an actress: 'Tonight she is Imogen . . . and tomorrow night she will be Juliet'.[43]

40 Ibid. 265.
41 Ibid. 162.
42 Ibid. 192.
43 Wilde, *Dorian Gray* (n 34) 54.

As an actress, Sybil fascinates him because she multiplies her personalities through her different roles, and is not confined to one identity. 'When is she Sibyl Vane?' asks Henry Wotton, to which Dorian answers, 'Never'. It is the multiple possibilities which the domain of art offers and which Sybil represents, the possibility of leaving one's love 'in the forest of Arden' only to find her again 'in an orchard in Verona', which charms Dorian.[44] However, when Sybil abandons her acting in favour of love in the real world with Dorian, he loses interest in her: 'You used to stir my imagination. Now you don't even stir my curiosity . . . Without your art you are nothing'.[45] Dorian's reaction to Sybil Vane enacts the second premise of Wilde's aesthetic philosophy in fictional form: the actress is more fascinating than the woman because art is superior to life; theatre does not imitate reality but 'invents a type' which 'life tries to copy' in vain.[46]

These two principles – that art exists as an autonomous entity, and that art is not subordinate to life because it is not a mere reflection of life – form the premise of Wilde's aesthetic philosophy and constitute his repudiation of the realist aesthetic. Carson's arguments, however, aligned themselves with the realist position that literature could be interpreted as a window into the reality of an author's life, thoughts and desires. The following sections will revisit the trials in light of Wilde's artistic principles and Carson's hermeneutic assumptions in order to show that they in effect constituted a confrontation not so much between a legal position and a literary position, but between two different literary conceptions of the relationship between text and reality.

(III) The interpretative battle over 'The Priest and the Acolyte'; 'Phrases and Philosophies for the Use of the Young'; and Wilde's letters

Edward Carson, who defended the Marquess, used various pieces of literary writing – some were Wilde's own, some were by authors with whom Wilde was believed to be associated – as evidence against the playwright. He attempted to demonstrate that the short story 'The Priest and the Acolyte' portrayed illicit same-sex desire; that an intention to corrupt young minds lurked behind the maxims in 'Phrases and Philosophies for the Use of the Young'; that Wilde's letters to Bosie expressed a forbidden intimacy between the two men; and that Wilde's novel *The Picture of Dorian Gray* was a 'sodomitical' book. Carson's strategy was to establish a link between literature and reality: he aimed to show that someone who approved of such homoerotic works and who wrote such works himself would be the kind of person likely to commit acts of gross indecency in real life. In Carson's own words, the reader of these literary texts would 'naturally and reasonably infer

44 Ibid. 74.
45 Ibid. 85.
46 Wilde, 'The Decay of Lying' (n 30) 179.

. . . that he, Mr. Wilde, was either in sympathy with, or addicted to, immoral and sodomitic habits'.[47]

This reading strategy can be said to be based upon a realist conception of literature: underpinning Carson's interrogation is the belief that literary works did not have an independent existence from the reality of their author's life, and that they were a reflection of this reality. Indeed, the possibility of using literature as legal evidence in the trial hinged on this realist assumption: the works were useful to Carson because he believed that they could be interpreted as proof of Wilde's desire and action in real life. Such an interpretative strategy was, of course, antithetical to Wilde's own conception of art and literature. 'If a man approaches a work of art with any desire to exercise authority over it and the artist, he approaches it in such a spirit that he cannot receive any artistic impression at all,' Wilde writes in 'The Soul of Man under Socialism'.[48]

By defining the real meaning of Wilde's writings as the insight they gave into a dark world of sexual deviancy and immorality, Carson sought to exercise precisely such an authority over them. Wilde further notes that this kind of reader 'becomes the avowed enemy of art'.[49] The battle lines were drawn; what was at stake in the Wilde trials was no less than the battle between the realist conception of art and Wilde's own aesthetic vision. We will now examine the literary works presented as evidence in the courtroom, which form the terrain of this battle.

Carson opened his cross-examination of Wilde with a brief reference to Bosie's 'Two Loves', and then proceeded to 'The Priest and the Acolyte', a short story about a priest who falls in love with a boy attending him at mass. Carson interrogated Wilde in two ways: first, he questioned whether Wilde thought the story was blasphemous. Such a question was premised on a realist aesthetic because it conflated the domain of art and the domain of ethics, a conflation which, as discussed in Section (I), Wilde was insistent should be kept separate. Wilde argues that 'Aesthetics are higher than ethics . . . even a colour-sense is more important, in the development of the individual, than a sense of right and wrong'.[50]

For Wilde, ethics belongs to life and is irrelevant to art, which is only concerned with beauty. To discuss ethics and beauty together would be to commit a categorical error. Carson then questioned Wilde on the same-sex implications of the story: 'I think you would admit, Mr. Wilde, that anyone who was connected with or who would allow himself publicly to approve of that article would be posing as a sodomite?'[51] This question assumed a correspondence between literature and life, for it attempted to link a piece of fiction to immoral attitudes and behaviours in life.

47 Holland (n 1) 255.
48 Oscar Wilde, 'The Soul of Man under Socialism' (1891) 125–63 at 150.
49 Ibid. 151.
50 Wilde, 'The Critic as Artist' (n 37) 277.
51 Holland (n 1) 72.

Wilde opposed Carson's realist reading of literature by presenting his own conception of literature; the content and dramatic style of his response are reminiscent of his essays such as 'The Decay of Lying' and 'The Critic as Artist', in which Wilde's characters also expound his views through dialogue with an interlocutor holding a different, more conventional, view of art. Indeed, one could argue that Wilde's astute responses to the cross-examination of his work in court stemmed from his familiarity with the dialogue form in literature; as a writer trained in the classics he often expressed his opinions through exchanges between his characters modelled on the Socratic dialogue. To the question of whether he thought 'The Priest and the Acolyte' was immoral or blasphemous, Wilde answered: 'Worse, it is badly written'.[52]

His response refused to establish a link between art and life and insisted on art's autonomous existence; the only way to judge a work of art is by artistic standards, not by any reference to external categories in reality such as blasphemy or immorality. When Carson persisted with the question, Wilde noted that the story's ending 'violated every canon of artistic beauty'.[53] His emphasis on beauty displaced Carson's focus on blasphemy by shifting the terms of the cross-examination from life back to art. Similarly, when asked whether someone who approved of or was connected with the story could be regarded as posing as a sodomite, Wilde responded that his only view was that this person 'had very bad literary taste'. Both of Carson's questions attempted to construe art as a window into reality, but Wilde countered this attempt by solely referring to aesthetic notions such as 'the literary point of view', beauty and taste.[54]

Wilde told the court that 'it is impossible for a man of letters to judge of a piece of writing otherwise than from its fault in literature' and that he 'couldn't criticise a book as if it was a piece of actual life'. Underpinning his response is Vivian's argument in *Intentions* that 'Art finds her own perfection within, and not outside of, herself. She is not to be judged by any external standard of resemblance'.[55] When the trial transcripts are read in the context of Wilde's aesthetic writings, it becomes possible to discern the parallels between his courtroom testimony and his literary works. Instead of being forced to admit to the text's sodomitical potential, Wilde parried attempts to read his life into the story with his unswerving insistence that an answer about beauty was 'the only answer' he could give in court.[56]

The next text which Carson presented to the court was 'Phrases and Philosophies for the Use of the Young', a series of maxims written by Wilde himself and which first appeared in *The Chameleon*, an Oxford undergraduate magazine. These include many aphorisms for which Wilde is known today, aphorisms such as: 'Wickedness

52 Ibid. 69.
53 Ibid. 70.
54 Ibid. 68.
55 Wilde, 'The Decay of Lying' (n 30) 178.
56 Holland (n 1) 70.

is a myth invented by good people to account for the curious attractiveness of others' and 'Religions die if they are proved to be true'. Carson attacked Wilde by accusing him of deliberately publishing false maxims. He was relentless in his cross-examination; the question 'Is that true?' was repeatedly fired at Wilde like bullets from a pistol.

The epistemological basis of this question is clear: any admission of the truth of the maxims on Wilde's part would immediately shift the focus back to an external reality, beyond the literary world, in which this truth must exist. Specifically, the truth to which Carson's questions referred – the truth about Wilde's sexual preferences and practices – was the truth which the law sought, and this truth was structured by a binary logic, a logic of either/or: Wilde was either telling the truth or telling lies; he either had sexual relations with other men or he did not; he was either guilty or not guilty; he would either be convicted or would be freed.[57]

The battle between Carson's realist interpretation and Wilde's aesthetic vision now turned on the question of the 'truth' of Wilde's maxims. Wilde responded to Carson's notion of legal truth with his own notion of artistic truth. For Wilde, truth in art is not the same as truth in life, so that even though he believed his maxims to be true he could simultaneously assert that they were 'not true in the actual sense of correspondence to the actual facts of life'.[58] Wilde argued that: 'In art there is no such thing as a universal truth. A Truth in art is that whose contradiction is also true'.[59] In other words, a work of art is capable of generating multiple interpretations, each of which is as true as another. As such, artistic truth is not constrained by the binary logic of truth in the courtroom; different readings of a text, even if contradictory, can have equal validity. For Wilde, the epitome of this artistic truth is the paradox: he repeatedly notes that his maxims in 'Phrases and Philosophies for the Use of the Young' 'represent wilful moods of paradox, of fun, nonsense, of anything at all'.[60]

A paradox is by definition a formulation which is capable of holding two contradictory notions as true at the same time and, as R.M. Sainsbury points out in his study of paradoxes, it is a profoundly disruptive formulation because it often reveals a crisis in an institution's intellectual framework. Wilde's aphorisms can be said to constitute a series of 'crises in thought' for Carson's legal interrogation because they did not conform to the logic of binary opposition on which his legal conception of truth is based.[61] Wilde claimed that the maxim 'If one tells the truth one is sure sooner or later to be found out' was a 'very pleasing paradox', and he argued that the phrase 'There is something tragic about the enormous number of

57 For a compelling argument of Wilde's subversion of binary oppositions in the context of sexual identity, see Jonathan Dollimore, *Sexual Dissidence: Augustine to Wilde, Freud to Foucault* (Oxford: Clarendon Press 1991) 3–21.

58 Holland (n 1) 74.

59 Oscar Wilde, 'The Truth of Masks' (1891) 280–305 at 304.

60 Holland (n 1) 74.

61 R.M. Sainsbury, *Paradoxes* (Cambridge: Cambridge University Press 2009) 1.

young men there are in England at the present moment who start life with perfect profiles, and end by adopting some useful profession' should be regarded as 'an amusing paradox, an amusing play on words'.[62]

By insisting that the maxims were no more than 'paradoxes', 'beautiful nonsense' and half-truths 'put in a very perverse and paradoxical form', Wilde removed them from the domain of reality, where truth has a binary structure, to the domain of art, where multiple truths are capable of coexisting. He reminded the court that his maxims were recycled from his dramatic works –'several of them appear in my plays', he said – and by doing so he further underscored the difference between art and reality: the maxims were purely literary products in that they have their origins not in the real world, but in the world of Wilde's plays, or in the world of art. They therefore had to be appreciated on the basis of beauty alone, and not by reference to any impact they might have in real life.[63]

Frustrated by his inability to show the incriminating potential of 'The Priest and the Acolyte' or 'Phrases and Philosophies for the Use of the Young', Carson later turned to a piece of evidence which seemed to bear a more direct relation to Wilde's life: his letters to Bosie. In a letter to his lover written in January 1893, Wilde had addressed him as 'My own boy', and had described his lips as 'made no less for music of song than for madness of kissing'.[64] Carson believed that such an expression of affection would be unequivocally construed as a reflection of same-sex intimacy. However, against the accusation that the text indicated an unnatural and improper exchange, Wilde elevated it from the realm of everyday correspondence to the realm of art, and insisted that a person 'who was not an artist could never have written that letter'.[65] He added:

> *Wilde:* Yes, it is a beautiful letter. If you ask me whether it is proper, you might as well ask me whether *King Lear* is proper, or a sonnet of Shakespeare is proper. It was a beautiful letter. . .
> *Carson:* But apart from art?
> *Wilde:* Ah! I cannot do that.
> *Carson:* But apart from art?
> *Wilde:* I cannot answer any question apart from art.[66]

Wilde's text led not to a reality outside literature, but only to other literary texts, to Shakespeare's sonnets and to *King Lear*. The truth about Wilde's sexual life which Carson sought slipped out of his grasp continuously, and in its place he always found another literary text. By insisting on the text's literary quality, Wilde once

62 Holland (n 1) 76.
63 Ibid. 77.
64 Ibid. 104.
65 Ibid. 95.
66 Ibid. 105.

again cut off the text from the immediate context of the trial, thereby precluding the possibility of its interpretation as part of a pose as a sodomite. Art never expresses anything but itself, so that all that a literary text refers to is another literary text. Similarly, when interrogated on another letter to Lord Douglas, Wilde insisted that the letter was a 'prose poem' whose sole object was to be beautiful.[67] He reiterated his view of the letter as a 'prose poem in beautiful phraseology' in the second and third trials.[68] By demonstrating that the focus of the reader should not be on any easy correspondence between literature and reality, and that art should be the one and only point of reference, Wilde pre-empted Carson from forging links between his sexual life and his works.

(IV) The interpretative battle over *The Picture of Dorian Gray*

Out of all the literary evidence which Carson presented against Wilde, *The Picture of Dorian Gray* received the most intense scrutiny: Carson repeatedly attempted to establish a connection between the events and relations in the novel and the writer's actual life. Wilde, on the other hand, was put on the defensive and sought to justify the novel's style and subject by demonstrating art's self-referentiality. Carson selected four passages as proof of Wilde's sodomitical tendencies. The first passage concerned Basil's first meeting with Dorian. It is arguably suggestive of same-sex infatuation: Basil claims that the beautiful young man filled him with a 'curious terror', that he felt like he was 'on the verge of a terrible crisis', and that he was in danger of becoming 'absolutely devoted to him'. Towards the end of the chosen passage he tells Henry Wotton: 'I have always been my own master . . . till I met Dorian Gray'.[69]

Carson was confident that such confessions by one of the main characters in Wilde's novel would lead the court directly from the artistic text to the reality of the author's sexual behaviour and desires. He argued that since Wilde was writing about an 'improper feeling' between men, it followed that the writer must experience the same kinds of feeling in real life. The battle now turned on whether fiction functions as a window into reality.

Wilde countered this reading by shifting the basis of interpretation from his life back to the realm of art. First of all, he glossed Basil's feeling towards Dorian as 'the feeling of an artist towards a beautiful personality'.[70] He then explained that, far from being the description of illicit desire between men, the passage represented 'the most perfect description possible of what an artist would feel on meeting a

67 Ibid. 111.
68 H. Montgomery Hyde, *The Trials of Oscar Wilde* (New York: Dover Publications, 1962) 245.
69 Ibid. 84–85.
70 Ibid. 86.

beautiful personality that he felt some way was necessary to his art and life'.[71] The artist is concerned with nothing but art. This self-referentiality was crucial for countering Carson's accusation of sexual immorality, for it effectively evacuated the passage of sexual content and anchored its ambiguity firmly in the domain of aesthetics by insisting that the 'peculiar effect' Carson highlighted could only refer to the effect an object of beauty exerted on an artist.[72]

The second passage concerned Basil's reason for not exhibiting his portrait of Dorian. This passage seemed even more suggestive of an illicit desire: Basil tells Dorian that he adored him 'madly, extravagantly, absurdly', and that every colour in the portrait seemed to reveal a 'secret' he was anxious not to disclose.[73] Once again, Carson's reading of this passage was based on the realist notion that Wilde's art had no independent existence from life, so that the language of adoration and secrecy in the passage must refer to some shameful sexual secret in the author which he was trying to conceal from legal scrutiny.

Wilde countered Carson's reading with flair. He refused to be interrogated on the passages in their entirety, and insisted that Carson pinpoint specific sentences. Carson in turn singled out one of Basil's frankest admissions: 'I quite admit that I adored you madly, extravagantly, desperately. I was jealous of everyone'.[74] Carson repeatedly applied the sentiment expressed in the novel directly to Wilde's life: 'Have you yourself ever had that feeling towards a young man? . . . Have you ever adored a young man, some twenty-one years younger than yourself, madly? . . . Have you ever felt that feeling of adoring madly a beautiful male person many years younger than yourself?'[75] For a moment, Carson seemed successful in using Wilde's art as a means of proving the existence of illicit desire in his life. But his interpretative strategy ultimately only brought him back to the realm of art:

> *Wilde:* I have never adored any young man younger than myself or any person older than myself of any kind. I do not adore them. I either love a person or do not love them.
> *Carson:* Then, you never had that feeling that you depict there?
> *Wilde:* No, it was borrowed from Shakespeare I regret to say. (Laughter)
> *Carson:* From Shakespeare?
> *Wilde:* Yes, from Shakespeare's sonnets.[76]

Behind Wilde's text was not Wilde's life, but another literary work, one by Shakespeare. The 'evidence' which Carson adduced led not to the author's life

71 Ibid. 85.
72 Ibid. 86.
73 Ibid. 87.
74 Ibid. 89.
75 Ibid. 89–91.
76 Ibid. 92.

outside of the text, not to any truth about Wilde's own desires, but to another piece of writing. Persistent barrister that he was, Carson continued his cross-examination, believing that behind this text was the objective truth of Wilde's same-sex relations, which he was determined to uncover:

Carson: I believe that you have written an article pointing out that Shakespeare's sonnets were practically sodomitical?
Wilde: On the contrary, Mr. Carson, I wrote an article to prove that they were not so.
Carson: You did write an article to prove that they were not sodomitical?
Wilde: Yes, the statement had been made against Shakespeare by Hallam, the historian, and by others. I wrote an article to prove that they were not so, and I consider that I have proved it.
Carson: In your opinion they were not sodomitical?
Wilde: Certainly not.[77]

The 'article' which Wilde refers to here is *The Portrait of Mr. W.H.*, in which Cyril Graham seeks to prove to Erskine that Shakespeare's sonnets were written to a young male actor. Behind Shakespeare's sonnet was thus a further literary text; Carson's attempt to grasp the reality of Wilde's sexual behaviour only led him even deeper into Wilde's literary corpus.

Most significantly, *The Portrait of Mr. W.H.* is not simply another artistic text; it is one which uncannily anticipates Carson's interpretation of literature in court. In the short story, Cyril Graham interprets the sonnets in an attempt to show that Shakespeare displayed a homosexual infatuation towards a boy actor in real life, just as Carson interprets *The Picture of Dorian Gray* in an attempt to show that Wilde was the kind of person who would commit sodomy with other men. Moreover, just as Cyril Graham becomes increasingly obsessed and increasingly frustrated with his interpretative task, Carson seemed to become increasingly desperate and increasingly frustrated in his attempt to use Wilde's writings as a reflection of Wilde's actual desires.[78] 'It seemed to me that I was on the brink of absolute verification, but I could never really attain to it'; these words which express Cyril's inability to move from literature to life arguably applied to Carson as well.[79] Far from being a mere reflection of life, as Eliot suggests, art always seems to be one step ahead of the reality of the law.

The third passage Carson presented as evidence against Wilde concerned the role played by an unnamed French novel in Dorian's life. Wilde initially confirmed the French novel which Dorian read as J.K. Huysmans's *À Rebours*, a work of high

77 Ibid. 93.
78 For a further discussion of the interpretative assumptions inherent in Cyril Graham and Erskine's readings, and of the ways in which literary and sexual elements are related in the story, see William A. Cohen, *Sex Scandal: the Private Parts of Victorian Fiction* (Durham: Duke University Press, 1996) 191–237.
79 Oscar Wilde, 'The Portrait of Mr. W.H.' (1889) 31–103 at 70.

decadence about a dandy who, amongst other things, experiments with strange forms of sensory experience and has a number of same-sex encounters. Wilde's description of the novel seemed to point to a reality outside of art which Carson could use to his own advantage: since Des Esseintes, the protagonist of Huysmans's novel, is clearly described as having had same-sex encounters, his role as 'a kind of prefiguring type' for Dorian would prove beyond doubt that Wilde's own protagonist also engaged in acts of gross indecency, and this interpretation would, in turn, strongly suggest that Wilde himself was likely to engage in such behaviour. Carson again attempted to construe the French novel literally: 'was it a book, sir, dealing with undisguised sodomy?'[80]

Yet Carson's strategy failed once again, for Wilde then told the court that the French novel in *Dorian Gray* was in fact not *À Rebours*, but an 'imaginary book', which he would have liked to have written himself: 'when I quote from the book . . . and allude to passages in the book, those passages do not occur in the book. It was merely what I imagined'.[81] To underscore his point, Wilde pointed out that even though his own novel referred to the seventh chapter of *À Rebours*, Huysman's novel did not actually contain a seventh chapter, thereby precluding the possibility of mapping any sodomitical behaviour by Des Esseintes onto Dorian and, by extension, onto Wilde.[82]

Once again, adducing *Dorian Gray* as evidence led to another artistic text (*À Rebours)*, which in turn led to another text (the 'imaginary book'). Every time Carson believed evidence of Wilde's desires and actions in real life to be within his grasp, they slipped away and, in their place, he found another text. His attempt to read literature as a reflection of life only led him back, full circle, to literature, confirming Wilde's view that art has an autonomous existence and is not subordinate to reality.

The final passage which was read in court appears towards the end of Wilde's novel. There are whispers about Dorian's behaviour in London, and he is shunned by high society. In this passage, Basil confronts Dorian about his behaviour, which has brought about this social castigation:

> Why is your friendship so final to young men? There was that wretched boy in the guards who committed suicide. You were his great friend. There was Sir Henry Ashton, who had to leave England with a tarnished name. You and he were inseparable. What about Adrian Singleton, and his dreadful end? What about Lord Kent's only son, and his career? I met his father yesterday at St James's Street. He seemed broken with shame and sorrow. What about the young Duke of Perth? What sort of life has he got now? What gentleman would associate with him?[83]

80 Holland (n 1) 95–96.
81 Ibid. 97.
82 Ibid. 98.
83 Ibid. 102.

Carson was convinced that the passage could be construed as indicative of same-sex desire: 'Do you think that, taken in its natural meaning, it would suggest that what they were talking about was a charge of sodomy?' However, Wilde once again showed that it was problematic to read the novel as evidence of its author's own desire. Wilde's counter-interpretation ran as follows: he argued that even though the passage did suggest that Dorian was a man of very corrupt influence, it contained 'no statement about what the nature of his bad influence was'. Even though a sexual reading was possible, it was not definitive; the corrupt influence could equally be suggestive of drug addiction, or blackmail for some non-sexual secret, or financial ruin from gambling. Since, as we saw above, literature is capable of accommodating not one true meaning but multiple true meanings – 'a truth in art is that whose contradiction is also true' – it follows that there were too many possible readings of this passage to allow Carson to prove beyond reasonable doubt that it must be suggestive of any sodomitical tendencies in its author.

Wilde explicitly told Carson that his attempt to read literature as legal evidence was a futile task because it was based on the realist assumption that life provided the only definitive meaning to a work of art: 'you must remember that novels and life are different things . . . You are not to ask me if I believe that they really happened; they are motives *in fiction*'.[84] Carson's mistake, from beginning to end, was to assume that Wilde's novel functioned as a mirror of Wilde's life, and that this life could somehow be retrieved through his fiction.

(V) Conclusion

This chapter has argued that Wilde's responses to Carson's cross-examination are premised on an aesthetic philosophy drawn from his writings, and that trials themselves can be understood as a clash between the 'realist' and the 'aesthetic' visions of the relationship between literature and reality. The confrontation between Wilde and Carson suggests that law and literature are based not so much on two distinct sets of interpretative practices (one literary, one legal) as on two views of the relationship between a text and the world (one realist, one aesthetic), both of which are firmly rooted in the literary domain. The law is also underpinned by a literary approach to reality, even though its literary approach is markedly different from Wilde's own. Furthermore, as a text both reflecting and enacting Wilde's aesthetic philosophy, the trial transcript can arguably be read not only for its biographical value or as historical source material on the regulation of sexuality in late-Victorian England, but as an integral part of Wilde's aesthetic corpus, to be given a place alongside such aesthetic manifestoes as 'The Decay of Lying' or 'The Critic as Artist'.

Over a century has passed since the trials, and one question still remains. Wilde knew from an early stage that the Marquess had strong incriminating evidence

84 Ibid. 103 (my italics).

against him; his friends and supporters repeatedly discouraged him from initiating an open battle in court and, when it became clear that the second trial was inevitable, they urged him to flee to France. Curiously, Wilde insisted on confronting the Marquess even though he realised that the chances of winning the case were slim, and even though he knew that the cost of losing would be formidable, not only in financial terms but also in terms of his personal reputation. Why, then, did he stubbornly insist on going to court? Critics have been unable to agree on Wilde's motive. Frank Harris, a fellow Irishman who knew Wilde personally, attributed this seemingly foolish decision to Bosie's influence on the playwright. Writing of a meeting between himself, George Bernard Shaw and Wilde, Harris remembers that Wilde had been inclined to go abroad as Harris advised, until Bosie angrily chided him for suggesting a non-legal course of action: 'Such advice shows you are no friend of Oscar's'.[85]

Harris came to the conclusion that 'it was not Oscar who had ever misled Douglas, but Lord Alfred Douglas who was driving Oscar whither he would'. Another critic posits a different interpretation of Wilde's conduct, and argues that Wilde refused to flee England in order to safeguard his reputation as a gentleman.[86] Finally, the biographer Richard Ellmann speculates that Wilde was as much 'the prey of his own consciousness' as he was of Lord Queensberry.[87] Ellmann notes that: 'we are by nature our own enemies . . . we seek events that unconsciously befit us, which consciously we fear'.[88] For Ellmann, Wilde was to some extent seeking his own destruction.

In conclusion, this chapter proposes one further interpretation of Wilde's seemingly baffling conduct, an interpretation based on the understanding of the Wilde trials as literature. Given that one of the main principles of Wilde's aesthetic philosophy is the supremacy of art over life, a trial in which he knew his writings would be construed as evidence against him, and which therefore provided a platform for him to expound his aesthetic vision, would have held a curious attraction for the writer. He knew that a trial in which he was the protagonist would attract great attention, and he would have envisaged that his carefully formulated aphorisms, his witty ripostes, and his passionate defence of aestheticism – in short, his literary language – would forever become integrated into the fabric of legal history through such a high-profile trial. The event would represent nothing less than a transformation of legal discourse into literary discourse through the intrusion of Wildean language, concepts and ideas into the courtroom. Here, then, was a chance to proclaim his artistic vision to the world. 'Life imitates Art far more than Art imitates Life': an occasion for turning a real-life court case into a literary

85 Frank Harris, *Oscar Wilde: His Life and Confessions* (London: Robinson Publishing 1916) 117.

86 Mark Girouard, *The Return to Camelot: Chivalry and the English Gentleman* (New Haven: Yale University Press 1981) 263.

87 Richard Ellmann, *Oscar Wilde* (London: Hamish Hamilton, 1987) 413.

88 Ibid. 414.

event, for turning the law itself into a form of literature, for making life imitate art, would have represented the ultimate triumph of Wilde's aesthetic philosophy.[89] Peter Raby has argued that 'Wilde's art, and his role as Artist, was itself conceived in the form of an extended dialogue, conducted within a variety of contexts'; it is not inconceivable that Wilde thought of the trials as another context for dramatic dialogue, as much as he acknowledged them to be a forum in which his work was judged.[90]

In the aftermath of Wilde's disgrace, it is easy to forget that Wilde's testimony about his writings in the libel trial was in fact a very compelling one: what ultimately led to his downfall was less his failure to justify his literary output and more the subsequent evidence of the rent boys with whom he had had sexual relations. As Mr Justice Charles pointed out to the jury in his summing up of the evidence, one cannot assume that a literary text is a reflection of its author's life because the writer may not share the views or habits of the characters he creates, and 'it would be unfair . . . when you are trying a man, to allow yourselves to be unfavourably influenced against him by the circumstances that he has written a book of which you, in so far as you have read any extracts from it, may disapprove'.[91] Even today one is struck by the force of Wilde's rhetoric when reading what the court referred to as 'the literary part of the case'.[92]

Wilde once noted that: 'No man dies for what he knows to be true. Men die for what they want to be true, for what some terror in their heart tells them is not true': perhaps he chose to go to court because he saw an opportunity of showing both himself and the world the truth of his conception of literature and art. This reading of Wilde's motive is of course pure speculation, based on imagination, make believe and even fantasy, all of which belong to the domain of art, not of law. However, one might argue that it is precisely because it springs from the domain of art that it offers a useful way of thinking about Wilde's relationship with the law.

89 Wilde, 'The Decay of Lying' (n 30).
90 Peter Raby, *Oscar Wilde* (Cambridge: Cambridge University Press, 1988) 10.
91 Hyde (n 68) 215–216.
92 Ibid. 196.

Chapter 5

The *Well of Loneliness* trials: lesbianism and the return of the repressed

Radclyffe Hall's *The Well of Loneliness*, like Flaubert's *Madame Bovary*, occupies a seemingly anachronistic place in the history of European fiction: Flaubert's novel was published in the mid-nineteenth century but has a distinctly 'modernist' style marked by shifting points of view and a focus on interiority, and Hall's novel was published in the time of high modernism but is based on a distinctly 'realist' mode of narration. Indeed, Hall's was critical of the modernist narrative method of her contemporaries such as Virginia Woolf and James Joyce: in a talk given at Sion College entitled 'True Realism in Fiction', she castigated them as writers 'suffering from a leaking subconscious'.[1]

She further established her own artistic philosophy as a contrast: whilst modernist writers dealt with 'subjects that with normal people sank naturally to the subconscious mind', Hall's own novels encapsulated her belief that 'all realism must mean something, must not be idly employed, and must lead somewhere', a belief which was rooted in the understanding of the nature of fiction from an earlier part of the Victorian period. The case of *The Well of Loneliness* concludes my study of literary trials and masculinity, allowing me to test the argument about the constructions of gender and the intertwining of literary and legal discourses beyond the Victorian period, whilst also serving as a reminder that periodisation in literary history and the use of labels such as 'realist' and 'modernist' in criticism, although useful, are themselves practices with a degree of arbitrariness which should be kept in view.

The events leading up to the legal case began with the publication of a damning review of *The Well of Loneliness* in the *Sunday Express* by the paper's editor, James Douglas. Its title, stating that the novel was 'a book that must be suppressed', was enlarged, capitalised and in bold, a format which was presumably meant to convey outrage at the novel's publication, as well as the urgency of banning it. As with the cases of obscenity we have seen, the premise for his condemnation was the likely mimetic effects of Hall's novel on its readers, who were imagined to be youthful and therefore vulnerable: Douglas points out that it could fall into the hands of 'young women and young men' and hence posed the risk of 'devastating the

1 F.A.D., *The Bookman* (April 1927) 24.

younger generation', 'wrecking young lives' and 'defiling young souls'.[2] As David Bradshaw has pointed out, 'for all his ludicrous hyperbole and self-important posturing, the well-connected Douglas was a prude to be reckoned with', and Hall's publisher, Jonathan Cape, was wary that the *Sunday Express* review would lead to prosecution.[3]

When it became clear that the Home Office would take action, Cape wrote to the Home Secretary, Sir William Joynson-Hicks, offering to withdraw the book. However, he was unwilling to concede defeat to the censors so readily. He secretly sent the moulds for printing to Paris, and in September 1928 the novel was reprinted by the Pegasus Press in France in its original English version. The published copies were then exported back to England. One shipment to a bookseller, Leopold Hill, was impounded at customs, but was subsequently released. The police then obtained search warrants under Lord Campbell's Act and seized copies at Hill's shop and also at the premises of another major bookseller on Charing Cross Road in London. Cape and Hall soon found themselves before the Chief Magistrate, Sir Henry Chartres Biron, at the Bow Street Magistrates' Court. Biron convicted the publisher and ordered all copies of the novel to be destroyed. Cape and Hall appealed against Biron's decision, but to no avail.[4]

In this chapter, I will situate the trials of *The Well of Loneliness* in the context of how female same-sex relations were understood in the early twentieth century, and will examine them as the terrain on which law and literature clashed over the construction of lesbian identity.[5] In the first section, I will argue that the text constructs lesbian relations in a hetero-normative mode in order to ensure acceptability to a largely heterosexual readership. I will further contend that its representation of lesbianism is premised on an insufficiently acknowledged denigration of male homosexuality, and that Hall's narrative displaces the offensiveness of gender deviancy from the figure of the lesbian onto the figure of the male homosexual as part of a strategy to establish lesbianism's cultural acceptability. I will deepen this line of analysis in the second section through an investigation of lesbian-homosexual relations in the novel in a psychoanalytic frame. In the final section, I will analyse the way in which *The Well of Loneliness* was interpreted through the eyes of the law in the obscenity trial, and will posit that the magistrate's reading of Hall's novel unexpectedly constituted the route through which the

2 James Douglas, 'A book that must be suppressed' *Sunday Express* (19 August 1928) 10–11.

3 David Bradshaw, 'James Douglas: The sanitary inspector of literature' in David Bradshaw and Rachel Potter (eds), *Prudes on the Prowl: Fiction and Obscenity in England, 1850 to the Present Day* (Oxford: Oxford University Press, 2013) 90–111 at 91.

4 For a more extensive discussion of the events leading up to the trials, see Michael Baker, *Our Three Selves: The Life of Radclyffe Hall* (London: Hamish Hamilton, 1985) 149–201.

5 I will focus on the trials in the English context. For a helpful discussion of the obscenity trial on *The Well of Loneliness* in the United States, see Kim Emery, '*Well* meaning; pragmatism, lesbianism, and the U.S. obscenity trial' in Laura Doan and Jay Prosser (eds), *Palatable Poison: Critical Perspectives on The Well of Loneliness* (New York: Columbia University Press, 2001) 355–72.

figure of the male homosexual, which the narrative had sought to repress, returned to haunt it.

(I) Lesbianism, heteronormativity and homophobia in *The Well of Loneliness*

A number of scholars of the history of female sexuality have observed that the final decades of the nineteenth century and the first decades of the twentieth century were a time when a distinct lesbian sexual identity came into being. Sharon Marcus has shown that during the mid-Victorian period, female friendships took diverse and malleable forms that do not readily fall on either side of the deep divide between homosexuality and heterosexuality in our own century; she further argues that the category of 'the lesbian' began to emerge in the 1880s and took hold in England in the 1930s.[6] Laura Doan's wide-ranging study of the origins of modern English lesbian culture gives even greater historical precision to Marcus's observation, by pinpointing the controversy generated by the publication of Hall's novel as a crucial moment in the formation of the concept of the 'lesbian' which we know today: 'some of the styles and accoutrements we now associate unquestionably with lesbianism . . . did not signal unequivocally something about sexuality until the cultural dissemination of Hall's photographic portrait . . . set her apart from her fashionable friends'.[7]

The insight of critics such as Doan and Marcus has important consequences: since lesbian identity only started to emerge in the 1880s and did not crystallise until after the novel's publication and the trials in 1928, it follows that the public conception of lesbianism was still in a state of flux in the years leading up to the trials. A study of the representation of 'the lesbian' in literature and the law therefore has to be attuned to the fuzziness or amorphousness of conceptions of female same-sex desire at this time.

The parliamentary records provide one starting point for an examination of the ways in which lesbian relations were understood. The question of whether such relations ought to be legally regulated arose in the course of the debate on the Criminal Law Amendment Bill in the 1920s. The committee on the bill discussed the possible inclusion of a clause criminalising them, and this clause became a point of great contention in both Houses of Parliament. The records attest to the multiple, overlapping and often conflicting views of how lesbian desire manifested itself during these years. When the legislator Frederick Macquisten introduced the clause to the House of Commons, he began by describing lesbianism in medical terms, noting that the topic was 'more a matter for medical science and for

6 Sharon Marcus, *Between Women: Friendship, Desire and Marriage in Victorian England* (Princeton: Princeton University Press, 2007) 261.

7 Laura Doan, *Fashioning Sapphism: The Origins of a Modern English Lesbian Culture* (New York: Columbia University Press, 2001) xiv.

neurologists'. He attributed it to the effects of 'dreadful nerve deterioration', and compared Sapphic practices to 'the use of cocaine and other drugs'.[8]

This medical vocabulary co-existed, and jarred, with a moral template which was itself self-contradictory: on the one hand, the female invert was the victim of a biological condition for which she was not to blame, yet on the other hand she was a sexual predator who had recklessly 'forgotten all the dictates of Nature and morality' who ought to be condemned. He further argued that the 'horrible grossness of homosexual immorality' formed part of the 'undercurrent of dreadful degradation' in English society which Parliament ought to rectify. In addition to considerations of medicine and morality, Macquisten's speech expressed grave concerns about the family, and in particular about the danger lesbian desire posed to the heterosexual man's place in the family. He purported to have spoken to a man whose 'home had been ruined by the wiles of one abandoned female, who had pursued his wife'. Another Member of Parliament claimed to know a man who fell victim to the lesbian menace, and told his fellow legislators that 'the whole of his married life was ruined because his wife had been taken from him by a young woman'.[9]

Deviant female sexuality threatened to undermine the stability of families and usurp the rightful place of the husband, thereby posing a direct threat to a normative masculinity which, as we have seen, is premised on domesticity and the authority of the *paterfamilias*. This menace was depicted in a vampiric mode: lesbianism was 'an evil' which was 'capable of sapping the highest and the best in civilisation'.[10] Female same-sex relations as illness, as a form of immorality, as evil or vice, as threat to masculinity . . . the complementary, yet multiple, representations highlight the instability of the term 'lesbian' prior to the trials. They also reflect a tension between the conception of lesbianism as a category of forbidden acts and as the basis for a core identity.

Macquisten described lesbianism as a set of 'gross practices', which implies that he understood it as a form of behaviour rather than the basis for an identity, but his equation of lesbianism with nervous bodies, cunning or immoral sexual predators and figures of threat to family and conventional masculinity arguably point to the conception of a recognisable sexual type. To complete the story of the draft clause on the 'lesbian vice', it was eventually rejected by the House of Lords, mainly as a result of concerns about the possible rise of blackmailing, the difficulty of finding evidence to prove the proposed crime and the hasty way in which the clause was introduced.[11] When the bill was finally passed as law in 1922, it included no reference to the problem of female same-sex relations.

8 *The Parliamentary Debates: Official Report*. House of Commons, vol 145, 8th vol of Session 1921 (25 July 1921–5 August 1921), cols 1799–800.

9 *Parliamentary Debates*, vol 145, col 1803.

10 Ibid. col 1800.

11 *The Parliamentary Debates: Official Report*. House of Lords, vol 46, 3rd vol of Session 1921 (26 July 1921–19 August 1921), cols 567–77.

In light of the complexity and the contradictions in the way female same-sex relations were understood in the early decades of the twentieth century, literature and the law can be understood as two discourses vying for hegemony in defining 'the lesbian' during this period, *The Well of Loneliness* trials constituted one terrain on which this battle was fought. Hall's novel was deemed obscene because it represented female same-sex relations in a way which the court found unacceptable, and the law reacted to its publication by positing its own construction of the 'lesbian'.

In this section, I will examine the novel's construction of lesbian identity, with a focus on how this representation was premised on, sustained by, even dependent upon, a negative depiction of male homosexuality. As we will see in the analysis of the court's reading of the novel, the figure of the male homosexual will make an important, if unexpected, appearance on the stage during the trials. The intertwining of these two identities, lesbian and homosexual, is reflected in the comparisons between Hall and Wilde, which many commentators have made. In the diatribe against Hall in the *Sunday Express*, Douglas concluded by noting that literature had 'not yet recovered from the harm done to it by the Oscar Wilde Scandal. It should keep its house in order'.[12] After Cape's decision to withdraw the book from circulation, the medical journal *Lancet* prophetically noted that the availability of *The Picture of Dorian Gray* in the 1920s suggested that 'Miss Radclyffe Hall's book may at some future date be restored to circulation'.[13]

The commentator of *Truth* condoned the withdrawal with a reminder of how 'literary merit attempted in the Wilde case to throw its cloak over gross misconduct, and all but succeeded'.[14] Alan Sinfield continued this tradition of comparison in *The Wilde Century*, in which he argued that the effect for gay men of the events in 1895 'was comparable to that produced for lesbianism by Radclyffe Hall's *Well of Loneliness*'.[15] Jeffrey Weeks also noted that the *Well* trials 'had in many ways for women an equivalent social impact to the one the Wilde trial had for men'.[16] There seems to be a recognition that male homosexuality directly or indirectly influenced the construction of lesbian identity. How did *The Well of Loneliness* articulate a lesbian identity in the early decades of the twentieth century, and to what extent, and in what way, did gay male identity play a role in its articulation in fiction and in law?

Hall relies heavily on the language of late nineteenth-century sexology to construct lesbian identity in the novel. Michael Baker has noted that Hall was 'heavily influenced' by her extensive reading in sexological theories and 'swallowed

12 Douglas (n 2) 11.

13 'The Well of Loneliness', *The Lancet* (1 September 1928) 484.

14 A Truthful Tory, 'The suppressed novel', *Truth* (29 August 1928) 381.

15 Alan Sinfield, *The Wilde Century: Effeminacy, Oscar Wilde and the Queer Moment* (New York: Columbia University Press, 1994) 3.

16 Jeffrey Weeks, *Coming Out: Homosexual Politics in Britain From the Nineteenth Century to the Present* (London: Quartet Books, 1977) 101.

them wholesale', taking to heart in particular Havelock Ellis's ideas on sexual inversion.[17] Stephen Gordon's father, Sir Philip Gordon, turns to the writings of Richard von Krafft-Ebing and Karl Heinrich Ulrichs in his attempt to understand his daughter's development. After her father's death, Stephen seeks to understand her own desires by turning to sexological texts: she discovers a book by Krafft-Ebing in his 'special bookcase', in which she finds notes written in 'her father's small, scholarly hand'. Intrigued, 'she began to read . . . For a long time she read; then went back to the bookcase and got out another of those volumes, and another'.[18] Although Ellis declined to give evidence in the trial, he praises Hall for presenting the 'relation of certain people' in a 'completely faithful and uncompromising form' in his preface to the novel, and therefore gives the sexological foundation of the novel a degree of formal recognition.[19]

The construction of lesbian identity in sexological terms focuses on Stephen's body as the site for the expression of an inner masculinity: her oversized hands, her broad shoulders, her small breasts all bear witness to her inversion. Stephen is in effect a man trapped in a woman's body. The novel's emphasis on the protagonist's clothing as an expression of her gendered identity also derives from its affinity to sexological discourse. In *Psychopathia Sexualis*, von Krafft-Ebing identifies two kinds of inversion, congenital and acquired. The female congenital invert falls into one of four categories: psychico-hermaphrodism, homosexuality, viraginity and gynandry.[20] The viragin invert, whose characteristics seem to match those of Stephen most closely, is marked by, amongst other things, a disdain for feminine items such as perfume and a preference for male garments. Havelock Ellis also notes that there is 'a very pronounced tendency among sexually inverted women to adopt male attire when practicable'. He explains that 'male garments are not usually regarded as desirable chiefly on account of practical convenience, nor even in order to make an impression on other women, but because the wearer feels more at home in them'.[21]

Stephen Gordon seems to be a case study for female inversion; her penchant for neckties, suits and cufflinks mark her as different from 'normal' women. One of the earliest clashes between Stephen and Anna, her mother, is sparked by clothing: Anna insists on 'large hats trimmed with ribbons or roses or daisies . . . supposed to be softening to the features' for her daughter, but the 'far from becoming' effect on Stephen's face and her subsequent resistance to them caused 'constant warfare between them on the subject of clothes'.[22] This episode highlights the indissociability

17 Baker (n 4) 217.

18 Radclyffe Hall, *The Well of Loneliness* (1928) (London: Virago, 2005) 207.

19 H. Havelock Ellis, 'Commentary' in *Palatable Poison* (n 5) 35.

20 Richard von Krafft-Ebing, *Psychopathia Sexualis: With Especial Reference to Antipathic Sexual Instinct: A Medico-Forensic Study* (F.J. Rebman (trans), Chicago: Keener, 1901) 430–75.

21 H. Havelock Ellis, *Studies in the Psychology of Sex, 7 vols* (3rd edn, Philadelphia: F.A. Davis, 1920) II, 245.

22 Hall, *The Well of Loneliness* (n 18) 70–71.

of clothing and the body in the process of gender construction: they are complementary modes of representing the lesbian and reinforce one another, so that the conflict over clothing causes Stephen to say: 'It's my face . . . Something's wrong with my face'.

Sexology also informs the relational aspects of the text's representation of lesbianism; Stephen's innate masculinity expresses itself through the characteristics of the women with whom she falls in love. Stephen not only looks like a man, but is depicted as possessing masculine qualities necessary for her to be the dominant, active partner in a relationship, and she is only attracted to women who play a complementary, passive, conventionally feminine role. Ellis observes that the female invert is often drawn to women who are conventionally beautiful, and this observation is confirmed by Stephen's attraction to Angela and Mary. Alison Hennegan also points out in her introduction to the Virago edition of the novel that Stephen is only able to love 'real' women, that is to say, women who display the traditional qualities of femininity such as passivity, docility, and obedience.[23]

This point is crucial to the novel's representation of lesbianism: the sexological underpinnings of the novel mean that even though it depicts sexual and emotional relationships between people who are biologically female, these relationships have a heterosexual structure, in that one partner is coded as masculine, whilst the other is coded as feminine. In gender terms, the novel presents a structure of lesbian relations which replicates the norms and conventions of cross-sex relations: one woman is the active/masculine partner and the other woman is the passive/feminine partner. Lesbian interaction is presented in a hetero-normative mode. This is particularly evident in the relationship between Stephen and Mary Llewellyn. Stephen is presented as the man in the relationship, and Mary the woman. Stephen's anatomical attributes and her demeanour translate into a manly physical and moral strength with which she shelters Mary. Even as a child, Stephen was 'tall for her age' and had 'over-broad shoulders'.[24]

In contrast, Mary is small, delicate, and is repeatedly described as child-like; she looks like 'little more than a schoolgirl'.[25] The first time Stephen holds Mary within her gaze, she is in a state of passivity, having fallen asleep in a state of 'complete exhaustion'. She is 'very young', small, and 'pale', and her smallness and frailty make her unsuitable for war, such that Mrs Breakspeare is initially reluctant to accept her into her group. Stephen, by contrast, is constantly aware of her own disproportionately large limbs. The contrast in the physical appearances between Stephen and Mary is a visible reminder of their different roles in the relationship. Moreover, Stephen takes on all the tasks of a dutiful husband: she provides for Mary through her inheritance, and also becomes obsessed with her writing to

23 Hall, *The Well of Loneliness* (n 18) xvi.
24 Ibid. 22.
25 Ibid. 324.

ensure a steady income to financially 'protect the woman she loved'.[26] Everything that she does is done to build 'a harbour of refuge for Mary'.[27]

Mary, in her turn, exhibits the dependence which complements Stephen's protectiveness: as the Breakspeare Unit is about to disband, Mary clings onto Stephen: 'I've always been waiting for you . . . don't send me away, I want to be near you . . . Stephen, say you won't send me away'.[28] After they arrive in Paris, Mary performs all the 'womanly tasks': she types up Stephen's work, answers her letters and oversees the housework. When Stephen returns from Morton after her meeting with her mother, she finds Mary waiting at the door with a question about the strength of her love, or 'woman's eternal question'.[29]

Despite their sexed identity, their gender identities replicate the cross-sex relationship with which the reader of the novel is assumed to be familiar. Michèle Aina Barale has argued that the cover art of the various editions of the novel, whilst purporting to express its transgressive sexuality in pictorial or photographic form, in fact allows a series of cross-sex identifications for the potential purchaser, so that the images of lesbianism are presented in ways acceptable to the predominantly heterosexual readership. As such, the images at once enable 'heterosexual readers to engage with a narrative of a sexuality not their own' but also to 'buttress and enlarge heterosexuality's domain'.[30] She interprets the representations in the cover art as a sales strategy, as it is assumed that no heterosexual reader would buy the novel if it presented deviant desire in a repulsive or unfamiliar form. For Barale, the imagistic representations indicate that 'lesbian sexuality is permissible only when it is available for heterosexuality's consumption'. The discussion in this section demonstrates that the text's strategy of presenting deviant sexuality in a recognisable form to ensure acceptability extends beyond the cover art to the story itself; the hetero-normative construction of lesbian relationships is fundamental to the narrative. *The Well of Loneliness* may be poison, but its hetero-normative template for same-sex love can be interpreted as an antidote to make it palatable.

The antidote of hetero-normative structures, however, has highly unpleasant side effects. What has not been sufficiently acknowledged by critics is the role played by the figure of the male homosexual in the novel's representation of lesbianism. Since lesbian relations have been made palatable to the reader, the offensiveness of their deviancy has to be displaced. In other words, the novel needs another representation of transgressive desire against which the normality of female inversion can be defined. Male homosexuals make up this other group in the novel; they are forced to bear the mark of Cain so that Stephen's own mark of inversion can be re-read as the mark of masculine valour and hence as 'a very

26 Ibid. 346.
27 Ibid. 360.
28 Ibid. 295.
29 Ibid. 325.
30 Michèle Aina Barale, 'Below the belt: (un)covering *The Well of Loneliness*' in Diana Fuss (ed), *Inside/Out: Lesbian Theories, Gay Theories* (New York: Routledge, 1991) 235–59 at 236.

becoming scar'.[31] In his essay entitled 'Outlaws: Gay Men in feminism', Craig Owens identifies a persistent strand of homophobia in feminist criticism; he argues that, whilst homophobia directed by men against men has been the focus of criticism in academia, it is also necessary to ask: 'what about homophobia directed by women against men?'[32] My question here is both a variation and an extension of Owens's: what about homophobia directed by lesbians against gay men in this instance? How are homosexuals depicted in the novel, and how does this depiction help to normalise the lesbian relations in the narrative?

As the most visible gay character in the novel, Jonathan Brockett provides one entry point into the problem. Terry Castle's argument that the character of Brockett is based on one of Hall's close friends, the playwright Noël Coward, has been taken up as academic orthodoxy. Castle reads the two writers' relationship into the novel, and depicts Brockett as one of the most likeable characters in the novel's otherwise gloomy universe. He represents all that is positive in the world: 'humour, friends, love, work, sex, and peace of mind'.[33] Although Castle does pay lip service to an 'authorial ambivalence' towards this character, her biographical reading of the novel leads her to conclude that Brockett is 'the book's most wholesome, valuable, even therapeutic presence'. Castle's positive depiction of Brockett is unsurprising, because it is situated within the broader context of the friendship between Coward and Hall as an allegory of 'the rich yet neglected cultural relationships that have existed between gay men and lesbians in England and America since the turn of the century'.[34]

However, this biographical reading obscures a more obvious fact, which is that Stephen views Brockett very negatively. The narrator explicitly says that Stephen often 'disliked him intensely'.[35] Loathing would not be too strong a word to describe her attitude towards him. By attempting to recuperate an aspect of the author's real life from the text, Castle unwittingly repeats Carson's hermeneutic method in the first Wilde trial, through which the reader seeks an interpretation of a fictive text by reference to the author's life. If we return to the novel, however, we will find that Hall's relationship with Coward is no more present in *The Well of Loneliness* than is Wilde's relationship with Bosie in *Dorian Gray*.

Stephen resents Brockett almost from the beginning of their acquaintance. He is constantly described as an intrusion into her life: he insists on 'thrusting his friendship on Stephen', and much to her dismay, his friendship takes the form of 'ringing her up almost daily at one time, of worrying her to lunch or dine with him, of inviting himself to her flat in Chelsea, or what was still worse, of dropping in

31 Hall, *The Well of Loneliness* (n 18) 333.

32 Craig Owens, 'Outlaws: gay men in feminism' in Scott Bryson and others (eds), *Beyond Recognition: Representation, Power, and Culture* (Berkeley: University of California Press, 1992) 218–39 at 219.

33 Terry Castle, *Noël Coward and Radclyffe Hall: Kindred Spirits* (New York: Columbia University Press, 1996) 53.

34 Ibid. 109.

35 Hall, *The Well of Loneliness* (n 18) 235.

on her whenever the spirit moved him'.[36] The episode in which he invites himself to Stephen's residence for dinner gives a particularly clear indication of her attitude towards him. He is in high spirits, but Stephen is 'tired to death and did not want him', and has in fact 'grown to dread him in this mood; there was something almost aggressive about it; it would seem to her that he thrust it upon her'.[37] His intrusiveness is constant and pervasive, and he is described as always prying 'into everyone's secret without shame or mercy'.

Whilst Castle is right in pointing out Brockett's role as a truth-bearer – he forces Stephen to confront the failure of her second novel and is always brutally honest in his evaluation of her work – her reading overlooks Stephen's resentment of such frankness. Stephen is wary of talking to him, for their conversations make her feel as though 'he had peeped through a secret keyhole into her mind, had been spying upon her trouble'.[38] When he asks her about her personal life in Paris, Stephen immediately believes that he is 'putting his eye to the keyhole' and distances herself. She makes 'a mental note to be careful', for 'Brockett's curiosity was always most dangerous when apparently merely childish'. After he takes her on a tour of the city, the narrator tells us that he watches her 'surreptitiously' in the car. His powers of penetration outrage her: she asks: by 'what right did this curious man spy upon her?' and concludes that he has 'no right' to do so.[39]

Such character traits form a contrasting backdrop to Stephen's constancy, reliability and spirit of self-sacrifice. Furthermore, even though Stephen finds Brockett clever and talented, his genius is dark, untrustworthy and even sinister, as reflected in the language of monstrosity and cannibalism through which it is described. Stephen compares him to Moloch (which, significantly, means 'shame'), the demon god who demanded the sacrifice of children in his honour, and notes that he is successful only because he feeds his genius 'upon live flesh and blood'.[40] The metaphor of monstrosity manifests itself in multiple ways. It is present in Brockett's advice to the protagonist: 'People are the food that we writers live on; get out and devour them, squeeze them dry, Stephen!'[41] It also lurks in his words of care and comfort; they often conceal an attempt to 'squeeze a kind of beef-tea from all those with whom life brought him into contact – a strong brew, and one that served to sustain and revivify his inspiration'.[42] His inspiration is parasitic, even murderous. He is depicted as a 'creature' who is 'fiendishly' clever, whose plays are 'cruel', and whose genius is 'carnivorous'.[43] Such references to destruction,

36 Ibid. 228.
37 Ibid. 230.
38 Ibid. 235.
39 Ibid. 240.
40 Ibid. 235.
41 Ibid. 233.
42 Ibid. 299.
43 Ibid. 235.

evil, monstrosity and death form part of the nexus of connotations by which the male homosexual becomes defined.

Most importantly, Brockett is consistently described as effeminate, and as we shall see below his effeminacy has important implications for the articulation of lesbian identity. This effeminacy expresses itself in different ways. When he is excited, Brockett's voice takes on an 'effeminate timbre that Stephen always hated and dreaded'.[44] When Valerie Seymour asks Brockett to 'be a man' and make some tea for Stephen and Mary at one of her receptions, he trails behind and asks Stephen to do it instead, because she is 'so much more efficient'.[45] Such effeminacy irks Stephen, making her wonder 'how she could tolerate this young man – why, indeed, she chose to endure him'.[46] Brockett is frail and nervous: the hustle and bustle of London is prone to 'get on his nerves', and Stephen notices that he is 'apt to be nervous in motors'.[47]

He also incessantly complains of bodily pains: when he first introduces Stephen to Valerie, he moans about a 'curious pain' in his right eye, complains about his injured spine, and appears 'very intolerant of all pain'.[48] Owing to his feminine caprice, he has the tendency to disappear from people's lives without warning, which means that he cannot be depended upon. He runs away to Paris not long after his reacquaintance with Stephen to calm his nerves, and later disappears again to a mountain in the Austrian Tyrol to write his plays.[49] During the early days of their acquaintance, Stephen regarded such absences to be a 'breach of good manners', which was highly 'disconcerting', for they made her feel as if 'she had never known him, so completely did he go out of her life'.[50] His disappearances make his friendship unreliable.

Stephen's disgust at gay male sexuality is not directed at a single individual but at an entire minority group. This is made apparent by the episode at Alec's, the gay bar which Stephen visits with Mary and their female friends. There is no doubt that gay men are considered a class below lesbians in the novel, for 'more pitiful than her lot was theirs', and the all-male bar is described as 'the meeting-place of the most miserable of all those who comprised the miserable army'.[51] These men are 'stamped under', are 'abhorred, spat upon' and had sunk 'lower than their enemies knew, and more hopeless than the veriest dregs of creation'. They constitute those who are 'despised of the world', and who must 'despise themselves beyond all hope, it seemed, of salvation'. There is no sense of irony or

44 Ibid. 245.
45 Ibid. 253.
46 Ibid. 245.
47 Ibid. 239.
48 Ibid. 248.
49 Ibid. 252.
50 Ibid. 228.
51 Ibid. 393.

sympathy in such descriptions of male homosexuality. Stephen's final assessment of Alec's brings to light the novel's homophobia:

> When one comes to a place like this, one feels horribly sad and humiliated. One feels that the odds are too heavily against any real success, any real achievement. Where so many have failed who can hope to succeed? Perhaps this is the end.[52]

Although Stephen fights for the female invert's right to existence, she flatly gives up on the male invert and is content to believe that misery is 'the end' for him. These are men who have no hope, but who must 'yet laugh shrilly from time to time, must yet tap their feet to the rhythm of the music, must yet dance together in response to the band', and lest the reader misses the point, their dance is explicitly named the 'Dance of Death'. Alec's is a kind of inferno into which these miserable men are cast. The hetero-normative mode by which female same-sex relations are depicted means that the deviancy of lesbianism needs to be displaced or transferred to another group, the male homosexuals. Their effeminacy, hopelessness and abjection form the dark background against which Stephen's positive, manly qualities such as reliability, constancy and physical strength can shine. The very text which established itself as the mainstream novel of female same-sex love, and which continues to be taught as a pioneering narrative in courses on gay and lesbian studies, is also one which constitutes gay men as the abandoned, the non-human and the already-dead. Hall denigrates gay men and fights for lesbians' right to exist in the same breath.

(II) Fetishism and the construction of gendered identities

The contrast, and the interdependence, between Stephen's masculinity and the male homosexual's undesirability come into sharper focus when analysed through a psychoanalytic lens. One justification for the recourse to a psychoanalytic mode of reading is the dynamic of fetishism explicitly at work in Hall's fiction: her female inverts often display a fetishistic fixation on hands. In an earlier novel, *The Unlit Lamp* (1924), the protagonist's desire is almost always signalled by her attention to another woman's hands. *The Unlit Lamp* tells the tragic story of Joan Ogden, a woman who gives up a university education at Cambridge and a life of happiness with her lover to take care of her mother. In the novel, she finds a 'new found intimacy' developing between herself and Elizabeth, her former governess, after Elizabeth burns her hands while attempting to rescue someone covered in flames.[53] When her mother asks Joan about the accident, her reply compresses the significance of the entire incident into a body part: 'It's her hands'.[54]

52 Ibid. 395.
53 Radclyffe Hall, *The Unlit Lamp* (1924) (London: Virago Press, 1986) 100.
54 Ibid. 102.

Later, as she keeps Elizabeth company during her convalescence, Joan's focus is on her 'helpless hands on their supporting pillow'.[55] Elizabeth never fully recovers from her burns, and Joan weeps when she sees them 'hideously seamed and puckered with large, discoloured scars'.[56] After the accident, then, the hands acquire a libidinal charge and become a point of fixation for Joan. Years later, the significance of the hands does not diminish, even as Elizabeth herself ages:

> And there lay her beautiful hand, all scarred and spoilt; a brave hand, but spoilt none the less. Was it only the scars, or had the texture of the skin changed a little too, grown a little less firm and smooth? *She stared at it hopelessly.*[57]
>
> She felt that her sorrow must choke her . . . Elizabeth's youth was slipping, slipping; it would soon have slipped out of sight. *Joan stooped on a sudden impulse and kissed the scarred hand.*[58]

The passages reveal a dynamic of displacement and substitution: instead of Elizabeth's face or body, Joan stares at her hands, 'beautiful' despite the accident and the passage of time, and it is also the hand that she kisses when she is overcome by love and sadness. Elizabeth's surprise when she wakes up and finds Joan next to her bed attests to the displacement at work: 'you were kissing my hand!' she exclaims. Reading Joan's manual fixation in light of Freud's discussion of fetishism, her adoration of the mutilated hand can be interpreted as being in the same order as foot binding, which Freud describes as 'the Chinese custom of mutilating the female foot and then revering it like a fetish after it has been mutilated', as though 'the Chinese male wants to thank the woman for having submitted to being castrated'.[59] The fixation bears witness to the 'divided attitude' of the fetishist: whilst the mutilation, be it of the foot (the Chinese man) or the hand (Joan), corresponds to the affirmation of castration, the adoration of the body part functions as the simultaneous disavowal of the same recognition.

In *The Well of Loneliness,* Stephen Gordon exhibits a similar fixation. When Angela Crosby first expresses the possibility of a relationship which goes beyond friendship, Stephen diverts all of her attention to Angela's hand and refuses to let go:

> Go on holding like that to my hand – hold it tighter – I like the feel of your fingers.
>
> Stephen, don't be absurd!
>
> Go on holding my hand, I like the feel of your fingers.[60]

55 Ibid. 105.
56 Ibid. 109.
57 Ibid. 211(my italics).
58 Ibid. 212 (my italics).
59 Sigmund Freud, 'Fetishism' (1927) in James Strachey (ed and trans), *The Standard Edition of the Complete Psychological Works of Sigmund Freud, 24 vols* (London: Vintage, 2001) XXI, 149–59 at 157.
60 Hall, *The Well of Loneliness* (n 18) 143.

Angela reacts to Stephen's fixation by crying out in alarm: 'Stephen, you're hurting, you're crushing my rings!' As with the example of Joan and Elizabeth, Angela's protest reflects the strength of Stephen's fixation, and the curiously strong attachment signals its fetishistic nature. However, the fetishistic fixation also poses a challenge to a psychoanalytic reading, in part because castration is only possible for the male subject: within the Freudian schema, it is the male viewer who refuses 'to take cognizance of the fact of his having perceived that a woman does not possess a penis' when confronted with the sight of the female genitals, and disavows the difference by deflecting his gaze onto a nearby object or body part.[61]

Freud arrives at his conclusion after the examination of exclusively male patients, and claims that the manifestation of a similar panic when 'Throne and Altar are in danger' only affects 'a grown man', not a grown woman.[62] Since Freud's narrative of castration functions as an explanation of sexual difference, within the narrative the woman is necessarily represented as already castrated. 'Female fetishism' would therefore be an oxymoron, and even though a number of feminist critics in the late twentieth century have sought to retrieve the basis for precisely such a female fetishism in Freud's discussion of the masculinity complex, the significance of their analysis is limited to their interpretative contexts and does not significantly further the understanding of the dynamic in Hall's novel.

In a frequently cited essay, Naomi Schor interprets female fetishism in George Sand's novels as part of a wider strategy of undermining the very notion of sexual difference itself; she argues that Sand's 'bisexuality' enables a 'perverse oscillation' within the text which refuses to anchor the subject on either side of the axis of castration.[63] As we have seen, however, the representation of lesbian relations in *The Well of Loneliness* is premised precisely on the difference between conventional codes of the masculine and the feminine. Another critic, Elizabeth Grosz, argues for the possibility of a specifically lesbian fetishism, yet her conclusion that it is the lesbian's partner, that is to say, another woman, who functions as the fetish object does not account for the specific fetishistic attachment to hands that we see at work in Hall's novels.[64] Finally, Teresa de Lauretis's argument that Stephen Gordon's obsession with male attire arises from their function as the 'visible signifiers and accoutrements of masculinity' accounts for Stephen's fixation on clothing but neglects the equal attention she pays to body parts.[65]

61 Freud, 'Fetishism' (n 59) XXI, 153.

62 Ibid. 152–53.

63 Naomi Schor, 'Female fetishism: the case of George Sand' in Susan Rubin Suleiman (ed), *The Female Body in Western Culture: Contemporary Perspectives* (Cambridge: Harvard University Press, 1986) 363–73 at 369. See also Schor's *Breaking the Chain: Women, Theory, and French Realist Fiction* (New York: Columbia University Press, 1985) and Sarah Kofman, *The Enigma of Woman: Woman in Freud's Writings* (Catherine Porter (trans), Ithaca: Cornell University Press, 1985) 202–206.

64 Elizabeth Grosz, 'Lesbian fetishism?' in Emily Apter and William Pietz (eds), *Fetishism as Cultural Discourse* (Ithaca; Cornell University Press, 1993) 101–119.

65 Teresa de Lauretis, 'Perverse desire: the lure of the mannish lesbian' in *Palatable Poison* (n 5) 109–26 at 122.

It is therefore necessary to rethink the significance of Stephen's manual fixation. What does it mean, in terms of the articulation of lesbian identity, for her to exhibit a fetishistic attachment? It is possible to posit a two-part answer. The first part relates to the hetero-normative construction of lesbian identity, and more specifically to Stephen's masculinity. A number of critics have discussed the significance of Stephen's masculine attributes. Heather Love has argued that Stephen's is a 'failed masculinity',[66] which condemns her to a 'sense of nonfit' with her body.[67] For Love, Stephen's masculinity is an embodiment of her feeling as an 'unwanted being'.[68] Love's analysis usefully foregrounds the feeling of being cast as a gender deviant in Hall's time, yet her focus on loss, negativity and regret is, as Love herself notes, against the grain of contemporary readings of the novel, in that it pays inadequate attention to the very real positive, masculine qualities highlighted above.

Other critics have interpreted Stephen's masculinity more affirmatively, usually as an assertive and effective construction of gendered identity. In her classic essay, Esther Newton argues that the mannish lesbian appears in male body drag as a way of breaking out of the asexual model of romantic friendship inherited from the Victorian period which defined female interaction.[69] Judith Halberstam has argued that Stephen's sartorial turn to men's clothing enacts a rejection of the body as a basis for articulating identity, and that she 'literally redresses the wrongs of her embodiment by taking on male clothing, meticulously tailored and fashioned to fit her masculine spirit'.[70] Heike Bauer has posited that Stephen's masculinity can be read as an integral part of her status as a 'superinvert', whose superiority is reflected in 'her physicality, intellect, artistic sensibility and economic independence'.[71]

The dynamic of fetishism provides a further configuration of Stephen's masculinity and also brings back into focus the inadequately acknowledged role of male homosexuality in the text, which enables and sustains this masculinity. Since only the male subject fetishes in the Freudian *schema*, the female invert's display of the masculine perversion *par excellence* can be read as part and parcel of her masculinity; her fetishism codes her behaviour as male, regardless of her biological sex. In other words, Stephen's fetishistic attachment to hands can be understood as a way of signalling her occupation of the male subject position within the

66 Heather Love, *Feeling Backward: Loss and the Politics of Queer History* (Cambridge: Harvard University Press, 2007) 122.

67 Ibid. 119.

68 Ibid. 123.

69 Esther Newton, 'The mythic mannish lesbian: Radclyffe Hall and the new woman' in *Palatable Poison* (n 5) 89–109 at 100.

70 Judith Halberstam, '"A writer of misfits": "John" Radclyffe Hall and the discourse of inversion' in *Palatable Poison* (n 5) 145–62 at 158.

71 Heike Bauer, *English Literary Sexology: Translations of Inversion, 1860–1930* (New York: Palgrave Macmillan, 2009) 130.

narrative. It is significant that in both Joan's relationship with Elizabeth and Stephen's relationship with Mary, only one partner exhibits such a fetishistic dynamic, and it is always the partner who also displays her masculinity through other attributes, such as her attire, her valour and her moral uprightness. The other partner is presented in a much more traditionally feminine way. Such a difference between the women is part of the re-inscription of the masculine–feminine order of relations into the same-sex relationships. Stephen's fetishism suggests that she plays the male role in the relationship, so that even though in sexual terms the relationship involves two women, in gender terms the partnership is given a structure akin to a conventional cross-sex relationship.

This interpretation of Stephen's fetishism as part of her masculinity is bolstered by the narrative focus on the stockings of which she is so fond. Not long after Mary first moves into Stephen's residence in Paris she notices that, in addition to her masculine apparel, Stephen has a fine selection of stockings:

> Finally she discovered the stockings where they lay by themselves in the one long drawer, and these she proceeded to unfurl deftly, with a quick and slightly important movement. *Thrusting a fist into toes and heels she looked for the holes that were non-existent.*[72]

Stephen's penchant for stockings can be productively read in an intertextual relation with Freud's discussion of their psychoanalytic significance. He writes about a patient who had difficulty putting on his stockings because 'he was disturbed by the idea that he must pull apart the stitches in the knitting i.e. the holes, and to him every hole was a symbol of the female genital aperture'.[73] Slightly further on in the same paragraph, he refers to another patient who repeatedly put on and took off his stocking; he notes that the hole in the stocking again symbolised the female genitals into which his foot, symbolising the penis, was inserted. Freud sees a linguistic connection between the holes in the stockings and the female genitalia; in both cases 'a hole is a hole' to the male patient.[74]

If holes in patients' stockings function as a symbol of castration, then the fact that the holes in Stephen's are 'non-existent' can be understood as the representation of Stephen as phallic and therefore as masculine. Mary is disappointed that Stephen's stockings are not torn or ripped and 'would not require darning', for she regards darning as one of her talents. She notes that Stephen 'must be very well served', and the narrator tells us that this observation is true: 'she was served, *as are certain men*, with a great deal of nicety and care by the servants'.[75] The lack of holes of the stockings signifies the wholeness of their owner, by virtue of which she is coded as one of the men in the hetero-normative order.

72 Hall, *The Well of Loneliness* (n 18) 324 (my italics).
73 Sigmund Freud, 'The Unconscious' (1915) XIV, 159–217 at 200.
74 Ibid. 201.
75 Hall, *The Well of Loneliness* (n 18) 325 (my italics).

The second part of the answer to the question of the significance of Stephen's fetishistic attachment brings us back to the homophobia which sustains the hetero-normative structure of lesbian relations. In addition to discussing the importance of fetishistic fixation as a simultaneous affirmation and disavowal of castration, Freud also makes reference to male homosexuality in his essay on fetishism, a reference which can be understood as a corollary of his theoretical speculations on homosexuality elsewhere in his writings.[76] For Freud, male same-sex object choice is the outcome of castration anxiety: the subject cannot overcome the discovery that his mother does not possess a penis and is horrified and disgusted that he may share a similar fate. The unbearable thought that his mother's penis has been taken away causes him to choose the compromise of an effeminate boy, who in effect represents a woman with a penis. Freud argues that both fetishism and homosexuality are responses to the threat of castration: for the fetishist, the displacement of the gaze onto the substitute object endows women with 'the characteristic which makes them tolerable as sexual objects'.[77] Fetishism thereby 'saves the fetishist from becoming a homosexual'. He continues:

> Probably no *male* human being is spared the fright of castration at the sight of a female genital. Why some people become homosexual as a result of that impression, while others fend it off by creating a fetish, and the great majority surmounts it, we are frankly not able to explain.

Fetishism is here presented as an alternative to homosexuality; they are mutually exclusive responses to the threat of castration. In his study of the representation of same-sex desire in psychoanalytic theory, Kenneth Lewes argues that, for Freud, fetishism occupies 'a position equal to' that of homosexuality, which it 'resembles in many ways'.[78] However, Freud's word choice in these passages betrays the fact that they are not regarded as alternatives of equal desirability. By noting that the fetish object 'saves the fetishist' from the trap of homosexuality, by claiming that it can 'fend off' such a threat, and by portraying same-sex object choice as an obstacle one would want to 'surmount', the fetish is valorised over homosexuality, and is presented as a defence against a less positive outcome. One would rather be a fetishist than a homosexual (although of course the further implication is that the ideal is to be neither). Homophobia underlies and sustains Freud's discussion on

76 See Sigmund Freud, 'Analysis of a Phobia in a Five-Year-Old Boy' (1909) X, 5–149 and 'Leonardo da Vinci and a Memory of his Childhood' (1910) XI, 59–139.

77 Freud, 'Fetishism' (n 59) XXI, 154.

78 Kenneth Lewes, *The Psychoanalytic Theory of Male Homosexuality* (New York: Simon and Schuster, 1988) 36. For a further discussion of Freud and homosexuality, see Paul Robinson, 'Freud and homosexuality' in Tim Dean and Christopher Lane (eds), *Homosexuality and Psychoanalysis* (Chicago: University of Chicago Press, 2001) 91–98.

fetishism. Freud's implicit homophobia alerts us to the possible prejudices inherent in texts which purport to be politically neutral.[79]

Stephen's fetishistic fixation on hands extends to Brockett: her attention is drawn to his 'soft, white hands' whenever she sees him.[80] The unequal comparison between homosexuality and fetishism in Freud's text can point us towards the significance of this extension in the novel. Stephen feels 'a queer little sense of outrage creeping over her when she looked at his hands', because they are 'as white and soft as a woman's' and so 'went so ill with him somehow'.[81] She observes that when he is excited, his 'soft, white hands' would grow restless 'making their foolish gestures'.[82] She also notes that, whilst his gestures befit the 'soft, white hands of a woman', they are 'so ill-befitting the rest of his body'.[83] After Brockett comes back from the war, Stephen notices that 'his hands remained unchanged; those white and soft-skinned hands of a woman'.

In light of the gender dynamic of fetishism in Freud's writings, in which the fetishist plays the masculine role and the person in possession of the fetishised body part occupies the female gendered position, the homophobia inherent in her fetishistic attachment to his hands becomes clear: since Stephen occupies the position of the male subject in displaying this male perversion, it follows that Brockett occupies the position of the female subject within this dynamic. He is the woman from whom the viewer displaces his gaze, and hence is represented in the novel as castrated. Within this dynamic of fetishism, the effeminacy of the gay man is part of his representation as a castrated man. His hands are therefore not simply soft and white, but womanly, with the Freudian connotations of lack, insufficiency and incompletion.

A similar dynamic of homophobic fetishism placing the homosexual in a female subject position operates in the episode at Alec's. After a quick survey of the clients of the all-male bar, she quickly hones in on their accessories:

> On more than one hand was a large, ornate ring, on more than one wrist a conspicuous bracelet; they wore jewellery that might only be worn by these men when they thus gathered together.[84]

The displacement of the gaze from figure to accessory is accompanied by the language of deficiency and dispossession: the perverse investment in the ring and the bracelet is 'what was left' of these abject beings, who are 'bereft' of the dignity and the company of normal men. They are but shards and fragments of real

79 For a related argument, see Kofman (n 63) 82–89 and Emily Apter, *Feminizing the Fetish: Psychoanalysis and Narrative Obsession in Turn-of-the-Century France* (Ithaca: Cornell University Press, 1991) 211–12.
80 Hall, *The Well of Loneliness* (n 18) 245.
81 Ibid. 227–28.
82 Ibid. 245.
83 Ibid. 235.
84 Ibid. 393.

men; they bring to Alec's not complete male bodies but 'what was left of themselves'. Male homosexuals, in Hall's lesbian universe, are coded as womanly not in the sense of embodying positive feminine qualities, but in the sense of lacking the ultimate signifier of normal masculinity. They do not have the qualities of the heterosexual male, which of course Stephen, in contrast to them, possesses. The text therefore consistently represses the male invert, casting him as the other of the female invert and therefore as undeserving of pity or sympathy. He carries on his shoulders all of her negative attributes.

However, the relationship between fetishism and homosexuality in Freud's writings does not end with homophobia. Whilst it is true that there is a valorisation of fetishism over homosexuality, it is important to recognise that fetishism is not presented as a simple repudiation of its alternative. Freud takes pains to emphasise that the logic of fetishism is the logic of 'compromise'. There is both acknowledgement and disavowal of the absence which so terrifies the subject; he has both 'retained the belief' in the maternal phallus, but has 'also given it up'.[85] This dual mode of presence and absence, denial and affirmation, gestures towards an understanding of the relationship between lesbians and gay men in Hall's novel, which is more complex than a simple repudiation of the latter by the former. Rather, the two groups are always imbricated; the group that is rejected is foundational to the self-identity of the group that does the rejecting, and constantly returns to haunt it as its double. In *The Well of Loneliness*, the figure of the homosexual which the text seeks to reduce to abjection constantly returns to assert its affinity to the figure of the lesbian.

Again, thinking about the novel in a psychoanalytic mode brings this complex intertwining of identities to the forefront. The narrative's designation of the male homosexual as the other of the lesbian is never complete; every attempt at creating difference between the two kinds of inverts in fact simultaneously highlights their resemblance. On the level of bodily detail, the effeminacy of Brockett's hands may signify castration, yet it also echoes the overly large hands which so distress Stephen. Despite the apparent differences, the hands of both characters betray their sameness. The depiction of the lesbian body as a 'monstrous fetter' imposed on the spirit, as a 'strangely ardent yet sterile body', can equally apply to the male invert.[86] The sartorial detail reveals even more clearly how the two groups echo one another. Brockett is every bit as fastidious about his clothing as Stephen: he is careful to choose platinum '[cuff-]links set with tiny diamonds' to match his shirts,[87] only wears gloves made of reindeer hide[88] and, as Stephen's mentor, Puddle, notices, his clothes are always 'a trifle too careful'.[89] Yet Puddle, like Stephen,

85 Freud, 'Fetishism' (n 59) XXI, 154.
86 Hall, *The Well of Loneliness* (n 18) 187.
87 Ibid. 227.
88 Ibid. 230.
89 Ibid. 227.

refuses to see the commonality of their condition: 'Like to like. No, no, an intolerable thought!'[90]

Such resemblance, so forcefully denied, confronts Stephen directly at Alec's. Puddle's denial is significant since she, too, is an invert, although she does not publicly acknowledge her desires. Stephen initially continues her refusal to acknowledge her kinship to her male counterparts:

> But Stephen would not dance, not among these men, and she laid a restraining hand upon Mary. Despite her sense of their terrible application, she could not dance in this place with Mary.[91]

The homophobia in this passage is barely concealed; Stephen's refusal to dance is fuelled by her hatred of these men. However, her insistence on the difference between her own respectability and their degradation, between self and other, is disrupted by a young man who, whilst attempting to pass her, leans forward and gazes at her. He then whispers: *Ma soeur*. Stephen's reaction to this appellation of sameness is revealing:

> For a moment she wanted to strike that face with her naked fist, to obliterate it. Then all of a sudden she perceived the eyes and the memory came of a hapless creature, distracted, bleeding from bursting lungs, hopelessly pursued, glancing this way, then that, as though looking for something, some refuge, some hope – and the thought: 'It's looking for God who made it'.
>
> Stephen shivered and stared at her tightly clenched hands; the nails whitened her flesh. *Mon frère*, she muttered.

Stephen acknowledges the similarity between herself and the male invert, but with intense animosity and reluctance. Her encounter with someone so disconcertingly familiar echoes Freud's discussion about 'doubles' in a footnote to his essay on the uncanny. He writes of 'an elderly gentleman in a dressing-gown and a travelling cap' coming into his train compartment, and confesses that he 'thoroughly disliked his appearance'. He then realises, with 'dismay', that the intruder is nothing more than his own reflection in the looking glass of the door. His colleague Ernst Mach has a similar experience, and describes his own image as a 'shabby-looking school-master'. Freud ponders over the significance of these encounters with the self:

> Instead . . . of being *frightened* by our 'doubles', both Mach and I simply failed to recognize them as such. Is it not possible, though, that our dislike of them was a vestigial trace of the archaic reaction which feels the 'double' to be something uncanny?[92]

90 Ibid. 224.
91 Ibid. 394.
92 Sigmund Freud, 'The Uncanny' (1919) XVII, 218–53 at 248 (original italics).

The dislike which marks such confrontations stems from the recognition that what is external to the self is in fact part of the self. The other is the self and the self is the other; the sameness which inhabits the difference makes the encounter uncanny. Like the scene described by Freud, it is possible to interpret Stephen's confrontation at Alec's as an uncanny encounter with her 'double', and hence as the text's failure to institute absolute difference between the male and the female invert: even though Stephen longs to strike at the face, 'to obliterate it', the 'memory' of their repressed resemblance returns as she gazes into the eyes of the invert and recognises herself in this 'hapless creature' who is 'looking for something, some refuge, some hope'.

The series of contrasts which the novel sets up, such as Brockett's effeminacy versus Stephen's valour, or the normality of lesbian relations versus the dysfunctionality of gay male ones, breaks down at this moment. The uncanny 'proceeds from something familiar which has been repressed', and Stephen's recognition of herself in the image of the other marks this encounter as the site at which the repressed kinship between the gay man and the lesbian returns – hence her acknowledgement of the male invert as her brother, no matter how reluctantly the words 'mon frère' are spoken.[93]

This kinship is further emphasised in her conversation with Adolphe Blanc, a gay Jewish designer. When he explains to her that she should not abandon people like the inverts at Alec's, Stephen feels that 'this man was actually speaking her thoughts'.[94] 'Strange' is this feeling. And strangeness is, of course, part of what constitutes the uncanniness of the congruence between *heimlich* and *unheimlich*, the 'homely' or the familiar and the 'unhomely' or the eerily unfamiliar. Just as '*heimlich* is a word the meaning of which develops in the direction of ambivalence, until it finally coincides with its opposite, *unheimlich*', Stephen's strange encounters at Alec's show how a familiar, comfortable, 'homely' representation of female same-sex relations merges with its 'unhomely' opposite despite the text's energetic insistence on difference.[95]

Nicholas Royle has pointed out that the uncanny is always characterised by 'a sense of ghostliness', and the repressed other of the male invert returns to haunt Stephen literally once again at the end of the novel.[96] After she gives up Mary to Hallam, Stephen finds herself confronting the voices of reproach from the other inverts she has encountered. She sees her friends Wanda, Jamie and Barbara, and then the ghosts of male inverts appear:

> Aye, and those lost and terrible brothers from Alec's, they were here, and they also were calling: 'Stephen, Stephen, speak with your God and ask Him why He has left us forsaken!' She could see their marred and reproach-

93 Ibid. 247.
94 Hall, *The Well of Loneliness* (n 18) 396.
95 Freud, 'The Uncanny' (n 92) 226.
96 Nicholas Royle, *The Uncanny* (Manchester: Manchester University Press, 2003) 16.

> ful faces with the haunted, melancholy eyes of the invert . . . And these terrible ones started pointing at her with their shaking, white-skinned, effeminate fingers.[97]

The appearance of the ghosts at the end of the novel marks the final return of the repressed; the denial of resemblance no longer seems to be able to silence a group which has been unjustly represented. Their accusation that 'You and your kind have stolen our birthright; you have taken our strength and have given us your weakness!' takes on new meaning in this context: what their fingers of accusation point to is not only Stephen's sacrifice of Mary to the heterosexual world, but also her prejudice, her injustice, her homophobia towards male homosexuals. Yet the narrative once again tames these unruly ghosts, and the uncanny doubling that marked the encounter at Alec's is finally restabilised in the novel. As the apparitions descend upon Stephen, their voices merge into one: 'We are coming, Stephen – we are still coming on, and our name is legion – you dare not disown us'. The distinction between male and female inverts disappears as the former becomes subsumed into the latter under the general 'We', until at last there is 'one voice, one demand'.[98]

But this voice, which claims to speak for all inverts, this voice 'into which those millions had entered' is a female one, that of Stephen. And the reader who reaches the end of the novel has just heard it; it is articulated in the form of Hall's novel. The male homosexual's voice is once again denied. Shuttled between the hetero-normative world and the lesbian textual universe which replicates its norms as part of a plea for acceptance, the male invert in Hall's novel becomes a pure object of representation, a sexual subaltern that cannot speak. *The Well of Loneliness* presents female same-sex relations in a hetero-normative mode, but their respectability is made possible by the sacrifice of another group onto which the transgressive force of deviancy from gender norms is displaced.

(III) Judicial silencing and the return of the repressed

The issue of the vexed relationship between lesbians and homosexuals will return, in a different and unexpected form, in the obscenity trials. Douglas's irate review paradoxically ensured publicity for Hall's novel. Crowds gathered at Bow Street on 16 November 1928 to hear the verdict of the trial, and scores of people had to be turned away. At the end of his judgment, which took over an hour to deliver, Magistrate Biron concluded:

97 Hall, *The Well of Loneliness* (n 18) 446.
98 Ibid. 446.

> I have no hesitation whatever in saying that it is an obscene libel, that it would tend to corrupt those into whose hands it should fall, and that the publication of this book is an offence against public decency, an obscene libel, and I shall order it to be destroyed.[99]

I will argue that Biron's judgment is in effect a silencing of the lesbian in the novel, and that this silencing also marks the return of the repressed male invert. On one level, the silencing took place literally: when Hall interrupted the delivery of the judgment by stating 'I protest . . . I . . . emphatically protest . . . I am the author of this book', Biron brushed her aside contemptuously and threatened to remove her from the courtroom.[100] The novel's depiction of lesbian relations in a realist mode meant that the court treated it as a 'sincere' representation of Hall's views on sexuality or a transparent window into her mind, such that 'it needed no more help from the author in identifying its "voice" '.[101] Hall was furious at being gagged in this manner: even though she 'remained silent' for the remainder of the judgment, she 'left the court in a rage' as soon as it ended, 'clenched her fingers excitedly' when her friends asked her for her reaction, and 'protested vehemently' against the magistrate's reading.[102]

The witnesses were also denied their say in the trial. Norman Birkett, the defence lawyer, had assembled a formidable group of witnesses, including E.M. Forster, Desmond McCarthy (the editor of *Life and Letters*), Leonard and Virginia Woolf, Vita Sackville-West and other 'distinguished authors and authoresses who would have said that they had read the book and in their view it was not obscene'.[103] However, Biron claimed that it was 'entirely a question for the Magistrate to decide whether a book was obscene or not', and declared that evidence in the form of witness testimony was inadmissible. The dynamic of judicial silencing goes beyond the literal imperative for Hall to stay quiet and extends to a textual level, to the way the law substituted its own articulation of lesbian identity for the one presented in the novel.

To understand the conditions which made possible this act of silencing, we need to return briefly to the wider context of the trial. The anecdotes about men whose lives had been ruined by the predatory female invert referred to at the beginning of the chapter suggest that the masculinity of a female invert like Stephen Gordon can be read as a challenge to the 'normal' masculinity in the period; Stephen's inversion means that she repeatedly finds herself in competition with heterosexual men for other women's affection.[104] When she tries to woo Angela, she describes

99 Biron (n 108) 49.

100 Vera Brittain, *Radclyffe Hall: A Case of Obscenity?* (London: Femina Books, 1968) 101.

101 Adam Parkes, 'Lesbianism, history, and censorship: *The Well of Loneliness* and the suppressed randiness of Virginia Woolf's *Orlando*' (1994) 40 *Twentieth Century Literature* 434–60 at 438–39.

102 *Daily Express* (17 November 1928) 2.

103 Brittain (n 100) 92.

104 For a discussion of Stephen's affinity to a masculinity traumatised by war, see Susan Kingsley Kent, '*The Well of Loneliness* as war novel' in *Palatable Poison* (n 5) 216–32.

Ralph, Angela's husband and therefore her rival, as 'a nagging, mean-minded cur of a man' who 'doesn't understand the first rudiments of loving'.[105] Later on, Stephen's mother, Anna Gordon, expresses her outrage at Stephen's resemblance to Sir Philip: 'You dare to look like your father, and your face is a living insult to his memory'.[106] Such an outrage can be interpreted as a loving wife's disgust at the invert's attempt to usurp the orthodox masculinity of her husband.

Perhaps the most obvious episode which reflects this challenge is Stephen's competition with Martin Hallam for Mary's affection. Stephen issues a direct challenge to him: 'I defy you to take her from me!' The intensity of the gender conflict is reflected in the fact that their deep friendship fails to prevent the 'bitter hostility' which arises from their common object choice: the female invert is out to assert her 'right to possess' what has traditionally belonged to the heterosexual man, and her challenge rouses 'all the combative manhood' in him.[107] The competition for Mary between Stephen and Martin can be read as emblematic of the threat which lesbians posed to normative masculinity; Stephen epitomised the threat of 'the whole of her kind' to heterosexual men. In this context, it is no surprise that Biron was only willing to accept the representation of female inversion 'as tragedy'.[108] He believed that 'no reasonable person' could deny that a book which defended or upheld female inversion was obscene; the reasonable person here is implicitly assumed to be male and heterosexual.

By the time the trial of *The Well of Loneliness* took place in 1928, Biron found himself confronted at once by social anxiety about the lesbian menace, and also by the lack of criminal law provisions dealing with female same-sex desire. He therefore had to find alternative legal authority in order to rule that the 'bible of lesbianism' ought to be considered as obscene. For Biron to bring lesbianism within the scope of criminal law, he had to posit it as an act rather than an identity, for it is a fundamental premise of criminal law that only conduct, and not character, is punishable. As Courtney Stanhope Kenny notes in his Cambridge law lectures, which were still widely reprinted in the late 1920s, a crime has to be evidenced by 'vicious conduct', because the court will 'never inflict penalties upon mere internal feeling' and 'a merely mental condition . . . is practically never made a crime'.[109] Love between women was therefore insufficient for incrimination; a way of reinterpreting female behaviour was needed. In his attempt to convert lesbianism into criminal conduct, Biron drew on what he believed to be the closest legal parallel:

105 Hall, *The Well of Loneliness* (n 18) 148.
106 Ibid. 203.
107 Ibid. 432.
108 Sir Henry Chartres Biron (1928) 'Judgment' in *Palatable Poison* (n 5) 39–49 at 42.
109 Courtney Stanhope Kenny, *Outline of Criminal Law: Based on Lectures Delivered in the University of Cambridge* (Cambridge: Cambridge University Press, 1902; reprinted 1926) 37–38.

> These unnatural offences between women which are the subject of this book involve *acts which between men would be a criminal offence*, and involve acts of the most horrible, unnatural and disgusting obscenity.[110]

Biron interpreted *The Well of Loneliness* through the lens of the Labouchère Amendment of the 1885 Criminal Law Amendment Act, which prohibited 'the commission by any *male* person of any act of gross indecency with another *male* person'.[111] As we saw in the last chapter, there has been much discussion of the way a gay male identity was forged in the Wilde trials, but it remains crucial to remember that, in strictly doctrinal terms, the Labouchère Amendment criminalises sexual acts, and the legal provision's firm focus on such acts has important implications here: the representation of female same-sex relations crystallised into a series of definable, punishable sexual acts through Biron's decision to view the case through the lens of Amendment. The law's construction of lesbianism was upheld on appeal, during which the court concluded that the novel condoned 'unnatural *practices*'.[112]

Biron's legal interpretation has far reaching gender implications, because it in effect used the law's construction of gay identity as the template for its construction of lesbian identity in the trials. The deployment of the legal provisions on gay male relations in the context of the trials turned lesbianism into a series of acts and thereby gave it an indictable form even in the absence of specific legislation targeting it. The court's recourse to a construction of deviant male sexuality as a tool for incrimination can be read as a return of the repressed; the representational injustice which male homosexuality suffered in Hall's novel returns to pronounce a guilty verdict.

Elisabeth Ladenson has argued that the magistrate's reference to gay identity was only made 'in passing' and that the depiction of 'female inversion was enough' to fall under the definition of obscenity.[113] However, if we follow Biron's reasoning, it is possible to see that that the law's equation of female and male same-sex relations was in fact precisely the factor that led to the conviction; Biron's reference to the Labouchère Amendment was central to his argument and was not made merely in passing. In what must count as one of the strangest ironies in the history of literary trials, the male invert which Hall's novel tries to repress returned, with a vengeance, in the form of the law in Biron's judgment.

The return of the repressed was an outcome of Biron's interpretation of the novel. How, exactly, did he import the model of male-male relations into a novel about female inversion? Biron's judgment is underpinned by an interpretative

110 Biron (n 108) 41–42 (my italics).

111 Criminal Law Amendment Ac 1885 (48 & 49 Vict. c.69) s 11 (my italics).

112 Brittain (n 100) 126.

113 Elisabeth Ladenson, *Dirt for Art's Sake: Books on Trial From Madame Bovary to Lolita* (Ithaca: Cornell University Press, 2007) 118.

praxis which was in fact the antithesis of close, patient reading. He was content to rely on loose paraphrasing and to set aside textual detail in order to reach his conclusion. 'Without going into this in any great detail,' he remarked near the beginning of his reading, and the phrase appeared again as 'I need not go into this book in all its details' towards the end of the judgment.[114] He was content to dispense with the particular in favour of the general, noting that he 'need not elaborate' on textual specifics, and based his ruling not on Hall's meticulous choice of detail but on his overall impression of selected episodes or 'something to that effect'.[115] However, it would be a mistake to characterise this mode of reading as simple carelessness or sloppiness. Rather, as we shall see, it constituted a hermeneutic strategy for imposing onto the novel his own model of female same-sex desire as criminality based on the male model of the 1885 Act.

The first episode Biron analysed was that of Stephen's relationship with Angela. In the novel, Stephen's mother, Anna Gordon, finds her suspicions confirmed when Ralph sends her a note with Stephen's love letter to Angela attached. Stephen's defence of her love, which also reads as a plea for the female invert, forms a site on which the battle for the representation of female same-sex relations is fought within the novel; Stephen's own notion is pitted against that of her mother's. Stephen frames same-sex love in a hetero-normative mode when she attempts to justify it in terms which her mother can understand:

> As my father loved you, I loved. As a man loves a woman, that was how I loved – protectively, like my father. I wanted to give all I had in me to give. It makes me feel terribly strong . . . and gentle. It was good good *good*.[116]

By focusing on the universality of love, Stephen explains her relationship with Angela as having a parallel structure to cross-sex relationships; Stephen loves Angela just as her father loved her mother. And this love, as we have seen, is coded as hetero-normative: Stephen loves 'protectively' as does a man, like her father. Yet Anna refuses to accept the analogy. In fact, Stephen's abomination consists of precisely her attempt to represent lesbianism in hetero-normative terms:

> In that letter you say things that may only be said between man and woman, and coming from you they are vile and filthy words of corruption – against nature, against God who created nature.[117]
>
> I have loved – do you hear? I have loved her father, and your father loved me. That was love.[118]

114 Biron (n 108) 43, 47.
115 Ibid. 46, 48.
116 Hall, *The Well of Loneliness* (n 18) 204 (original italics).
117 Ibid. 203.
118 Ibid. 204.

Anna's rejection of Stephen's model is coupled with her alternative representation of same-sex desire: she tells Stephen that her relationship is not one of love, but one of 'lusts', of the 'unnatural cravings' emanating from her 'unbalanced mind and undisciplined body'. For Stephen's mother, love is the domain of the heterosexual; lust, that of the invert.

Anna's reaction provides the point of entry for Biron's reading. Biron glossed the Stephen–Angela relationship as one in which a girl was 'indulging in these horrible practices and endeavouring to induce a married woman to share these horrible practices with her'. In one stroke, the novel's own representation of female same-sex relations was cast aside and replaced by the notion of lesbian menace. When Stephen refuses to accept her mother's 'terrible slur upon her love', Biron asked: '"this terrible slur upon her love" – what does that mean?' Like Anna, he refused to acknowledge the hetero-normative model which Stephen posits in this passage; the way Sir Philip loves Anna, the way a man loves a woman, was emphatically rejected as the analogy of how Stephen could love Angela. He posited the notion of lesbianism as acts of lust: he configured Stephen as a '*practitioner* of unnatural vice' who was guilty of engaging in 'unnatural *practices* between women'.[119]

He continued: 'I am asked to say that this book is not a defence of *these practices*. What does it go on to say? What is the result of these horrible *practices*?'[120] He therefore converted the hetero-normative love which defined lesbianism in the novel to same-sex acts. This conversion was key to representation of female same-sex relations in gay male terms, for such acts could then be categorised, proven and, most importantly, criminalised under the terms of the Labouchère Amendment. The 'acts of the most horrible, unnatural and disgusting obscenity' which he found in the novel were but another name for the 'acts of gross indecency' in the 1885 Act.[121] Biron therefore silenced the novel by imposing his own, legal formulation of female same-sex relations over the one it posits.

The need to contain the lesbian menace is even more evident in his interpretation of the 'Mary incident'. As we have seen, Stephen's relationship with Mary is coded hetero-normatively: Stephen plays the role of the protective husband, whilst Mary plays the role of the dutiful wife. But for Biron, the occupation of the male position by the female invert formed an unacceptable challenge to normative masculinity. The basis of his reading is reflected in his choice of passages for analysis; the parts of the book which Biron found most objectionable were those which challenge male authority most openly:

> Men – they are selfish, arrogant, possessive. What could they do for Mary Llewellyn? What could a man give that she could not? A child? But she would give Mary such a love as would be complete in itself without children.

119 Biron (n 108) 43.
120 Ibid. 44 (my italics).
121 Ibid. 42.

> Mary would have no room in her heart, in her life, for a child if she came to Stephen.[122]
>
> And Stephen as she held the girl in her arms, would feel that indeed she was all things to Mary; father, mother, friend and lover, all things; and Mary all things to her – the child, the friend, the beloved, all things.[123]

By occupying the position of the husband in the relationship with Mary, the novel shows that a female invert could potentially replace the man entirely. The passages begin by presenting men in negative terms: they are 'selfish, arrogant, possessive'. Then they proceed to dispense with the need for procreation; the love of Stephen and Mary could be 'complete in itself without children'. The position of the heterosexual man in the world of a girl like Mary is looking increasingly shaky. Finally, the novel asserts that the female invert could be 'all things' to Mary, just as Mary can be 'all things' to her: father, mother, friend, lover. In the short space of two paragraphs, the man is completely edged out of the picture.

Perhaps the most troubling aspect of this episode is that, unlike Angela and Anna, Mary is responsive to Stephen. Although Anna regards Stephen's resemblance to Sir Philip as an 'insult' to his memory, and Angela betrays Stephen to her husband, Mary is completely and utterly devoted to Stephen. This responsiveness is troubling because, as Esther Newton points out, Mary does not conform to the image of the mannish lesbian. She notes that 'Hall calls her "normal", that is, heterosexual'.[124] Newton sees Mary as a 'forgettable and inconsistent' character who weakens the novel because of her purported normality, but her heterosexuality in fact makes her one of the most unsettling characters for the male reader, for she represents the heterosexual woman who could potentially be stolen from the heterosexual man by the female invert. Her reaction to Stephen's affection confirms the very fears of those men who were anxious about losing their place to their female rival: 'And now Mary need no longer sigh with unrest . . . her rightful place was in Stephen's arms and there she would be, overwhelmed by the peace that comes at such times to all happy lovers'.[125]

The novel takes pains to assert that Stephen is not an isolated example; there are 'many exactly like her in this very city, in every city . . . they lived natural lives – lives that to them were perfectly natural'. Another passage which Biron highlighted makes a similar point: Valerie Seymour notes that 'inverts were being born in increasing numbers, and after a while their numbers would tell, even with the fools who still ignored Nature. They must just bide their time – recognition was coming'.[126] If this was the case, then competition for heterosexual women like

122 Hall, *The Well of Loneliness* (n 18) 302.
123 Ibid. 318.
124 Newton (n 69) 102.
125 Hall, *The Well of Loneliness* (n 18) 318.
126 Ibid. 413.

Mary was likely to become more intense. The rise of the female invert seemed to imply the fall of the heterosexual man.

It is in light of the lesbian menace that Biron's hermeneutic transformation of Stephen's relationship with Mary into culpable 'acts of gross indecency' derived from all-male relations should be understood, a transformation which was made possible by the rejection of close reading in favour of general paraphrasing and heavy-handed glossing: 'With the terrible bonds of her dual nature she could bind Mary fast' – that is, of course, indulge in obscene practices with her – 'The world would condemn but they' – that is, Stephen and her victim – 'would rejoice; glorious outcasts, unashamed, triumphant'. It is not surprising that, those being the meditations present to the mind of the heroine Stephen, she does debauch Mary.[127]

By turning Stephen's affection into acts which fall within the scope of the 1885 Act, Biron in effect turned the threat of the female invert which Stephen embodied into a criminal offence. The incongruity of this recurrent emphasis on lustful acts and practices, based on the male model, is especially evident when we remember the novel's decidedly unsexual nature. As generations of readers have noted, sex is conspicuously absent in Hall's novel. Birkett argued that Cape should be acquitted because 'nowhere is there an obscene word or lascivious passage' in the text.[128] Emery also points out that it is 'a singularly unsexy book, devoid not only of "lewd" language but of any direct description of sexual activity'.[129] There is no basis for inferring a purely sexual connection even from the scandalous line 'that night . . . they [Stephen and Mary] were not divided', for it can equally be a description of a more spiritual union.[130]

It seems that the novel is only as obscene as reader himself makes it. Hall herself leapt up in anger at the disparity between the novel's representation of same-sex desire, and the representation which the magistrate read into it: her outburst in the courtroom came right after Biron's unjustified and unjustifiable assertion that 'a number of women of position and admirable character, who were engaged in driving ambulances in the course of war, were addicted to this vice'.[131] Even though there is evidence of same-sex attraction in the war episodes in the novel, nowhere do they ever hint that the women in the Breakspeare Unit engaged in same-sex practices. 'Shame! It is not correct!' and 'It was simply shocking the way passages in my book were misinterpreted' was Hall's verdict on the magistrate's understanding of her novel.[132]

What Biron's hermeneutic strategy shows is that the law repeats the dynamic of repression which we have seen operative in the novel. Just as *The Well of Loneliness*

127 Biron (n 108) 46.
128 Brittain (n 100) 89.
129 Emery (n 5) 361.
130 Hall, *The Well of Loneliness* (n 18) 316.
131 Biron (n 108) 45.
132 '*Well of Loneliness* to be burned', *Daily Express* (17 November 1928) 1–2 at 2.

silences the male invert by turning him into a sexual subaltern unable to respond to its representation, so the law silences the female invert by recasting her in the mould of male same-sex desire, that is, in the mould of criminality, as a response to the mannish lesbian's threat to normative masculinity. It seems that Biron was intent on relegating female inverts to the position of 'desolate, hungry outcasts; unloved and unwanted, despised of the world', which is, of course, the position occupied by the male inverts in Hall's novel.[133]

The most complete act of textual silencing occurs in the last part of the judgment, in which Biron discussed the ending of the novel. His interpretation amounted to a radical act of judicial rewriting. To understand the significance of his act, we need to examine the final sections of the novel in greater detail, for they form no less than the narrative of the dissolution of the lesbian self under the pressure of the censorious world. Hall's novel ends with a scene of great self-sacrifice: unwilling to subject Mary to the prejudice of the world, Stephen stages an affair with Valerie Seymour so that Mary, heartbroken, would run into the arms of Martin for comfort and hence turn away from the world of the inverts forever.

In the third section of the final chapter, the narrator begins by telling the reader: 'she let herself in'. Since the sentence inaugurates a new section, it is not immediately clear who this 'she' is. This ambiguity is sustained as this person approaches Mary's room: the narrator notes that 'someone is slowly climbing the stairs' and that it was 'someone whom David [the dog] knew and loved well'. From the context, the reader may assume that it is Stephen returning after the staged affair with Valerie. Yet we are told that this person was 'not Stephen Gordon . . . Stephen Gordon was dead; she had died last night'. The passage therefore presents Stephen as a disembodied consciousness, a lost soul without a body. The exchange between the lovers is worth quoting in full:

> When she spoke her voice sounded unfamiliar: 'Where were you last night?'
> 'With Valerie Seymour. I thought you'd know somehow . . . It's better to be frank . . . we both hate lies . . .
> Came that queer voice again: 'Good God – and I've tried so hard not to believe it! Tell me you're lying to me now; say it, Stephen!'[134]

Upon the first reading, the identity of the 'she' who begins the conversation is unclear. Was it the 'someone' who had appeared in the room, or was it Mary, whom we are told had just woken up? It is not until we arrive at the question of 'Where were you last night?' that we know for certain that the speaker is Mary. When Stephen responds, the direct speech again presents her as a disembodied consciousness, a floating voice unidentified by markers such as 'she said' or 'Stephen confessed'. This dis-identification continues as the lovers part. 'Someone'

133 Hall, *The Well of Loneliness* (n 18) 320.
134 Ibid. 444.

pushes Mary away, and the narrator reiterates that this someone was 'not Stephen Gordon who stood there unmoved by such pitiful sobbing'. This process of de-subjectivisation then spreads to Mary: her body disappears, she is now a 'queer voice' within 'the folds of the thick black mist'. Even this last trace of identity then fades: the voice is 'muffled' by the darkness, and 'only a word here and there' can get through, until at last even the words degenerate into inarticulate noises of 'rough and pitiful sobbing'. Slightly further down the passage, Mary changes from a 'she' into an 'it' without an identity:

> But what was the figure [Mary] doing in the mist? *It* was moving about, distractedly, wildly. All the while *it* sobbed as *it* was moving about: 'I'm going . . .'
>
> Going? But where could *it* go?[135]

The lesbian subject's figurative death is signalled by the change in pronouns: after she gives up her lover, Stephen becomes a nameless 'someone', and Mary becomes an 'it'. This dissolution of the self is described as a process of self-inflicted violence: the subject brings upon herself 'pain, burning rockets of pain – their pain, her pain, all welded together into one great consuming agony. Rockets of pain that shot up and burst, dropping scorching tears of fire on the spirit'.[136] The final pages of the narrative depict the death of the lesbian subject when she is finally forced to succumb to the hegemony of heterosexual relations: from a fully-formed self, tall and strong, she is reduced to a voice and, finally, to an unidentifiable 'it'.

The novel thus represents female same-sex relations in a tragic mode: not even a hetero-normative structure can save the relationship of two women who love one another, and the break-down of the relationship leads to the dissolution of lesbian subjectivity. The lesbian is literally no more. As we noted above, Biron opined early on in his judgment that a novel which represented female inversion as tragedy would not be considered obscene libel. Following the magistrate's own logic, the novel's ending would potentially have been sufficient to secure an acquittal for the publishers. But something very curious occurred in this part of the judgment. Biron substituted a new ending for the one in Hall's novel, and he ruled that the publication of the novel constituted an obscene libel based on this new ending. By offering nothing more than a loose paraphrase of the ending, he summarised it as follows:

> In this particular incident what happens is this, that Stephen eventually pretends to be tired of Mary, goes off to Valerie and persuades Valerie to pretend to be misconducting herself with her in order that this may throw her into the arms of Stephen. Such is the end of the book.[137]

135 Ibid. 445.
136 Ibid. 446.
137 Biron (n 108) 48.

It is hard to envisage a greater injustice: by throwing out the details of the story, the magistrate turned Stephen from a selfless lover into a lying, scheming figure of vice. This new ending was clumsily written. As we have seen, the construction of Stephen's identity as invert is premised on her possession of positive, masculine attributes such as courage, valour and moral strength. Despite the many flaws of the novel, Stephen's self-sacrifice in Hall's original ending is at least consistent with the rest of her character. The ruse on which the ending turns in Biron's rewriting, however, is the act of someone more cunning, more ruthless and more sexually predatory than Stephen.

Given that the novel presents the female invert as the usurper of male privilege and qualities, its content prior to its ending would already have been deemed sufficiently immoral to justify a conviction. However, the novel's original ending, which re-inscribes the triumph of cross-sex relations through Stephen's decision to offer Mary to Martin, posed an obstacle to a verdict of obscene libel. To justify his ruling, Biron needed an ending which continued the representation of the female invert as menace. His own ending achieved precisely this result: by throwing Mary back into the arms of Stephen, the ultimate loser in the triangle becomes Martin, the 'normal' man. Stephen's betrayal becomes doubly unsettling for the male reader: not only does she reject Martin's initial proposal of marriage because of her inversion, but she prevents him from the 'normal' cross-sex union with the woman he loves, and who shows signs of reciprocating this love, by deliberately inciting jealousy in her. Despite its clumsiness, the new ending eliminated the original conclusion of the novel as an obstacle to conviction. This is a judicial silencing which can be described as totalitarian; Hall's Stephen disappears and is replaced by a completely new character with the same name.

In the twentieth-century case of *The Well of Loneliness*, we witness once more the repetition of problems of representation between legal and literary discourses. Here, the law in effect repeats the discriminatory stance of the novel: just as the narrative sought to silence the male homosexual, the law sought to silence the lesbian, and the irony is that it did so by imposing onto the novel's representation of female same-sex desire its own understanding which was rooted in the male model of criminality. The two discourses therefore show parallel tendencies of repression of sexual minorities, and Hall's novel was simultaneously conservative and progressive in its sexual politics. The return of the repressed brings the trial to a close. The homosexual may have obtained justice against the novel's act of repressive representation, but it is a cruel and unsatisfactory justice indeed: 'justice' here refers not to equality before the law for all sexual minorities, but to the way one minority obtained vengeance on another for the injustice she did to him in another discursive domain.

The Well of Loneliness trials, like the other trials that I have examined, demonstrate just how much was at stake in the shaping of masculinity in the nineteenth and early twentieth centuries. The courtroom became a forum in which the battle for the legitimacy of different forms of gendered identities was fought between literature and the law. The trials also reveal the discursive entanglements between the legal and the literary, showing that despite the overt confrontational positions between them in the courtroom, they are, despite themselves, intertwined discourses repeating each other's tropes, structures and modes of representation. The trials in this study move us away from the conventional model of opposition between law and literature which casts the literary text as simply an object upon which the law imposes its power, or which presumes that the legal text has more authority and legitimacy than its seemingly trivial counterpart. Rather, they show us that law and literature are interlinked discourses, linguistic domains that bear surprising resemblances to, and are implicated in, one another. Beyond their significance to their immediate historical and cultural contexts, the trials also point us to a new way of conceptualising the relationship between law and literature.

Bibliography

Primary sources

Parliamentary serials, court judgments and legal evidence

Dossier D2U8 174, Archive de Paris Article 23, *Bulletin des lois de la République Française*, 12th series, Deuxième semestre de 1881
Beamish v Beamish (1861) 9 HL Cas 273
Biron, Sir Henry Chartres, 'Judgment' in L. Doan and J. Prosser (eds), *Palatable Poison: Critical Perspectives on The Well of Loneliness* (New York: Columbia University Press, 2001) 39–50
The Confessional Unmasked: Showing the Depravity of the Romish Priesthood, and the Iniquity of the Confessional, and the Questions put to Females in Confession (London: The Protestant Electoral Union, 1867)
Desprez, Louis, 'Pour la liberté d'écrire' in René-Pierre Colin and Jean-François Nivet (eds), *Louis Desprez, 1861–1885* (Charente: Du Lérot, 1992)
Hansard 1857, 1888
Holland, Merlin (ed), *Irish Peacock and Scarlet Marquess: The Real Trial of Oscar Wilde* (London: HarperCollins, 2004)
London Street Tramways Co Ltd v London County Council [1898] AC 375
The Parliamentary Debates: Official Report 1921
'Pernicious literature. Debate in the House of Commons. Trial and conviction for the sale of Zola's novels. With opinions of the press' in George Joseph Becker (ed), *Documents of Modern Literary Realism* (Princeton: Princeton University Press, 1963) 350–83
R v Hicklin (1968) LR 3 QB 360
Vizetelly, Henry, *Extracts Principally from the English Classics: Showing that the Legal Suppression of M. Zola's Novels would Logically Involve the Bowdlerizing of Some of the Greatest Works in English Literature* (London: H. Vizetelly, 1888)

Books, essays, articles and newspapers

Ballanche, Pierre-Simon, *La vision d'Hébal* (Paris: Librairie Minard, 1969)
'Balzac and his writings', *Westminster Review* (July and October 1853)
Baudelaire, Charles, 'Madame Bovary, par Gustave Flaubert', *L'Artiste* (19 October 1857)
Bertillon, Jacques, *La statistique humaine de la France (naissance, mariage, mort)* (Paris: Germer Baillière, 1880)

Bonnetain, Paul, *Charlot s'amuse* (Geneva: Slatkine Reprints, 1979)

Bossuet, Jacques-Bénigne, *Traité de la concupiscence* (Paris: Éditions Fernand Roches, 1930)

Champfleury, Jules, 'A letter to Madame Sand about M. Courbet' in Linda Nochlin (ed), *Realism and Tradition in Art, 1848–1900* (New Jersey: Prentice Hall, 1966) 36–45

Cléry, Léon, *Souvenirs du Palais* (Paris: A. Lemerre, 1890)

Defoe, Daniel, *The Fortunes and Misfortunes of the Famous Moll Flanders* (Juliet Mitchell (ed), Harmondsworth: Penguin Books, 1988)

Douglas, James, 'A book that must be suppressed', *Sunday Express* (19 August 1928)

Eliot, George, *Adam Bede* (Margaret Reynolds (ed), London: Penguin Books, 1985)

Ellis, Havelock, 'Commentary' in L. Doan and J. Prosser (eds), *Palatable Poison: Critical Perspectives on The Well of Loneliness* (New York: Columbia University Press, 2001) 35

—— *Studies in the Psychology of Sex, 7 vols* (3rd edn, Philadelphia: F.A. Davis, 1920) II

F.A.D., *The Bookman* (April 1927)

Flaubert, Gustave, *The Letters of Gustave Flaubert, 1830–1857* (Francis Steegmuller (ed and trans), London: Belknap Press, 1980)

—— *The Letters of Gustave Flaubert, 1857–1880* (Francis Steegmuller (ed and trans), London: Belknap Press, 1982)

—— *Madame Bovary* (Margaret Cohen (ed), Eleanor Marx Aveling and Paul de Man (trans), New York: W.W. Norton, 2005)

—— *Oeuvres, 2 vols* (A. Thibaudet and R. Dumesnil (eds), Bibliothèque de la Pléiade, Paris: Gallimard, 1951) I

Fournier, H., *De l'Onanisme: causes, dangers et inconvénients pour les individus, la famille et la société. Remèdes* (2nd edn, Paris: J.B. Baillière et Fils, 1876)

Freud, Sigmund, 'A Child is Being Beaten', *Standard Edition* XVII, 175–204

—— 'Analysis of a Phobia in a Five-Year-Old Boy', *Standard Edition* X, 5–149

—— 'The Censorship of Dreams', *Standard Edition* XV, 136–49

—— 'Fetishism', *Standard Edition* XXI 149–57

—— 'Fragment of an Analysis of a Case of Hysteria', *Standard Edition* VII, 3–125

—— The Interpretation of Dreams, *Standard Edition* IV

—— 'Leonardo da Vinci and a Memory of his Childhood', *Standard Edition* XI, 59–139

—— 'Medusa's Head', *Standard Edition* XVIII, 273–75

—— and Joseph Bauer, Studies on Hysteria, *The Standard Edition of the Complete Psychological Works of Sigmund Freud, 24 vols* (James Strachey (ed and trans), London: Vintage, 2001) II

—— 'The Uncanny', *Standard Edition* XVII, 218–53

—— 'The Unconscious', *Standard Edition* XIV, 159–217

Garnier, Pierre, *Onanisme seul et à deux sous toutes ses formes et leurs conséquences*, (9th edn, Paris: Garnier Frères, 1895)

Hall, Radclyffe, *The Well of Loneliness* (London: Virago, 2005)

—— *The Unlit Lamp* (London: Virago Press, 1986)

Harris, Frank, *Oscar Wilde: His Life and Confessions* (London: Robinson Publishing, 1916)

Lebel, André, *Vade-Mecum des jeunes gens, ou guide pratique des maladies syphilitiques vénériennes à l'usage des gens du monde, précédé d'un essai sur l'onanisme et contenant l'exposition d'une méthode certaine de preservation* (5th edn, Paris: Morris et Comp., 1858)

Leroux, Pierre, *De l'humanité* (Paris: Fayard, 1985)

Lewes, G.H., 'Realism in art: recent German fiction', *Westminster Review* (July and October 1858)

Lilly, W.S., 'The new naturalism', *Fortnightly Review* (August 1885)
'London, Thursday, November 1', *Daily Telegraph* (1 November 1888)
Michelet, Jules, *Le prêtre, la femme et la famille* (Paris: Calmann Lévy, 1881)
'M. Zola on his English critics', *Pall Mall Gazette* (14 November 1888)
The Morning Advertiser (1 November 1888)
Nabokov, Vladimir, *Lectures on Literature* (Fredson Bowers (ed), London: Weidenfeld & Nicolson, 1980)
Plato, *The Symposium* (J.A. Brentlinger (ed), S.Q. Graden (trans), Amherst: University of Massachusetts Press, 1970)
Pouillet, T., *Étude médico-psychologique sur l'onanisme chez l'homme, précédé d'une introduction sur les autres abus génitaux* (Paris: Adrian Delahaye et Émile Lecrosier, 1883)
Proudhon, P.J., *Du principe de l'art et de sa destination sociale* (Paris: Garnier Frères, 1865)
Proust, Marcel, *Contre Sainte-Beuve; précédé de pastiches et mélanges et suivi de essais et articles* (Pierre Clarac and Yves Sandie (eds), Bibliothèque de la Pléiade, Paris: Gallimard, 1971)
'The Queen v. William Strange', *The Times* (11 May 1857)
Sainte-Beuve, C.A., 'Madame Bovary par M. Gustave Flaubert', *Causeries du Lundi* (1868–1870)
Saintsbury, George, 'The present state of the novel', *Fortnightly Review* (January 1888)
Sartre, Jean-Paul, *L'Idiot de la famille, 3 vols* (Paris: Gallimard, 1971) I [bib]'The sale of M. Zola's works – sentence', *The Times* (1 November 1888)
Simmias, 'Sans Dieu', *La Gazette de France* (5 September 1887)
Stead, W.T., 'The sacro-sanct male', *Review of Reviews* (1 June 1895)
A Truthful Tory, 'The suppressed novel', *Truth* (29 August 1928)
Ulbach, Louis (Ferragus), 'La littérature putride' (1868) in Henri Mitterand (ed), *Thérèse Raquin* (Paris: GF Flammarion, 1970)
Vizetelly, Edward, 'My life and publications', *Pall Mall Gazette* (24 March 1888)
Vizetelly, Ernest Alfred, *Émile Zola: Novelist and Reformer* (London: John Lane, 1904)
Von Krafft-Ebing, Richard, *Psychopathia Sexualis: With Especial Reference to Antipathic Sexual Instinct: A Medico-Forensic Study* (F.J. Rebman (trans), Chicago: Keener, 1901)
'The Well of Loneliness', *The Lancet* (1 September 1928)
'*Well of Loneliness* to be burned', *Daily Express* (17 November 1928)
Wilde, Oscar 'The Critic as Artist' in Linda Dowling (ed), *The Soul of Man Under Socialism and Selected Critical Prose* (London: Penguin Books, 2001) 213–80
—— 'The Decay of Lying' in Linda Dowling (ed), *The Soul of Man Under Socialism and Selected Critical Prose* 163–93
—— *The Picture of Dorian Gray* (Robert Mighall (ed), London: Penguin Books, 2003)
—— 'The Portrait of Mr. W.H.' in Linda Dowling (ed), *The Soul of Man under Socialism and Selected Critical Prose* (London: Penguin Books, 2001) 31–103
—— 'The Soul of Man under Socialism' in Linda Dowling (ed), *The Soul of Man Under Socialism and Selected Critical Prose* 125–63
—— 'The Truth of Masks' in Linda Dowling (ed), *The Soul of Man Under Socialism and Selected Critical Prose* 280–305
Wilson, H. Schultz, 'L'Assommoir', *Gentleman's Magazine* (December 1878)
Zola, Émile, 'Le naturalisme au théâtre' in François-Marie Mourad (ed), *Le roman experimental* (Paris: GF Flammarion, 2006) 129–66
—— 'Réponse à Ferragus', *Le Figaro* (31 January 1868)
—— *La Terre* (Henri Mitterand (ed), Paris: Gallimard, 1980)
—— *Thérèse Raquin* (Henri Mitterand (ed), Paris: GF Flammarion, 1970)
'Zola's novels', *Daily Telegraph* (1 November 1888)

Secondary sources

Altick, Richard D., *The English Common Reader: A Social History of the Mass Reading Public, 1800–1900* (Columbus: Ohio State University Press, 1957)

Angenot, Marc, *Le Cru et le faisandé: sexe, discours social et littérature à la Belle Époque* (Brussels: Labor, 1986)

Apter, Emily, *Feminizing the Fetish: Psychoanalysis and Narrative Obsession in Turn-of-the-Century France* (Ithaca: Cornell University Press, 1991)

Arata, Stephen, *Fictions of Loss in the Victorian Fin-de-siècle* (Cambridge: Cambridge University Press, 1996)

Aristodemou, Maria, *Law and Literature: Journeys from Her to Eternity* (Oxford: Oxford University Press, 2000).

Attridge, Derek, *The Singularity of Literature* (London: Routledge, 2004)

Auerbach, Erich, *Mimesis: The Representation of Reality in Western Literature* (William R. Trask (trans), Princeton: Princeton University Press, 1953)

Baguley, David, *Naturalist Fiction* (Cambridge: Cambridge University Press, 1990)

Baker, Michael, *Our Three Selves: The Life of Radclyffe Hall* (London: Hamish Hamilton, 1985)

Barale, Michèle Aina, 'Below the belt: (un)covering *The Well of Loneliness*' in Diana Fuss (ed), *Inside/Out: Lesbian Theories, Gay Theories* (New York: Routledge, 1991) 235–59

Baron, Jane, 'Law, literature and the problems of interdisciplinarity' (1998–99) 108 *Yale Law Journal* 1059–86

Barthes, Roland, *S/Z* (Richard Miller (trans), Oxford: Basil Blackwell, 1990)

—— *Image-Music-Text* (Stephen Heath (trans), Glasgow: William Collins, 1977)

Bauer, Heike, *English Literary Sexology: Translations of Inversion, 1860–1930* (New York: Palgrave Macmillan, 2009)

Beaumont, Matthew (ed), *Adventures in Realism* (Oxford: Basil Blackwell, 2007)

Beizer, Janet, *Ventriloquized Bodies: Narratives of Hysteria in Nineteenth-Century France* (Ithaca: Cornell University Press, 1993)

Ben-Yishai, Ayelet, *Common Precedents: The Presentness of the Past in Victorian Law and Fiction* (Oxford: Oxford University Press, 2013)

Bersani, Leo, 'Is the rectum a grave?' in *'Is the Rectum a Grave?' and Other Essays* (Chicago: University of Chicago Press, 2010) 3–31

Borie, Jean, *Le célibataire français* (Paris: Le Sagittaire, 1976)

Bradshaw, David, 'James Douglas: the sanitary inspector of literature' in David Bradshaw and Rachel Potter (eds), *Prudes on the Prowl: Fiction and Obscenity in England, 1850 to the Present Day* (Oxford: Oxford University Press, 2013) 90–111

Brantlinger, Patrick, *The Reading Lesson: The Threat of Mass Literacy in Nineteenth-Century British Fiction* (Bloomington: Indiana University Press, 1998)

Bristow, Joseph, *Empire Boys: Adventures in a Man's World* (London: Unwin Hyman, 1991)

Brittain, Vera, *Radclyffe Hall: A Case of Obscenity?* (London: Femina Books, 1968)

Brooks, Peter, *Realist Vision* (New Haven: Yale University Press, 2005)

—— *Body Work: Objects of Desire in Modern Narrative* (Cambridge: Harvard University Press, 1993)

Brombert, Victor, *The Novels of Flaubert: A Study of Themes and Techniques* (Princeton: Princeton University Press, 1968)

Burns, Colin, 'Zola et l'Angleterre' (1959) 12 *Cahiers naturalistes* 495–504

Busst, A.J.L., 'The image of the androgyne in the nineteenth century' in Ian Fletcher (ed), *Romantic Mythologies* (London: Routledge & Kegan Paul, 1967) 1–97

Castle, Terry, *Noël Coward and Radclyffe Hall: Kindred Spirits* (New York: Columbia University Press, 1996)
Cline, Sally, *Radclyffe Hall: A Woman Called John* (London: John Murray, 1997)
Cocks, H.G., *Nameless Offences: Homosexual Desire in the Nineteenth Century* (London: I.B. Tauris, 2010)
Cohen, Ed, *Talk on the Wilde Side: Towards a Genealogy of a Discourse on Male Sexualities* (New York: Routledge, 1993)
Cohen, William, *Sex Scandal: the Private Parts of Victorian Fiction* (Durham: Duke University Press, 1996)
Connell, R.W., *Gender and Power: Society, the Person and Sexual Politics* (Stanford: Stanford University Press, 1987)
—— *Masculinities* (2nd edn, Cambridge: Polity Press, 2005)
—— and James W. Messerschmidt, 'Hegemonic masculinity: rethinking the concept' (2005) 19 *Gender & Society* 829–59
Cook, Matt, *London and the Culture of Homosexuality, 1885–1914* (Cambridge: Cambridge University Press, 2003)
Corbin, Alain, *L'Harmonie des plaisirs: les manières de jouir du siècle des Lumières à l'avènement de la sexologie* (Paris: Flammarion, 2010)
—— Jean-Jacques Courtine and Georges Vigarello (eds), *Histoire de la virilité, 3 vols* (Paris: Éditions du Seuil, 2011) II
Counter, Andrew, *Inheritance in Nineteenth-Century French Culture: Wealth, Knowledge and the Family* (Oxford: Legenda, 2010)
Cross, Rupert and James W. Harris, *Precedent in English Law* (4th edn, Oxford: Clarendon Press, 1991)
Culler, Jonathan D., *The Literary in Theory* (Palo Alto: Stanford University Press, 2007)
—— *Flaubert: The Uses of Uncertainty* (London: Paul Elek, 1974)
Cummins, Anthony, 'Émile Zola's cheap English dress: the Vizetelly translations, late-Victorian print culture, and the crisis of literary value' (2009) 60 *Review of English Studies* 108–133
Danson, Lawrence, *Wilde's Intentions: The Artist in his Criticism* (Oxford: Oxford University Press, 1997)
Decker, Clarence R., 'Zola's literary reputation in England' (1934) 49 *PMLA* 1140–53
de Lauretis, Teresa, 'Perverse desire: the lure of the mannish lesbian' in L. Doan and J. Prosser (eds), *Palatable Poison: Critical Perspectives on The Well of Loneliness* (New York: Columbia University Press, 2001) 109–126
Derrida, Jacques, 'Force of law: the "mystical foundation of authority"' (1990) 11 *Cardozo Law Review* 920–1046
Doan, Laura, *Fashioning Sapphism: The Origins of a Modern English Lesbian Culture* (New York: Columbia University Press, 2001)
—— and Jay Prosser (eds), *Palatable Poison: Critical Perspectives on The Well of Loneliness* (New York: Columbia University Press, 2001)
Dolin, Kieran, *A Critical Introduction to Law and Literature* (Cambridge: Cambridge University Press, 2007)
Dollimore, Jonathan, *Sex, Literature and Censorship* (Cambridge: Polity Press, 2001)
—— *Sexual Dissidence: Augustine to Wilde, Freud to Foucault* (Oxford: Clarendon Press, 1991)
Dousteyssier-Khoze, Catherine, *Zola et la littérature naturaliste en parodies* (Paris: Eurédit, 2004)
Dumesnil, René, *'Madame Bovary' de Flaubert: Étude et Analyse* (Paris: La Pensée moderne, 1968)

Durant, Alan, 'Reading cases in interdisciplinary studies of law and literature' in Marco Wan (ed), *Reading the Legal Case: Cross-Currents between Law and the Humanities* (Abingdon: Routledge, 2012) 11–29

Eagleton, Terry, *Heathcliff and the Great Hunger: Studies in Irish Culture* (London: Verso, 1995)

Edelman, Lee, 'Seeing things: representation, the scene of surveillance, and the spectacle of gay male sex' in Diana Fuss (ed), *Inside/Out: Lesbian Theories, Gay Theories* (New York: Routledge, 1991) 93–119

Ellmann, Richard, *Oscar Wilde* (London: Hamish Hamilton, 1987)

Eltis, Sos, *Revising Wilde: Society and Subversion in the Plays of Oscar Wilde* (Oxford: Clarendon Press, 1996)

Emery, Kim, '*Well* meaning; pragmatism, lesbianism, and the U.S. obscenity trial' in L. Doan and J. Prosser (eds), *Palatable Poison: Critical Perspectives on The Well of Loneliness* (New York: Columbia University Press, 2001) 355–72

Evans, Jim, 'Change in the doctrine of precedent during the nineteenth century' in Laurence Goldstein (ed), *Precedent in Law* (Oxford: Clarendon Press) 35–72

Felman, Shoshana, *The Juridical Unconscious: Trials and Traumas of the Twentieth Century* (Cambridge: Harvard University Press, 2002)

—— *Writing and Madness* (Martha Noel Evans, Shoshana Felman and Brian Massumi (trans), Ithaca: Cornell University Press, 1985)

Ferguson, Robert A., 'Untold stories in the law' in Peter Brooks and Paul Gewirtz (eds), *Law's Stories: Narrative and Rhetoric in the Law* (New Haven: Yale University Press, 1996) 84–99

Finn, Michael R., *Hysteria, Hypnosis, the Spirits and Pornography: Fin-de-siècle Cultural Discourses in the Decadent Rachilde* (Newark: University of Delaware Press, 2009)

Flint, Kate, *The Woman Reader, 1837–1914* (Oxford: Clarendon Press, 1993)

Forth, Christopher E., *The Dreyfus Affair and the Crisis of French Manhood* (Baltimore: Johns Hopkins University Press, 2004)

—— and Bertrand Taithe (eds), *French Masculinities: History, Culture and Politics* (Basingstoke: Palgrave Macmillan, 2007)

—— '*La Civilisation* and its discontents: modernity, manhood and the body in the early Third Republic' in C.E. Forth and B. Taithe (eds), *French Masculinities* 85–103

Foucault, Michel, *The History of Sexuality, 3 vols* (Richard Hurley (trans), London: Penguin, 1978) I

Gay, Peter, *The Bourgeois Experience: Victoria to Freud. Volume 2: The Tender Passion* (New York: Oxford University Press, 1986)

Genette, Gérard, 'Silences de Flaubert' in *Figures: essais* (Paris: Éditions du Seuil, 1966) 223–45

Girouard, Mark, *The Return to Camelot: Chivalry and the English Gentleman* (New Haven: Yale University Press, 1981)

Goldstein, Jan, 'The uses of male hysteria: medical and literary discourse in nineteenth-century France' (1991) 34 *Representations* 134–65

Goodrich, Peter, *Oedipus Lex: Psychoanalysis, History, Law* (Berkeley: University of California Press, 1995)

—— *Law in the Courts of Love: Literature and Other Minor Jurisprudences* (London: Routledge, 1996)

Gordon, Rae Beth, *Ornament, Fantasy, and Desire in Nineteenth-Century French Literature* (Princeton: Princeton University Press, 1992)

Griffin, Ben, *The Politics of Gender in Victorian Britain: Masculinity, Political Culture and the Struggle for Women's Rights* (Cambridge: Cambridge University Press, 2012)
Grosz, Elizabeth, 'Lesbian fetishism?' in Emily Apter and William Pietz (eds), *Fetishism as Cultural Discourse* (Ithaca; Cornell University Press, 1993) 101–119
Halberstam, Judith, '"A writer of misfits": "John" Radclyffe Hall and the discourse of inversion' in L. Doan and J. Prosser (eds), *Palatable Poison: Critical Perspectives on The Well of Loneliness* (New York: Columbia University Press, 2001) 145–62
Hall, Catherine, 'The early formation of Victorian domestic ideology' in Robert Shoemaker and Mary Vincent (eds), *Gender and History in Western Europe* (London: Arnold, 1998) 181–97
Harrison, Nicholas, *Circles of Censorship: Censorship and its Metaphors in French History, Literature, and Theory* (Oxford: Clarendon Press, 1995)
Hertz, Neil, *The End of the Line: Essays on Psychoanalysis and the Sublime* (New York: Columbia University Press, 1985)
Holcombe, Lee, 'Victorian Wives and property: reform of the Married Women's Property Acts, 1857–1882' in Martha Vincus (ed), *A Widening Sphere: Changing Roles of Victorian Women* (London: Methuen & Co., 1980) 3–29
Hughes, Michael J., 'Making Frenchmen into warriors: martial masculinity in Napoleonic France' in C.E. Forth and B. Taithe (eds), *French Masculinities: History, Culture and Politics* (Basingstoke: Palgrave Macmillan, 2007) 67–85
Jacobus, Mary, *Psychoanalysis and the Scene of Reading* (Oxford: Oxford University Press, 1999)
Jauss, Hans Robert, 'Literary history as a challenge to literary theory' (1970) 2 *New Literary History* 7–37
Jefferson, Ann, *Reading Realism in Stendhal* (Cambridge: Cambridge University Press, 1988)
Kalsem, Kristin, *In Contempt: Nineteenth-Century Women, Law & Literature* (Columbus: Ohio State University Press, 2012)
Kaplan, Morris B., *Sodom on the Thames: Sex, Love and Scandal in Wilde Times* (Ithaca: Cornell University Press, 2005)
Kendrick, Walter, *The Secret Museum: Pornography in Modern Culture* (Berkeley: University of California Press, 1987)
Kenny, Courtney Stanhope, *Outline of Criminal Law: Based on Lectures Delivered in the University of Cambridge* (Cambridge: Cambridge University Press, 1902; reprinted 1926)
Kent, Susan Kingsley, '*The Well of Loneliness* as war novel' in L. Doan and J. Prosser (eds), *Palatable Poison: Critical Perspectives on The Well of Loneliness* (New York: Columbia University Press, 2001) 216–32
King, Graham, *Garden of Zola: Émile Zola and his Novels for English Readers* (London: Barrie and Jenkins, 1978)
Kofman, Sarah, *The Enigma of Woman: Woman in Freud's Writings* (Catherine Porter (trans), Ithaca: Cornell University Press, 1985)
Korey, Marie Elena and Richard Landon (eds), *Vizetelly and Compan(ies): A Complex Tale of Victorian Printing and Publishing* (Toronto: University of Toronto, 2003)
Kristeva, Julia, 'Word, dialogue, and novel' in Toril Moi (ed), *The Kristeva Reader* (Oxford: Basil Blackwell, 1986) 34–62
Krueger, Christine L., *Reading for the Law: British Literary History and Gender Advocacy* (Charlottesville: University of Virginia Press, 2010)
LaCapra, Dominick, *'Madame Bovary' on Trial* (Ithaca: Cornell University Press, 1982)
Lacey, Nicola, 'Psychologising Jekyll, demonising Hyde: the strange case of criminal responsibility' (2010) 4 *Criminal Law and Philosophy* 109–133

—— *Women, Crime and Character: From Moll Flanders to Tess of the d'Urbervilles* (Oxford: Oxford University Press, 2008)

Ladenson, Elisabeth, *Dirt for Art's Sake: Books on Trial From Madame Bovary to Lolita* (Ithaca: Cornell University Press, 2007)

Lapalus, Sylvie, *La Mort du Vieux* (Paris: Tallandier Éditions, 2004)

Laplanche, Jean and Jean-Bertrand Pontalis, 'Fantasy and the origins of sexuality' in Victor Burgin, James Donald and Cora Kaplan (eds), *Formations of Fantasy* (London: Methuen, 1986) 5–28

Laqueur, Thomas W., *Solitary Sex: A Cultural History of Masturbation* (New York: Zone Books, 2003)

—— *Making Sex: Body and Gender from the Greeks to Freud* (Cambridge: Harvard University Press, 1990)

Leighton, Mary Elizabeth and Kirsten Macleod, 'The trials of naturalism: Zola in the British literary and cultural imagination of the *Fin de Siècle*' (2001) 15 *Excavatio* 322–36

Leclerc, Yvan, *Crimes écrits: la littérature en procès au dix-neuvième siècle* (Paris: Plon, 1991)

Levine, George, *Realism, Ethics and Secularism: Essays on Victorian Literature and Science* (Cambridge: Cambridge University Press, 2008)

—— *The Realist Imagination: English Fiction from Frankenstein to Lady Chatterley* (University of Chicago Press, 1981)

Lewes, Kenneth, *The Psychoanalytic Theory of Male Homosexuality* (New York: Simon and Schuster, 1988)

Love, Heather, *Feeling Backward: Loss and the Politics of Queer History* (Cambridge: Harvard University Press, 2007)

MacNeil, William, *Novel Judgements: Legal Theory as Fiction* (Abingdon: Routledge, 2012)

Manchester, Colin, 'Lord Campbell's Act: England's first obscenity statute' (1998) 9 *Journal of Legal History* 223–41

Manderson, Desmond, *Kangaroo Courts and the Rule of Law: The Legacy of Modernism* (Abingdon: Routledge, 2012)

Marcus, Sharon, *Between Women: Friendship, Desire and Marriage in Victorian England* (Princeton: Princeton University Press, 2007)

Matlock, Jann, *Scenes of Seduction: Prostitution, Hysteria, and Reading Difference in Nineteenth-Century France* (New York: Columbia University Press, 1994)

Maugue, Annelise, 'The new Eve and the old Adam' in Geneviève Fraisse and Michelle Perrot (eds), *A History of Women in the West, 5 vols* (Cambridge: Belknap Press, 1993) IV, 515–33

—— L'Identité masculine en crise au tournant du siècle (Paris: Éditions Rivages, 1987)

McLaren, Angus, *The Trials of Masculinity: Policing Sexual Boundaries, 1870–1930* (Chicago: University of Chicago Press, 1997)

McMillan, James F., *France and Women 1789–1914: Gender, Society and Politics* (London: Routledge, 2000)

Merkle, Denise, 'Horizons d'attente victoriens et réécriture de Zola: 1880–1890' (1997) 9 *Excavatio* 103–110

Meyer, Moe, 'Under the sign of Wilde: an archaeology of posing' in Moe Meyer (ed), *The Politics and Poetics of Camp* (London: Routledge, 1994) 75–110

Miller, D.A., *Place for Us: Essay on the Broadway Musical* (Cambridge: Harvard University Press, 2000)

—— *The Novel and the Police* (Berkeley: University of California Press, 1988)

Miller, J. Hillis, *The Ethics of Reading: Kant, De Man, Eliot, Trollope, James, and Benjamin* (New York: Columbia University Press, 1989)

—— 'The fiction of realism: *Sketches by Boz*, *Oliver Twist*, and Cruikshank's illustrations' in Ada Nisbet and Blake Nevius (eds), *Dickens Centennial Essays* (Berkeley: University of California Press, 1971) 85–153

Monneyron, Frédéric, *L'Androgyne romantique* (Paris: ELLUG, 1994)

Mosse, George L., *The Image of Man: The Creation of Modern Masculinity* (New York: Oxford University Press, 1996)

Mullin, Katherine, 'Pernicious literature: vigilance in the age of Zola (1886–1889)' in David Bradshaw and Rachel Potter (eds), *Prudes on the Prowl: Fiction and Obscenity in England, 1850 to the Present Day* (Oxford: Oxford University Press, 2013) 30–52.

Mulvey, Laura, *Visual and Other Pleasures* (Bloomington: Indiana University Press, 1989)

Newton, Esther, 'The mythic mannish lesbian: Radclyffe Hall and the new woman' in L. Doan and J. Prosser (eds), *Palatable Poison: Critical Perspectives on The Well of Loneliness* (New York: Columbia University Press, 2001) 89–109

Nochlin, Linda, *Realism* (Harmondsworth: Penguin Books, 1971)

—— *Representing Women* (London: Thames and Hudson, 1999)

—— and Thomas B. Hess (eds), *Woman as Sex Object: Studies in Erotic Art, 1730–1970* (London: Allen Lane, 1973)

Nussbaum, Martha C., *Poetic Justice: The Literary Imagination and Public Life* (Boston: Beacon Press, 1995)

—— and Alison L. LaCroix (eds), *Subversion and Sympathy: Gender, Law, and the British Novel* (Oxford: Oxford University Press, 2013)

Nye, Robert A., *Masculinity and Male Codes of Honor in Modern France* (Oxford: Oxford University Press, 1993)

Owens, Craig, 'Outlaws: gay men in feminism' in Scott Bryson and others (eds), *Beyond Recognition: Representation, Power, and Culture* (Berkeley: University of California Press, 1992) 218–39

Parkes, Adam, 'Lesbianism, history, and censorship: *The Well of Loneliness* and the suppressed randiness of Virginia Woolf's *Orlando*' (1994) 40 *Twentieth Century Literature* 436–60

Powell, Kerry, *Acting Wilde: Victorian Sexuality, Theatre, and Oscar Wilde* (Cambridge: Cambridge University Press, 2009)

Prendergast, Christopher, *The Triangle of Representation* (New York: Columbia University Press, 2000)

—— *The Order of Mimesis: Balzac, Stendhal, Nerval, Flaubert* (Cambridge: Cambridge University Press, 1986)

Raby, Peter, *Oscar Wilde* (Cambridge: Cambridge University Press, 1988)

Ramona Naddaff, 'Confronting the frugal editors: the *Revue de Paris*' *Madame Bovary*' (2007) 3 *Law, Culture and the Humanities* 266–92

Robert, Guy, *La Terre d'Émile Zola* (Société d'édition les Belle Lettres, 1952)

Robertson, Geoffrey, *Obscenity: An Account of Censorship Laws and Their Enforcement in England and Wales* (London: Weidenfeld & Nicolson, 1979)

Robinson, Paul, 'Freud and homosexuality' in Tim Dean and Christopher Lane (eds), *Homosexuality and Psychoanalysis* (Chicago: University of Chicago Press, 2001) 91–98

Rodensky, Lisa, *The Crime in Mind: Criminal Responsibility and the Victorian Novel* (Oxford: Oxford University Press, 2003)

Rolph, C.H., *Books in the Dock* (London: Deutsch, 1969)

Royle, Nicholas, *The Uncanny* (New York: Routledge, 2003)

Rubinstein, David, *Before the Suffragettes: Women's Emancipation in the 1890s* (Brighton: Harvester Press, 1986)

Sainsbury, R.M., *Paradoxes* (Cambridge: Cambridge University Press 2009)
Sanders, Valerie, *The Tragi-Comedy of Victorian Fatherhood* (Cambridge: Cambridge University Press, 2009)
Sarat, Austin, Matthew Anderson and Cathrine O. Frank (eds), *Law and Humanities: An Introduction* (Cambridge: Cambridge University Press, 2009)
Schehr, Lawrence R., *Parts of an Andrology: On Representations of Men's Bodies* (Stanford: Stanford University Press, 1997)
Schor, Naomi, 'Fetishism and its ironies' in Emily Apter and William Pietz (eds), *Fetishism as Cultural Discourse* (Ithaca: Cornell University Press, 1993) 92–100
—— 'Female fetishism: the case of George Sand' in Susan Rubin Suleiman (ed), *The Female Body in Western Culture: Contemporary Perspectives* (Cambridge: Harvard University Press, 1986) 363–73
—— *Breaking the Chain: Women, Theory, and French Realist Fiction* (New York: Columbia University Press, 1985)
Schramm, Jan-Melissa, *Testimony and Advocacy in Victorian Law, Literature and Theology* (Cambridge: Cambridge University Press, 2000)
—— '"The anatomy of a barrister's tongue": rhetoric, satire, and the Victorian bar in England' (2004) 32 *Victorian Literature and Culture* 285–303
Sedgwick, Eve Kosofsky, 'Anality: news from the front' in Jonathan Goldberg (ed), *The Weather in Proust* (Durham: Duke University Press, 2011) 166–83
—— *Between Men: English Literature and Male Homosocial Desire* (New York: Columbia University Press, 1985)
Sinfield, Alan, *The Wilde Century: Effeminacy, Oscar Wilde and the Queer Moment* (New York: Columbia University Press, 1994)
Smith, Alison, *The Victorian Nude: Sexuality, Morality, and Art* (Manchester: Manchester University Press, 1996)
Steegmuller, Francis, *Flaubert and Madame Bovary: A Double Portrait* (revised edn, Chicago: University of Chicago Press, 1977)
Stora-Lamarre, Annie, *L'Enfer de la Troisième République: censeurs et pornographes, 1881–1914* (Paris: Imago, 1990)
Surkis, Judith, *Sexing the Citizen: Morality and Masculinity in France, 1870–1920* (Ithaca: Cornell University Press, 2006)
Sussman, Herbert, *Victorian Masculinities: Manhood and Masculine Poetics in Early Victorian Literature and Art* (Cambridge: Cambridge University Press, 1995)
Thomas, Donald, *A Long Time Burning: the History of Literary Censorship in England* (London: Routledge & Kegan Paul, 1969)
Tosh, John, *A Man's Place: Masculinity and the Middle-Class Home in Victorian England* (New Haven: Yale University Press, 2007)
—— 'Hegemonic masculinity and the history of gender' in Stefan Dudink, Karen Hagemann and John Tosh (eds), *Masculinities in Politics and War: Gendering Modern History* (Manchester: Manchester University Press, 2004) 41–61
Ward, Ian, *Sex, Crime and Literature in Victorian England* (Oxford: Hart Publishing, 2014)
—— *Law and the Brontës* (Basingstoke: Palgrave Macmillan, 2012)
—— *Law and Literature: Possibilities and Perspectives* (Cambridge: Cambridge University Press, 1995)
Weeks, Jeffrey, *Coming Out: Homosexual Politics in Britain from the Nineteenth Century to the Present* (London: Quartet Books, 1977)
Weil, Kari, *Androgyny and the Denial of Difference* (Charlottesville: University of Virginia Press, 1992)

Weinberg, Bernard, *French Realism: the Critical Reaction, 1830–1870* (London: Oxford University Press, 1937)
Weisberg, Richard, *Poethics, and Other Strategies of Law and Literature* (New York: Columbia University Press, 1992)
Welsh, Alexander, *Freud's Wishful Dream Book* (Princeton: Princeton University Press, 1994)
White, Nicholas, *The Family in Crisis in Late Nineteenth-Century French Fiction* (Cambridge: Cambridge University Press, 1999)
Wiener, Martin, *Men of Blood: Violence, Manliness and Criminal Justice in Victorian England* (Cambridge: Cambridge University Press, 2004)
Yeazell, Ruth Bernard, *Art of the Everyday: Dutch Painting and the Realist Novel* (Princeton: Princeton University Press, 2008)
Zander, Michael, *The Law-Making Process* (6th edn, Cambridge: Cambridge University Press, 2004)

Index

For Product Safety Concerns and Information please contact our EU
representative GPSR@taylorandfrancis.com
Taylor & Francis Verlag GmbH, Kaufingerstraße 24, 80331 München, Germany

www.ingramcontent.com/pod-product-compliance
Ingram Content Group UK Ltd.
Pitfield, Milton Keynes, MK11 3LW, UK
UKHW022125190926
475702UK00013B/1643
9781138606166